VERIZON

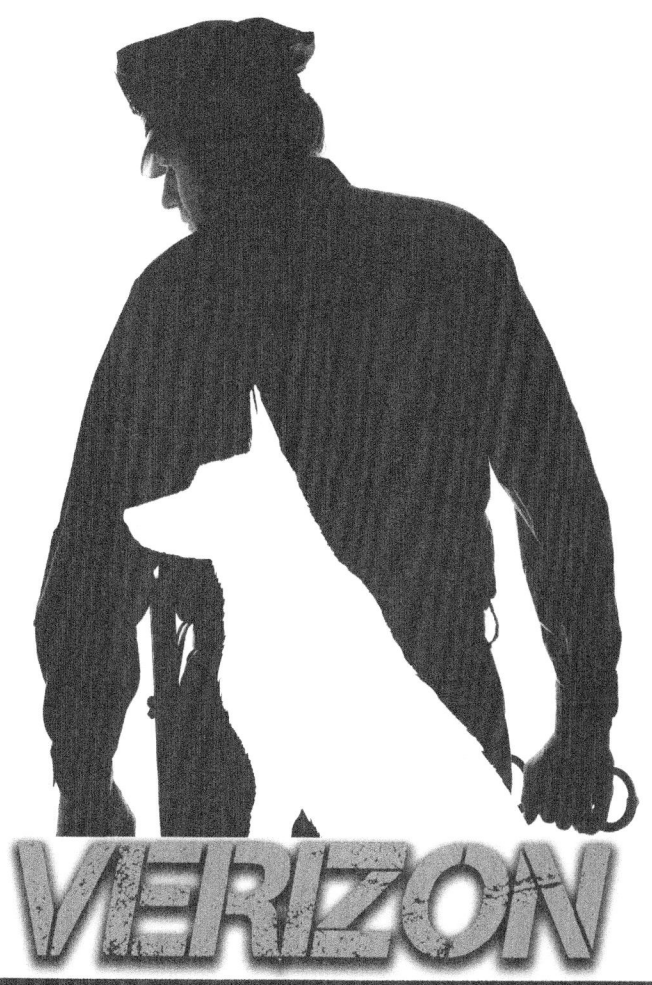

Camden's real-life Ocean's eleven gang and their audacious £100 million heist

Terry Ellis

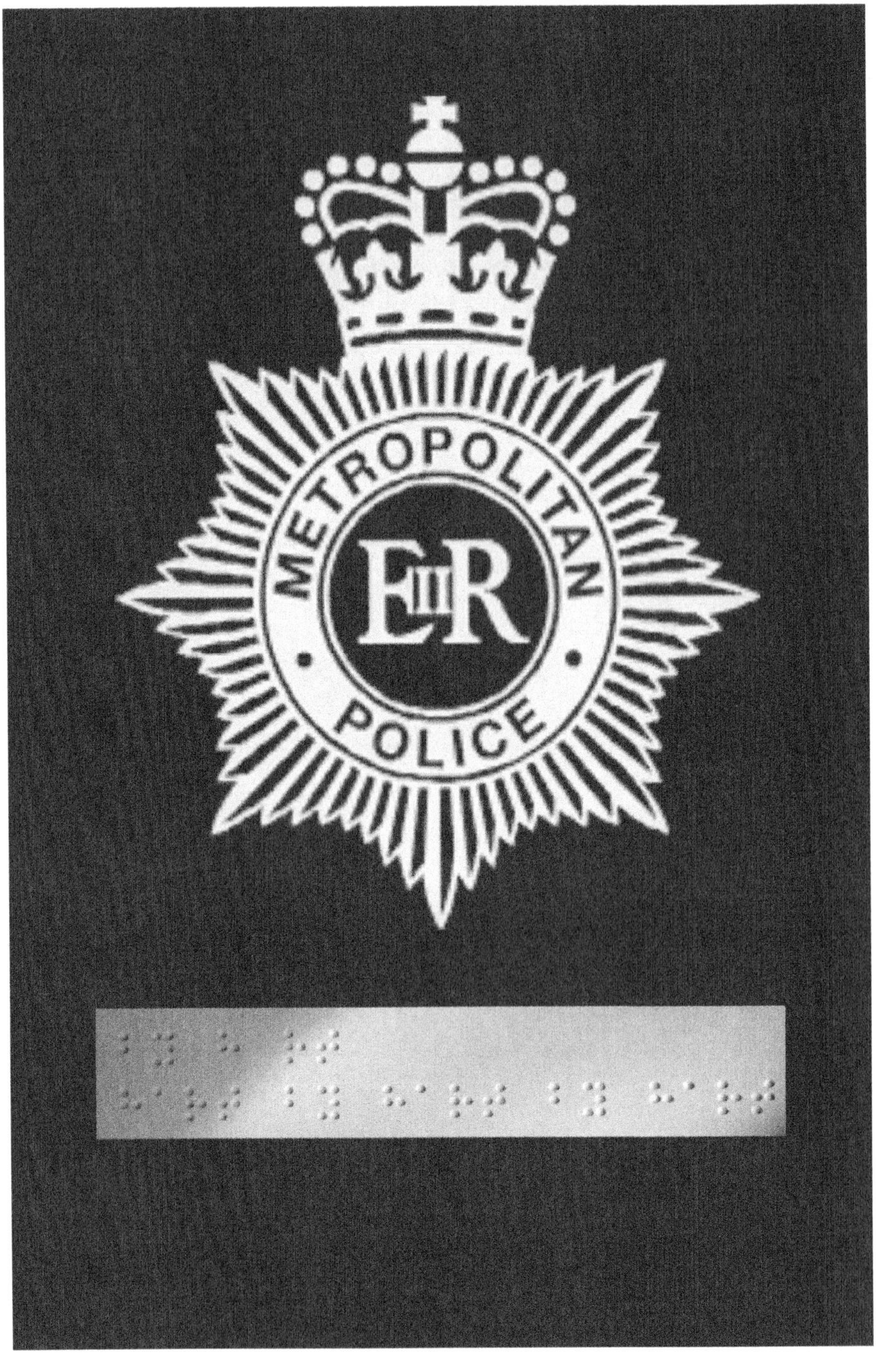
METROPOLITAN
EIIR
POLICE

METROPOLITAN POLICE

POLICE OFFICER

Warrant No:

275321

TERRY ELLIS
Constable

This is the warrant and authority for executing the duties of their office

Signature

Commissioner of Police of the metropolis

Copyright © 2021 Terence David Ellis

All rights reserved.

No part of this publication may be reproduced, stored in a retrieval system, or transmitted, in any form or by any means, without the prior permission in writing of the author, nor be otherwise circulated in any form of binding or cover other than that in which it is published and without a similar condition including this condition being imposed on the subsequent purchase

ISBN-13 9798709077416

Dedications

We would like to take the opportunity to thank several people and companies for their continued love and support of our work.

Writing these book has given us the opportunity to work alongside some truly special people, people without whom the books simply would not have had the success they have.

I would like to thank my good pal Gerard Love aka Gez from Corby.

A special thanks to my friend "The Wee Man" Paul Ferris for all of your support and guidance over the years

James English and his subscribers who have supported our work and given us a platform to promote it. Please check out the king of podcasts at: https://www.youtube.com/channel/UCkdiBNdMSiQeT8aD7gXWgvA or search Anything goes with James English.

Carol Wang our proof reader.

www.scoffmeals.com - our healthy meal prep supplier.

Anna Wheatley for putting up with Terry and keeping him on the straight and narrow.

Colette Goldthorpe from Nourish Wellness Sanctuary - a constant source of good vibes, positive thoughts an incredible friend and amazing coach.

Jason Allday at GHQ, a supporter of ours since before it was fashionable, he is also the writer of several great books - check him out by searching for him on amazon.

Brian Anderson also at GHQ - Brian has been a huge help through the magazine and by linking us with people to help further the books, he also has several great photography books available on Amazon.

And to each and every person that have made each book a bestseller on Amazon and provided so much positive feedback.

Chapter One

A Knock on the head

"The big lesson in life, baby, is never be scared of anyone or anything"

- Frank Sinatra -

They say that a knock on the head can change your whole life forever, which is a fair enough description when describing the changes in my personality after receiving a blow to my head when I was about 9 years old. I remember that moment in time as if it was only yesterday.

I was having a stone fight with my brother Steven and some friends on the waste ground that we used as our imaginary battlefield. I picked my team and Steve did likewise, we then split into two groups of five on each side. Our battlefield today was in Royal College Street on the corner of Fire Engine Hill. It was a piece of waste ground that had been cleared of all its buildings some years before and had been left to grow wild.

It was surrounded by a 15-foot wall that had two entrances. One was boarded up on the corner of Pratt Street, the other entrance was on the opposite side, on Georgiana Street. This entrance had two giant green gates which were padlocked and chained by us so that we could let in the illegal fly tippers so they could dump their loads, which normally consisted of builder's waste materials. It was a profitable arrangement for both sides, as we would unlock the gates and keep (dog) for them while they dumped their loads and in the process, giving us a shiny fifty pence piece after each tip.

In the middle of this wasteland sat a big red double-decker bus that had been dumped some months before, and us being kids, we explored it then claimed it as our own. It was the gangs camp, our fortress that we used for target practice, and a safe place to drink cans of lager and smoke cigarettes, contraband that we had stolen from our parents.

My mate Tony's Dad was an alcoholic, so we would sneak out the odd can of lager or a bottle of Strongbow cider. On a couple of occasions, I'd gone into his front room and dipped his Dad's pockets, because every time I went round there he was either asleep or passed out on the settee, so I would just nick his fags. It was frightening at times as he was a big Irishman and to anger him was more than our lives were worth, and God only knows what he would have done to us if he had caught us, he would probably have knocked our blocks off.

In some ways, the bus was our escape from the harsh reality of our homes, especially for Tony and me. The gang had managed to smash every window on the bus until someone set fire to it. But today we were using the bus as our shield because we were being bombarded with bricks and stones to the extent we were in fear of our lives. I shouted out to my brother for a ceasefire, which he reluctantly agreed to. After about five minutes we were allowed off the bus, hesitantly we all disembarked one by one, while the odd stone was still being thrown to cries of 'stop! we are coming out'. But just as I stepped clear of the bus, my brother threw a half-brick that came hurtling towards me and right down on my head, splitting it open. The blood gushed everywhere, my hands were soaked red.

But then something strange happened to me. My legs just started moving forward, I couldn't stop myself, I started running really fast but I had no control over my limbs. It was like an out-of-body experience but in slow motion. I could see the panic in my friends and brother's faces. However, and luckily for me, there was a six-foot concrete post sticking out of the ground, so I reached out and grabbed hold of it as I ran past, which stopped me in my tracks allowing my brother and friends to catch up with me and thankfully hold me down until my legs stopped running and I'd regained control. Steve had taken off his t-shirt to stem the flow of blood. They then all carried me to the bus stop where we hopped on the number 46 bus going to the Royal Free Hospital.

It wasn't long after this that I noticed that I had started to be more aggressive than normal. My fear of getting hurt had been replaced by a sense of invincibility that I didn't really understand at the time. I put it down to me getting older and wanting to explore my surroundings, but I had definitely changed as I no longer cried when I got hurt, I just sucked it up. If I got into a fight at school I retaliated regardless of the person's size, age or reputation and regardless of the catalyst. I never backed down from anybody again or shied away from anything, danger now seemed to excite me and brought the explorer out in me.

I think this was the first ingredient that started my career as a criminal. The next was learned behaviours.

Chapter two
Learned Behaviours

"You never really learn much from hearing yourself speak"

- George Clooney -

I can remember that one weekend in the school holidays we broke into the old Fishmongers in Georgiana Street, just across the road from the canal. I don't know what we expected to find in there, but we came out with calculators, tool kits, and bags of 2 pence pieces. As a nine-year-old kid, it felt great to be earning so much money.

The excitement of climbing through the window and trying not to make a noise was what really excited me. Slowly checking out every room was brilliant. It took me about ten minutes until I was able to let the others know that it was all clear to come in, but that ten minutes was exhilarating. I'd never felt anything quite like it and I knew then, at that moment, that I'd found my calling in life.

On the way out of there, someone opened up a cabinet on the wall and noticed that there were car keys to all the vehicles hung up on little hooks. So, being inquisitive young kids, we opened up the garage doors and discovered an MG sports car, a Mini Cooper, and two vans.

I jumped in the MG, my brother got into the Mini and my two pals jumped in the vans.

We were having a great time driving around the car park, it was brilliant. I couldn't stop myself from smiling, it was the first time I'd ever driven a car and we were making the most of it. That is until I drove my MG sports into the back of the Mini Cooper, a van then smashed into the back of me, and the other van went into the back of that. The noise and the smell of the petrol and exhaust fumes were everywhere, it was the most fun I'd ever had.

After the first smash, we all looked at each other starry-eyed, excited, and wanting more. We started the engines again, put the cars in gear then floored the accelerators and as fast as it could go we shamelessly smashed them into each other like dodgem cars. My brand new MG sports car with its brown leather interior now had a bonnet that was bent double with smoke coming out of the engine and its gleaming steel bumpers were hanging off. My brother's head could just be seen over the steering wheel of the Mini.

We were having so much fun that we didn't notice a police car pull up full of the Old Bill. They had started climbing over and under the gates. It wasn't until I looked in my rear view mirror that I noticed them. I shouted out to the others, then as quick as you like I was out of the car and heading out of there. But my exit had been blocked as the Old bill were now running everywhere, especially after my brother and pals as they had jumped over the wall back onto our bit of wasteland. I took the opportunity to hide in a big old oil drum, my only saving grace was that it was clean and empty, so I jumped in and pulled the lid over and waited for what seemed like an eternity.

But not before I saw my brother jump back over the wall followed in hot pursuit by all the plod. I kept still for about five minutes then peered out again, I saw the police cars and flashing blue lights were all still there, but there were no police as they had chased my brother and pals. I took the opportunity and calmly put the lid on the ground and hesitantly got out.

I then quickly sprinted over to the front gate, rolled underneath it, then darted down the canal until I came out in Camden town. I was knackered as I'd run all the way to Dingwall's market but at least I was free.

I hoped my brother and pals were also in the clear as the damage and the break in would see us all in deep shit, especially if any of them got caught and it came to light that I was with them, then my dad would kill me.

I made my way home, but when I turned into my street all I could see were old bill cars, there were police officers in our front garden, my mum and brother were being backed into a corner, my mum had a broom in her hands and was fending them off, she was swearing and throwing bottles at them also my brother. The whole street was out as most of our gang lived in the same road. My brother and my pals had all been chased and had run into the safety of their own homes, (the dopey fuckers). So now the police had laid siege in all the front gardens, the street was surrounded and on lockdown it was Mayhem.

There was nothing I could do so I took the opportunity and crossed over the road and climbed the wall opposite where we lived. I climbed on top of the roof of the GPO as I would be able to see everything more clearly from there, I could also hide up there.

It was horrible watching my Mum being arrested for assault and my brother and pals all being placed in handcuffs. My poor Nan and sisters were all crying in the doorway, the whole neighbourhood was out watching, there was a traffic jam with buses and cars backed up to Crandall Road.

My pals Mums and Dads were out, all effing and blinding, the other kids in the street were shouting at the police, it was like a fucking circus.

That night my dad came down and had to bail my Mum and brother out of the police station. When he came back he gave me and my brother a good belting, six of the best each then sent us to bed promising to kill us both if we ever got into trouble again. I'd never been so frightened.

My nan had beaten the shit out of me with her umbrella and shut me in my room under the threat of death if I ever came out. My Mum was in bits crying and shouting at us, eventually she calmed down, but not my Nan she was livid.

We tried our best over the coming weeks to keep out of trouble. Steve seemed to have turned a corner as far as not getting in trouble ever again, he had learned a valuable lesson as my Dad had given him a black eye, so he was now determined to knuckle down and do good at school.

As for me I had dyslexia and didn't fully understand the meaning of it at the time, but it definitely had a major impact on my schooling, attendance and education. I felt embarrassed and ashamed as my brother always took the piss out of me because I couldn't spell, so I became disruptive, argumentative and excluded myself from school.

Unfortunately to my Mum's annoyance as I would bunk off school and spend all my time down the West End dipping purses and anything else I could get my hands on. Hamley's toy shop was my favourite place, as I used to play with all the toys, then I'd go down to Trafalgar Square and feed the pigeons. The embankment was also a good place to explore, I'd walk along the Thames riverbank, jumping on and off the docks and nicking stuff out the warehouses. Everything seemed so big and full of riches, the South London kids I met down there were also different, they always wanted to fight me.

It was my secret world away from my family and Camden Town and I couldn't' wait to get back to it. Each week I would always try and get home early and pretend I'd been at school so my Mum wouldn't notice, but eventually the school informed her that my attendance was one of the worst in the whole school, so she and I were called in. Once she knew the full extent of my truancy she went ape shit and she even threatened to put me into care and tell my Dad, she even said that I had to go and live with him, which thank God was only a threat as that would have been hell for me, as it meant no more West End, no more sneaking out in the middle of the night robbing shops with my new best friends elder brother David who was 14 years old, compared to me only 10.

Chapter Three

Expelled from school

"I've been making a list of the things they don't teach you at school. They don't teach you how to love somebody. They don't teach you how to be famous. They don't teach you how to be rich or how to be poor. They don't teach you how to walk away from someone you don't love any longer. They don't teach you how to know what's going on in someone else's mind. They don't teach you what to say to someone who's dying. They don't teach you anything worth knowing."

- Neil Gaiman, The Kindly Ones -

I eventually got expelled from school for fighting my teacher and a kid in my class, who I accidentally stabbed in the hand with a metal pencil case, cutting his hand open, it was my last act of defiance. And the last time I sat in a classroom with normal kids at a Primary School.

But at least now I could do as I pleased within reason. It was about this time I started to notice that my Mum was a professional shoplifter, she used to take me into the Co-op, Woolworths and Marks and Spencer's, give me bars of chocolate to eat whilst she pocketed everything she could carry. I'm talking about big joints of meat, steaks, chickens, turkey roasts, sausages, bacon, and bottles of anything. She was brilliant, we never went without food ever.

I remember one night she woke me up and told me to get dressed and be quiet. I hurriedly got dressed and went downstairs, she then showed me a box that I had stolen that day out of the warehouse across the road from where we lived, she said I want you to get through that window again and pick out these certain boxes and bring them home to me ok, the boxes had crystal glasses in and the other boxes she wanted to have knife and forks sets.

I spent the whole night running back and forth filling up our front room with hundreds of boxes, it was pitch black as I climbed through the window, I was scared as I kept thinking someone would either jump out on me or the police would come, I couldn't see anything either at first, but my eyes eventually got used to it my mum kept watch, telling me when I could come out and run back to the house.

It was hard work and I was sweating and by the morning I was exhausted.

My mum however spent the whole of the next day and evening selling them down the bingo.

She was so happy that she brought us all some clothes and made a fantastic dinner with all the trimmings, I learned a valuable lesson that night that it was ok to steal but bad to get caught.

So I went to work with David who at 14 was a seasoned shop breaker/ burglar who took me under his wing, we went on a spree that encompassed the whole of Camden and Kentish Town, we started with a cafe, then a shoe shop, sweet shops and by the end of the first month, we'd done about ten shops it was an exhilarating experience that's hard to explain.

As Every time we burgled a shop, it was like everything in there was mine, it belonged to me and if I could carry it, then I owned it.

It was surreal, the smell, sounds, and quietness, mixed in with my anxiety and the fear of being caught, it was a fantastic adrenaline Rush, wow!

It was so addictive I needed a fix every night and if I didn't get it, I felt down.

The late nights and then having to go to secondary school (sir William Collins School in Somerstown) was now harming my education, I had mood swings and a shit attitude, I hated having to go to school. I Despised my social worker, teachers, and the other kids for being smart and me being stupid because I just couldn't spell and no matter how hard I tried I just couldn't learn.

I was castigated by the teachers for not trying hard enough and ridiculed and being academically astute.

The frustration I felt was palpable and again it got me excluded from classes and then eventually expelled from school, especially after I punched my teacher in the face as he made me feel inadequate by making snide remarks about me being stupid, so I told him to fuck off, then I punched him.

It was instinctive and I regretted it straight away, but he was so angry that he grabbed me and shook me until I nearly passed out, he then frog marched me to the headmaster's office. Who had a zero-tolerance policy for striking a principal member of his Faculty, so gave me six of the best with a bamboo cane that stung my arse so severely and afterward, a meeting was called and I was expelled again.

Chapter Four

Man about the house

"Try not to become a man of success, but rather try to become a man of value."

- Albert Einstein -

My mum and dad showed their displeasure by sending me straight to bed with no dinner or tea then they grounded me for life.

It was a crazy time for me as I was threatened with being put in care and being taken away by my social worker, but I thought it was just more idle threats so I just shrugged them off as just another tool in their chest of threats that would never materialize.

That night I went out and nicked a car and drove it down fire engine hill and almost turned it over before smashing it into a parked car and a traffic meter, knocking the top of it.

Luckily for me, it was one o'clock in the morning so there were no cars around, I was shaking and I'd cut my forehead open, but apart from that I had no broken bones.

However the car was a write-off.

But just as I was about to leg it I noticed the parking meter head was up against the wall so I picked it up and took it home.

I hid it under my bed and the next day when my brother and sisters went to school, and my mum went off to afternoon bingo, I took the meter downstairs, into the back garden and took a sledgehammer to it and bang!! it cracked open and revealed its prize, £8 in ten pence pieces, I had found a new source of income.

The next day I teamed up with my mate and night after night we smashed every parking meter from Camden town to kings cross it was so easy, my first attempt at creating a new revenue stream out of nothing had started.

We had bags of coins, so many I was finding it hard to hide them at home,
so I stashed them down the canal in the old railway arches. I brought myself new jeans, trainer's, tops and a jacket.

Every day I went to burger king in parkway and ordered a burger, chips and a knickerbocker glory with loads of ice cream, afterward I'd go to the cinema.

I watched the chainsaw massacre, Dracula and all the Kung Fu films, it was brilliant, I looked the bollocks and I even gave my mum a few quid, it felt really good because my mum never complained about where I got my money from, so I took her acceptance of the cash as a signal that I could do whatever I wanted as long as I didn't get caught.

Chapter Five

Air raid shelter

"I still find it quite easy to find my way into a child's imagination. We're all Peter Pan ourselves in some respects. Everybody should keep some grip on childhood, even as a grownup."

- Tim Curry -

My next excursion was at the back of boots the chemist in Camden town, I found that the council estate padlock keys were mostly 660 and one key fitted them all and as luck would have it I'd nicked a bunch of keys from the caretakers shed in Bayham Street, I then tried the keys in the lock to the old air-raid shelter, the one behind boots and it worked we couldn't believe it.

Being inquisitive young kids we went in and then went down the spiral staircase until we came into the tunnels at the bottom, there were miles and miles of tunnels and bunk beds, it was like nothing I had ever seen before and at intervals, there were 2 ft. thick air-raid doors.

I couldn't wait to show my brother and the rest of the gang, there were millions of bunk beds and all the tunnels we lit with bright lights, for weeks we just took our bikes down there and rode them for miles.

It was so much fun, we had our very own underground world that we could explore unhindered, no adults or kids spoiling for a fight, or spoiling our fun, no traffic noise, pollution or old Bill telling us to go home.

I loved it down there, some days I would go down there with my Jack Russell dog called flash, he belonged to one of our neighbours who used to treat it really badly and one day when I was walking past I saw him kick it halfway across the hallway, so I said if you hate the dog so much why don't you give it to me, he told me to mind my own business, then told me to fuck off, so that night I threw a brick through his window.

The old guy was always chucking the dog out on the street, so when I saw him do it from my window a couple of days later I went down and put the dog in a box then hid him under our staircase, I feed it scraps from the dinner table, his name was flash and every time I went near it, he would go for me, he was a vicious little bastard at first, it took me about three weeks to train it out of him before I could sit in with him.

Once he started to trust me he was a fantastic companion he slept on my bed and went everywhere with me, if anyone came near me he would go for them, my mum hated him also my brother and sisters too because he would growl at them every time they came near him.

So being down the air raid shelter with just him was heaven as I know he wouldn't go for anyone, we lay on the bunk beds and I would just cuddle him and he would run up and down barking.

One day when we were on our way back I saw some maintenance workers who chased us for what seemed like forever, I almost shit myself but luckily I was on my bike, it was scary as they were really angry and screaming at me to stop. it was a relief to get back to the surface and some fresh air.

I told the boys and we agreed that we would drop it out for a couple of weeks before we ventured down there again.

Chapter Six
Putting the tunnels to good use

"There is always one moment in childhood when the door opens and lets the future in"
- Graham Greene -

This time we were not going down for fun we were here to work, as I had noticed that the tunnels passed every train station, so this particular evening when the trains stopped and the station was closed we took the opportunity to use our master key to gain access to the platforms.

Unfortunately it didn't work so we went back out and got a couple of hacksaws and sawed the locks off, then explored the station it was our best adventure and the best adrenaline rush I've ever had, as we now had to dodge and hide from the maintenance workers who worked on the lines.

This night we were down Warren Street I noticed that most stations had cigarette and chocolate machines on the platforms, so we tooled up, my tool of choice, a Crowbar.

I can't remember which station it was because we chose a station a couple of miles away from Camden Town.

We went up the spiral stairs then hacksawed the chain, trying not to make too much noise, then we crept along the platform up the escalators, then out into the main entrance hall of the station, which had two machines a cigarette and chocolate one lovely.

We managed to find a spot to lever it open and after about ten minutes we had bags of fags and confectionery that now had to be transported back to Camden and into the hands of our milkman friend (fence) as he had promised to buy all the cigs we could carry, which we now had, two bags full.

I lost count over this period of how many machines we robbed, but we all had new chopper bikes and had all started smoking and for young kids We were now living large.

We had also depleted the underground system of its merchandise, plus they had gotten wise to our Modus operandi.

They had changed all the locks on the station's but it didn't deter us as no sooner had they boarded up the entrance to the air-raid shelter, we just pried it open, for one last caper.

We decided to go on foot this time as we didn't want to lose any of the bikes.
We choose warren St., as it was probably the only station on the northern line that we hadn't done, well that and Camden town.

We all had rucksacks, beanie hats, and gloves on, the three of us then made our way to the target, it was quiet I could hear my heart beating, the sweat was running down my back and wearing the hat made it even worse, but we kept to the script.

At Warren Street, we climbed the spiral stairs and when we got to the top we listened out for the maintenance crew, we couldn't hear anything, in fact, you couldn't hear a pin drop, so I took the rucksack off, pulled out a hacksaw then slowly went to town on the chain.

I was sweating but nearly through the chain when a black guy came round the corner and grabbed my arm through the gated fence, I cried out.

Then pulled as hard as I could, my pals ran for their lives, but I was now trapped as another black worker came round the corner shouting and trying to grab me.

I picked up the hacksaw and chopped at his arm and hand which seemed to take him back as he lost his grip momentarily and let go of me.

I fell backward down the stairs and by the time I was upright, they were putting their key in the lock, so I regained my balance and sprinted down the stairs, round and round I went until I reached the bottom where I tripped and sprained my ankle the pain was excruciating but the thought of being caught drove me on.

In the distance, I could see the others and I wanted to call out for help, but I couldn't because I was scared.

I didn't want my pursuers to hear I was in pain, so I gritted my teeth and ran and ran until I caught up with the others who were now laughing at the fact I nearly shit myself when the guy came flying around the corner.

I was now laughing too as we came to the spiral staircase at Camden Town, we had had a narrow escape and this would definitely be the last time I came down the underground and here ever again.

My ankle was killing me I had lost my rucksack, jacket, beanie hat, and hacksaw and almost killed myself in the process.

But at least we were free.

It took a trip to the hospital where I was prescribed four days in bed, for my proxy sprained ankle to heal, when it did eventually heal I decided to pop down to king cross as my pal said he had a little coup, for us, which was slang for nicking something.

Chapter Seven
Getting acquainted with King's Cross station

"Life is like riding a bicycle. To keep your balance, you must keep moving."
- Albert Einstein -

I asked him what it entailed and I was gobsmacked at his proposal, he said he was walking along the railway lines at kings cross and a car transporter had come past, but because it was going so slow, he was able to jump on and sit inside some of the cars as they were all unlocked.

So I asked, "what's your point?"

He said the point is every car has a car stereo in, so all we have to do is jump on, and with a screwdriver and a couple of black bags we can take them out and sell them, but the train is moving and it will probably speed up as soon as it gets out of the train depot, then we will be fucked.

"Well then we will just have to take that risk" he said, "what do you reckon Terry".

"Of course, I'm up for it" I said.

So we agreed to meet the following day and wait for a car transporter to come past, it would be hit and miss but nothing ventured nothing gained.

I met Jeremy the next day and he was looking extremely pensive but confident at the same time that his plan would work.

We walked along the canal to king's cross then climbed over the fence and waited by the side of the railway line.

There were so many trains coming and going it was like spaghetti Junction; passenger trains, container trains, flatbeds but no car transporter in or out of the depot.

We decided to give it a miss and started to walk along the tracks and just as we reached Camley St., our train pulled alongside us, so we jumped aboard and for the forty minutes or so we went from car to car, me holding the bag and Jeremy unclipping the stereos after the first bag we had about 6 Radios in so I lowered it over the side and carefully placed it on the ground then returned to Jeremy who was sweating, but smiling from ear to ear, come on he said two more then let's jump-off.

The train was still moving at the same speed, as when we got on but we were now roughly 3 or 4 miles down the track it was now definitely time to jump off.

I let the bag down then Jerry scurried down the side of the train and started running along to keep up with the speed but tripped over and landed on his front almost smashing his face, I couldn't stop laughing.

As quickly as he went down he was back on his feet shouting for me to jump as the train was just about to enter a tunnel.

I started running back down the train until I came to the part of the train that was lower to the ground and hesitantly I took a deep breath and jumped hitting the ground feet first before falling backward on my arse and banging my head on the stones.

But no harm is done. I was still alive and we had about nine stereos, but we wouldn't know that until we walked back and picked up the other bag.

It took us nearly an hour to get back, but we had nine stereos at £10 each, so it was definitely worth nearly killing ourselves so we thought.

We did this move four more times until the car company started locking the car doors and removing the radios, our little earner was now scuppered (over).

With the money I was earning and my new job working on the rail express parcel van with Dave Osborne I was doing really well, Dave was always nicking hampers and parcels that he would give to me, so mum was happy as I was bringing home some catalogue clothes and all sorts, even food hampers, I was killing it and for the first time in my life I was happy.

I was earning money and everything seemed to be going well at home but my mum was still shoplifting which I'd started to hate, as I had visions of her being nicked and all of us being taken into care.

Chapter Eight

Fear of going into care

"The initial trauma of a young child may go underground but it will return to haunt us."
- James Garbarino -

I don't think she understood the psychological consequences of her actions on me, as she was totally oblivious of this fact.

Her shoplifting wasn't done with malice she did it to feed us, unfortunately, it still never changed the fact that I hated meeting her after bingo as she would always ask me to come with her.

But what could I do? She was my mum.

I tried my best to earn money so she didn't have to do it but as fast as I gave it to her she would spend it on bingo, fags, and us kids.

Tonight I was hoping to change all that, as Mickey, my pal had found us a nice little earner down the cross.

Another warehouse, our fourth one up to date, we had done the toy factory in saint Pancras Way, the clothing factory in royal college street.

The parcel depot on Camley Street and the ABC in Camden road, we had done the ABC 10 or more times over the months, it was a massive place, four floors high.

On the first floor there was comic's, marvel, the beano, and every conceivable magazine, and on the ground floor there were cakes, cream cakes, cheesecakes, jam donuts, chocolate eclairs, hundreds of different ones.

In the vans, there were blocks of cheese. Giant tins of beans, bread, everything, we nicked so much out of that place, it was silly how easy it was, because it was so well protected,

In fact, it was Like Fort Knox, There were always three Scotland's working (security guards) on duty in there every night and day, 7 days a week but we were able to bypass the front gate, easy, by coming over the church wall.

In fact, we climbed on top of the vicar's conservatory and dropped down onto the tops of the parked vans and lorries.

The last time I went in there, I was in the back of a lorry passing out the blocks of cheese when two night watchman sneaked up on me and caught me red-handed I was cornered, my pals legged it and I was grabbed by the scruff of the neck and marched towards the front gatehouse as another guard shouted out, "I'll call the police".

He then went back into the office, so I then started to cry and pleaded for them to let me go but the old fucker slapped me around the head and told me to shut the fuck up.

When we were about twenty yards from the main gate he loosened his grip, then kicked me up the arse and demanded "get in the fucking office you little cunt".

I was frightened that my dad would kill me this time especially if he had to bail me out from the police station, so with all my might I pulled away from the guard and ran as fast as I could, l leapt up onto the gate which was about 15 feet high, it had little squares in it that I could just about get my fingers in and up I went like a rat up a drain pipe.

The guards were trying to grab my feet but I managed to pull myself clear just in time, I flew over the top and dropped to the ground, the relief was palpable my adrenaline was pumping and I was laughing at the same time, fuck I had escaped my captors and I was overwhelmed, I couldn't contain my delight as I gave them both the finger whilst telling them to fuck off, then I ran for my life as they called me all the cunts under the sun.

But tonight Mickey had come up with what he said was going to be our best earner to date, that is if I could get us in there.

The target was on Camley Street, a clothes and Jeans warehouse, we had to approach it from the back, then go along the railway tracks, then climb up onto the roof.

We had gloves on and a long rolled-up rope, we looked like two commandos, both wearing black Jean's, black Jackets, and beanie hats.

We definitely looked the part as we climbed over the fence, we had decided to enter from the railway lines, as it gave us access to the Roof of the building.

When we got there we had to jump across a gap that was the height of the warehouse, which was about 60 foot, then walk along a tin gully in the middle of the roof, on each side of the gully there were glazed reinforced wire meshed windows.

We walked slowly to the end and looked over the parapet wall, so we could Look up and down Camley Street, the road was empty so I went to town on the glass window, ripping off the outer case when that was done I eased the glass with a crowbar cracking it straight across the middle, I was then able to pry it back.

It took me about ten minutes until I made a big enough gap to climb in, it was pitch black inside, but I could see a joist so I tied the rope onto it and slowly lowered myself down. Mickey said the alarm system only worked if you opened a door.

"So don't open any ok" were his instructions.

"Are you sure" I asked.

"Yes" he replied.

Adding that his mate had told him.

Which was a relief to hear as all we needed was the alarm going off, especially as we were in the middle of king's cross, there was old bill everywhere and they had a really fast response time and a zero-tolerance policy to burglars on their patch.

With the rope now tied, I lowered myself down, Mickey shone his torch so I could see, it was hard going, I was hanging about 50 feet in the air, my hands were hurting as I was gripping the rope so tight, there was a rack about 15 foot down, so I slowly lowered myself onto it.

I managed to slide down without too much fuss, Mickey was still shining his torch in front of me so I could see where I was going I climbed down the rack and took out my own torch, which really helped as I could now see all around me, there were loads of boxes.

I quickly dropped about 6 feet to the ground and then walked across the gangway to look inside the boxes, but no sooner had I opened a box then the bloody alarm went off.

It was so loud that I nearly had a heart attack.

I panicked and jumped back up onto the rack dropping my torch and I quickly climbed back up.

By this time Micky was shouting "hurry up Tel", so I pulled myself up to the top of the rack, grabbed the rope and tried to pull myself up, but I couldn't climb as It was impossible, I just never had the strength.

The rope was swinging everywhere I called out to Mickey to help me but he had run off so I was now fucked.

I could have cried, but I was so scared of getting caught by the old bill that I just had to find the strength, but it was no good the rope was so thin it killed my hands and I dropped back down, I was cursing Mickey and blaming him for my stupidity.

But I noticed a beam running up the wall so I walked across to the top of the racks and reached out and put my hands behind it and with my feet pressed against it I was able to shimmy up. I was sweating,
my hat had fallen off my torch was on the floor and I had almost shit myself with fear this had turned into a fucking fiasco.

My night had gone from bad to worse in ten seconds, I was now nearly at the top and as I reached out Mickey came back and said the old bill were just outside, "hurry the fuck up" he said.

"Then help me! you cunt!" I shouted back.

He then reached down and pulled me up, I could have kissed him but at the same time I felt like punching him because I thought he had left me, added to the fact the information his mate had given us was fucking wrong and now we were on the verge of both being nicked.

Mickey then ran to the edge of the roof, and looked over, "fuck!" He said "the filth are just pulling up, quick let's go".

I pulled myself out onto the roof my hand was cut but It was such a relief to get out of that hole in the glass that I couldn't care less I wanted to cry out loud! That I had made it.

There was no time to hang around, we both Ran along the gully then jumped the gap landing on our feet, we could barely see but there was just enough light to run across the tracks, we had been seen, as there was now 5 or six torches aimed in our direction which helped us see where we were going, but also meant that they could see us.

Then I heard "stop! standstill you little cunts".

The cops were almost on us but we managed to climb through a little hole in the fence the one we had come through.

The old bill had to climb over which gave us just enough time to run into saint Pancras churchyard, Mickey had run up ahead and I quickly lost sight of him.

I called out, but he was nowhere to be seen, so I ran across the graveyard and crawled into a crypt through a hole in the end, I pulled myself in, I could feel the cobwebs on my face as I tried to turn myself around, it was a tight squeeze but I managed to turn round and poked my head out, it was pitch black now.

I could hear the old bill running through the churchyard shouting to each other and shining their torches.

I was so scared I could hear my heart beating, all I wanted to do was run but I had to lay still.

I kept imagining the tombstone would collapse on top of me and I would be buried alive in the little confined space in the middle of a graveyard and no one would ever find me.

I kept hearing noises and seeing shadows moving towards me, dead people coming to get me.

Fuck this I panicked and crawled out of the confined space, and as quickly as I could and made my way towards the light and then the main road.

I squeezed through the iron railings and ran into the flats until I came out at the back of Crowndale Road, I headed up to college Place, then left into Pratt street, then another left, onto royal college street and home, Fuck me I'd made it.

When I walked in, my mum asked "where have you been?".

"I've just been in Tony's house playing on his Scalextric".

"Ok" she said, "it's time for bed".

"No problem mum, see you in the morning".

"Ok darling".

My hands and face were black but my mum hadn't even noticed.

Chapter Nine
A Tragic Loss and New Beginnings

"Life is a succession of lessons which must be lived to be understood"

- Helen Keller -

The next morning I met Mickey who had also made it home safely, he had some sad news for me, my mate Tom had been killed on Crandall Road by a lorry on his way to school, he was playing a game of dare, a silly game where he would run across the road as fast as he could.

Normally in front of a bus, but this morning he had foolishly tried to beat a lorry and had been crushed under its wheels and dragged along the road.

I don't know how I felt, I was empty, I would never see my friend again, it didn't seem real.

We had walked to school a thousand times, nicked milk off peoples doorsteps and ice poles from the sweet shop.

It was only a few days previously that we had bunked off school and gone down the west end, we had nicked a load of aftershave out of a chemist in Soho, and then did a runner out of burger king.

We had been chased through Chinatown then into Leicester Square where we separated, I ran down the underground but tom had carried on running, we met up the next day and had a laugh about it.

Now he was gone forever.

I mourned him with a few tears as I sat in the toilet, my toilet was my crying place, so no one could see me.

A few days later my mum informed us that we would be moving to Kilburn, 38 Grange place, none of us wanted to leave but we had no choice our roof was leaking and the damp was making us sick.

My nan had been offered a flat in Kentish town on Morden road above an off-license, which she grasped with both hands.

In our old house most nights we had to sit around the Coal fire or the paraffin heater just to keep warm, the house was always cold, the black and white telly was our only saving grace, some nights we were allowed to watch the late-night film.

The thought of moving into a flat with central heating was like winning the pools, mum also informed us we would be getting a new colour tv.

The flat was on the ground floor, it had a small garden. we also had a small shed at the front, it had two toilets, three bedrooms, and a massive front room.

I would miss living in Camden town though, getting a fresh start would be great, for the family.

I was also allowed back in school again, at sir William Collins in Summer town.

Which meant me getting a 31 bus every day back to Camden town.

So at least I could keep in touch with my pals, so really nothing had changed.

Kilburn was a shit hole, full of Irish natives and a pub on every corner, it was like winning the pools for me and my brother Steven, we started creeping around all the shops as they left their back doors open, so we had a field day.

I would creep in and empty the safes.

We nicked fags out of the storerooms and if wasn't nailed down, we would take it home, we had so much money that we found it hard to hide it at times.

We had new bikes in the shed, I bought a colour telly for our room, a stereo and we even managed to find an African grey parrot which we called George.

My mum even brought two kittens tom and Jerry both ginger.

On the main road and round the corner on Willesden road there was a bingo hall, so my mum was happy, it was right next door to Billy Mulligans on Willesden Lane.

There was a cinema and a nightclub called the National and the number 16 bus took us straight to Hyde park and speaker's corner.

We were living the dream I was 11 years old and life couldn't be any better, I'd made some new friends in Kilburn, one, in particular, was Anthony Moriarty who introduced me to a shirt company called the fifth column down the bottom of Kilburn high road.

They screen printed t-shirts, I loved working in there after school.

Some evenings, we used to go to Portobello Market it was brilliant seeing all the market stalls, it had a really friendly vibe as everyone was either pissed or stoned out of their heads, as the Notting hill carnival was on, I'd never seen anything like it, or smoked anything like it before I was as high as a kite most days and loving it.

There's nothing like Dingwall's market in Camden Lock, or Inverness market the atmosphere and people are brilliant they come from all around the world and all walks of life, I could walk through those markets with no money on me and by the time I came out the other end, I'd have a wallet or a purse and something to eat.

I loved Camden town and now I'd found another market that equalled it.

I was bunking off school most days, I managed to go once or twice a week, until one day, I was again expelled for fighting an older boy.

He was in the third form and two years older than me, I was expelled all because I wouldn't say sorry after knocking his front teeth out.

My mum wasn't too pleased as the social services were driving her mad about my behaviour as I was now seen as a problem child, disruptive and violent.

Chapter Ten
The Winch

"My mama always said, life is like a box of chocolates. You never know what you're gonna get."
- Forest Gump -

I'd been nicked for burglary, breaking into shops TDA (taking and driving away), criminal Damage.

I'd been to court a few times at Seymour Place Marylebone Road, so to redeem myself I had to go to a special school called the winch in Swiss cottage, which was for problem kids.

I hated it, they tried their best to make me feel welcome but after a couple of months I just didn't want to go anymore, as it bored me to tears.

So instead I started going out nicking lead off the roofs, off food shops, churches, and even my school, then scrapping it down the scrapyard in saint Pancras way.

My pals tony and Alan would work all through the night with me after creeping out when their parents were asleep it was great walking around in the middle of the night.

The streets were always empty and quiet, we could see if anyone was in or out.

The only problem was that we used to get filthy dirty. as black as the Ace of Spades.

After a few weeks of doing this, we were chased and I nearly fell off the roof unfortunately Alan broke his arm which put the kibosh on our nightly excursions after he admitted he was out nicking lead with me.

This time my social worker promised me that this was definitely my last opportunity to change my ways, she said that she was going to give me one last chance and God forgive me if I fucked up again.

My days were now numbered, so it was back to school for me which I fucking hated, but I was determined to be good this time.

Chapter Eleven
Abandoned

"Abandonment doesn't have the sharp but dissipating sting of a slap. It's like a punch to the gut, bruising your skin and driving the precious air from your body."

- Tayari Jones, Silver Sparrow -

One morning in the flat when I woke up my mum, she was anxious and looked apprehensive, I asked her what's the matter but said I had to pack a bag of clothes as we had to go and see something and I might be away for a few days.

I obliged and packed a few things.

I Asked again "Where are we going mum?".

"Never you mind" she said, "just hurry up and come on, we have to go, we have to meet your social worker".

"Why?" I asked.

"Because! That's all!" She snapped back at me.

We then walked to the end of our block to be met by my social worker who was sitting in her car.

We got in and drove to Swiss cottage and a place called Langtry walk-in on Rowley Way.

My social worker was leading the way, I didn't know what was going on so I just kept quiet and followed them in.

We were met by two women and three men and I was asked to take a seat as my mum had to go in the office and sign some papers when she eventually came out she said "you're gonna have to stay here for a while so be good".

She then kissed me and walked away, I didn't know what was going on.

I called after her "MUM... MUM?".

She didn't turn around she just carried on walking,

Then my social worker cunt faces (as I had decided to call her) said "you have to stay here for a while until we can arrange for you to go home".

"What do you mean I have to stay here? why"

"It's just for a little while"

"No" I said, "I want to go home".

Then the three men and women asked me to follow them.

"I want to go home" I replied.

"Come on, come with us".

"NO" I was more forceful this time, "I WANT TO GO HOME!"

My social worker then said "goodbye Terry".

"Fuck you, FUCK YOU! You bitch, fuck off you cunt!" I was so angry I just wanted to go home, all I could do was swear.

As soon as she went through the door and was out of sight one of the guys grabbed me then the second pulled me through the door, then the third one punched me in the face as they pulled me to the ground, all five of them sat on me, whilst telling me to calm down.

I was crying and trying to get up but it was useless they were too strong for me, then someone punched me in the back again and again until I stopped struggling.

One of them said "if you carry on like this, then we will do this all fucking night".

"Fuck you" I said, and I was punched again in the back and every time I swore one of them punched me.

So I bit my lip and just lay there crying until they pulled me up and took me to my room, saying "calm down, everything is going to be alright Terry, but you have to do your part, meaning no more violence or swearing".

As I sat there crying on my bed I was so confused, I'd never been punched in the face by an adult before, why had I been brought here?

Why did I have to stay here?

How long would it be? A week, maybe two?

I didn't know, but what I did know was I hated everyone, I wanted to kill these cunts and that fucking social worker of mine.

Then I thought why did my mum leave me here. Why! why! why! All I had was questions.

It took me a couple of days to get my head around the fact I wasn't going home anytime soon or maybe ever again.

If I'm honest at that particular moment, if they would have said its time for you to go home I would have refused point-blank.

I had no family, no mum, dad, brother or sisters anymore, the person I loved more than anything in my life had just abandoned me left me with these scum.

Without so much as a blink of the eye or a second thought.

To be beaten and abused like a discarded piece of shit was a bitter pill to swallow.

This was the day that I really understood hate, I hated with a vengeance, I hated everyone and everything,

I was 11 years old and I was angry, bitter and I didn't give a fuck anymore,

I was now on my own, my own man.

Once I accepted the fact that this was my new reality my defences went up, no one would ever let me down again.

Trust me it won't happen again!

As the days turned in to weeks and weeks into months I gave up on the hope that my mom would come back.

I stayed in Langtry walk for about 4 months until one morning I was woken up and told to pack my belongings.

"You're leaving us Terry"

"Why? Where am I going?" I asked.

"Don't ask silly questions, Just pack your bags, a van is waiting for you downstairs in the garages, so hurry up"

When I got in the van I asked again where they were taking me, but I only got the silent treatment, but it didn't take me long as I saw a sign on the wall, as we went through the gates.

Chapter Twelve

In front of a Judge

"Nobody gets justice. People only get good luck or bad luck"
- Orson Welles -

I was at Seymour Court Marylebone road where I was put in the front of a judge who said I had been assessed to go to Stanford house in Shepherd's Bush Goldhawk Road.

It would be my new home for the foreseeable future, a secure unit for young men, of my age and disposition he then said take him away.

I had heard of Stanford house before and was told it was a violent place, as rough as fuck and it held the worst kids in the capital.

After I left the courtroom, I was taken to a room that was guarded by a court official who told me to sit down and be quiet.

I asked him if I could please use the toilet as I haven't been all morning.

"Go down the corridor, first door on the right" he pointed as he gave me the instruction.

I walked to the toilet and walked in the wrong door, I was in the ladies, but noticed the window was open just far enough for me to climb through it if I forced it.

Before I could go in the screw shouted "no! not that door! the other one! the other one you idiot!"

I felt like saying who you calling an idiot you fucking mug, but I apologised instead.

I then went into the men's, I waited for a second then opened the door slowly, poked my head out, the guard was facing the other way, so I quickly stepped out and went into the ladies closing the door slowly.

I squeezed through the window and dropped to the floor, I wanted to shout out who's the fucking idiot now you prick.

The drop down was about 15 feet, it was easy as we were on the first floor.

After I landed I ran around the corner, there was a big double door and it was closed, I was now trapped in the courtyard of the court, with my entrance blocked, then the panic alarm went off.

"Oh fuck, I'm fucked" I thought, the alarm was so loud and I was just about to resign myself to the fact I was caught when the gates opened and a police van pulled in, the driver smiled at me, so I did likewise and took the opportunity to just walk out, I was free, I actually escaped from a court.

I walked up the road and jumped on a number 16 bus to Kilburn high road.

I kept smiling to myself and laughing then the conductor came and asked me for my ticket, I told him I'd lost my fare money.

He wouldn't have it and kicked me off the bus, it didn't matter as I was at the bottom of Kilburn high road anyway, so I just apologized and got off the bus.

I sneaked into my mum's place, so I could grab my dog flash, a blanket, a pillow and some food

Flash wasn't in, which was strange.

However I couldn't dwell on it, I made my way down to the shed under the flats where we lived, it was just big enough for me to lay down.

With the heat from my candle and my little radio, I was now as snug as a bug in a rug.

It was pissing down with rain outside and the wind was coming under the gap in the door, but at least no one would be round in this weather.

It took me ages to sleep because there was so much going on in my head, where was my dog /my Jack Russell flash?

Would I have to go to Stanford house?

Would the police be round tonight?

How would I clean myself and get clothes and food without being caught?

I woke up about 6am to the police banging on my mum's door, I heard raised voices, first, my mum's and then my dad's, fuck my dad never came to our flat in the daylight, as he always worked nights, he was a black cab driver.

So I could only assume the shit must have hit the proverbial fan!

The police searched the flat so I kept as quiet as possible even turning off the radio until I heard them all leave.

I waited for about twenty minutes before I put the Radio on, but just as I did I heard a key go in the lock of the door and my dad opened it and was standing there looking at me.

He wasn't as angry as I'd imagined him to be, he just beckoned me out and said come in the house. we need to talk.

I was expecting the police but they were gone, then I asked my mum where flash was!

She said that he went out after I went into care and just never came back.

"No" I said, then started crying.

My dad said the police had asked him to take me to Stanford house in Goldhawk Road Shepherd's Bush, otherwise, they would keep coming back.

I said "no, I'm not going there. no, NO".

Then I crawled up into a ball on the front room floor. He left me there until I was all cried out.

It took me about ten minutes to calm down, my dog was gone and my mum and dad didn't want me and now my own dad was going to take me to a secure unit for kids,

As I got in the back of the cab my mum said "be good and keep out of trouble, I love you darling" then she started crying as she walked away.

All I kept thinking about was my dog, where was he?

Dad and I didn't speak until I was outside the gates of Stanford house, then he said "it's for the best son"

"Yeah dad, yeah!" I said.

Chapter Thirteen
Stanford House

"In addition to feeling sick and tired and feverish and nauseated, I also felt forgotten. And there was no easy cure for that."

- Sarah Thebarge -

Two prison guards came out and took me into the main entrance. I could hear my dad's diesel engine start as he pulled away, but I didn't turn round. No fucking way. I was crying inside but I couldn't show that here, I walked through the main door along a long corridor then out into a massive square, it was filled with kids all just standing around and talking.

As I walked across the yard with the screw I could feel everyone's eyes on me.

I just kept walking I couldn't show any fear, then Halfway across one of the officer told me to go into an office.

I knocked on the door and heard a voice say "come in".

"Wait over there and shut the fuck up!".

There were three officers on duty, one was writing things down and the other two were talking amongst themselves,

I looked out the window and wondered what was in store for me.

I was scared but couldn't show it, I wanted to cry, run but I couldn't, I would only be brought back.

Inside I was screaming I would never see flash again or My brother or sisters, everyone I loved was gone and for the first time in my life the realisation that family doesn't mean fuck all hit me like a psychological sledgehammer.

The realisation that love doesn't conquer all, was my first reality check and one of many l would learn throughout my life.

And where was my god, the imaginable being I'd been told to pray to all these fucking years?

Where was he now that I needed him? Nowhere, I was on my own and that's just the way I liked it.

"Come here! stand there, what's your name?"

"Terry"

"Terry what?"

"Terry Ellis!"

"No!"

"It's Terry fucking Ellis sir!"

"Right! You little cunt, What's your name?"

"Terry Ellis sir!"

"Right!" I finally met the officers approval.

"You are going into Hanvey house, take your bedding and some clothes. Now fuck off, Hanvey is opposite O'Hare and next to that is church house and Hastings.

The CP is the secure unit, make sure you don't misbehave or you'll end up in there."

He then told one of the officers, to escort me over to Hanvey.

When we reached there, he just said "wait there"

Then two minutes later another officer came out and said "don't worry son. Follow me"

He took me into a little office and said "this is your new home until the foreseeable future or otherwise, you will either be assessed to go home or somewhere else.

It all depends on how you behave here , do you understand me?"

"Yes sir".

"Right follow me, this is the day room"

It had a tv and loads of chairs. Also a tennis table and a book shelf. There were large windows, which were all reinforced and shut permanently, the place was sterile and stank of disinfectant.

He then took me upstairs, there were three rooms, room 1 had 3 beds in, another with 4 beds and a big dormitory with 10 beds.

Each bed had a little locker to the right side of it, lino floors and a wash room.

No pictures, just empty magnolia walls and white high ceilings.

The place was empty so I just sat on my bed.

At 4pm school finished and my new house mates started coming in.

First a big black kid called Richard who was the oldest kid at 15 he was also the head house boy, his second in command was a tall effeminate boy called Phil and a white Irish kid called paddy.

All three of them surrounded me and said I had to pay a tax to sleep in my bed, which meant all my tuckshop money and sweets went to them.

Just for good measure Richard punched me in the face as Phil and paddy started punching and kicking me, so I took the only defensive measure I could and I just rolled up into a ball on the floor, until they eventually stopped.

It was my initiation that all the new kids had to go through, when they stopped I got up and looked around the room as all the other kids in the dormitory were now sitting or standing around in little groups as Richard and his bully pals went around the room from bed to bed Punching and intimidating them.

I sat back down and starred at them, I couldn't cry, I was all pained out, I had nothing left to give, plus no one was ever going to see me cry again, especially these fucking mugs.

The shock of being here in an environment that was feral and animalistic to me was something I just had to learn to live with,

I had to get used to the fact that I was here on my own, with no friends, no mum or dad to protect me.

They came again that night as I tried to sleep,, whack after whack came down on me , it felt as if everyone was on top of me.

I could barely breath but no sooner had it started, then it stopped. Only because the night screw had shone his light up the stairs and shouted "be quiet up there , you lot".

I wasn't the only kid being bullied as I could hear some of the other kids crying.

This went on until canteen night as one by one I saw the other kids going into Richard room , they give him his so called tax, as his sidekicks bill and fucking ben stood idly by in the doorway, smiling and smirking as they taxed all the kids.

I was then called down to get my weekly allowance of black Jack's, chocolate bars and crisps.

As I came up the stairs paddy called me over, then Phil beckoned me , but I just ignored them and went to my bed.

Before I could even sit down Richard was in my face, he snatched the bag out of my grip, as all its contents exploded onto the floor.

He started punching and kicking me until I fell onto the bed.

Phil and paddy came over and picked all the confectionary up , seeing them take it made want to kill them both, but I just sat there and consoled myself with the thought that their Guardian Richard wouldn't always be around.

I would just bide my time, the bullying and threats only lasted a couple of weeks until the next kid came into the dormitory, a small pale kid called nick.

He didn't stop crying morning , noon and night, I felt sorry for him, but he had to do his own journey, just like the rest of us.

Unlike me he called the night screw and told them about Richard and his cronies, but nothing seemed to happen as this behaviour was seen as part and parcel of the culture here.

It was a crazy place throughout the day everyone would put on a brave face , but as soon as the lights went out , the tears would replace their bravado, some kids were here because they had been brutalised by their parents or drunken dads, so some of the kids said they were happy to be here.

I listen for weeks as kids came and went, it was like a revolving door of misery for underage kids, who had been sexually abused, raped and beaten in their homes but instead of being put into a care home they had been sent here, to be bullied and abused further.

I had seen Richard chasing some of the younger kids around with his trousers off with a hard on , pretending he was playing with them, I wanted to stab him in the eye but he was so big, plus he was always with his crew.

He had been in the system for years and knew how to handle himself, violence and bullying was the only way to survive here and the weak were just meal tickets in this game of survival of the fittest.

One afternoon I was called over to the gym for a swimming lesson , me, Paddy, Phil and 5 or 6 other kids.

We were given a swimming lesson that lasted for about forty minutes by two screws who seemed to be just going through the motions, it was however the first time in weeks that I'd heard laughter, the young kids seemed so different away from the dormitory and Richard.

The dormitory environment was miserable, depressing and toxic.

After we finished the lesson , we were told that we could have 15 minutes for a recreational swim, on our own while the screw sat in the office.

Everyone was doing bombs and generally having a good time.

All I can remember was diving into the pool , then I felt a sharp pain in my back as I broke the surface I saw blood in the water.

I'd been stabbed by paddy with a sharpened metal afro comb , he was just smiling at me.

Then went to stab me again, so I grabbed his arm and pulled him under the water where I wrestled the comb from him.

I just stabbed him, the first stab was in the head, then the neck, back and side.

It felt so good, to hear him screaming and calling out for the screw , there was blood everywhere, but it felt too good to stop, I'd finally got the prick, I didn't want it to stop, I wanted to hurt him. Months of hurt and anger that I had backed up was coming out.

But someone pressed the panic alarm , it was so loud that it made me drop the comb, giving paddy an opportunity to swim to the side of the pool and get out.

The screws came from every direction , through every door at the same time, paddy was bleeding and he even pointed at me, the fucking grass.

I swam to the opposite side and got out of the pool, the officers grabbed my arms and took me to the changing room where I was told to dress, I put my trousers on over my wet trunks, trainer's and got ready, then a call came over the radio!

"Take him to the CP"

All four of them then grabbed me up, 2 on my arms , the other 2 took my legs.

It was about forty yards to the CP from the gym, I tried to get in a better position but they saw this as me trying to struggle, so one of them punched me in the stomach, then another punched me, they seemed to take it in turns to hit me as we went through the door of the unit.

I was held face down for a while as my shoes were ripped off, then someone said "corner cell", I was then taken into a room as the manager of the wing came in.

He said "fuck around down here will you?"

Whack, whack, whack he hit me with what can only be described as a small baton across my legs, before I was thrown across the room, as the door was pulled shut.

"Fuck!" I was in big trouble, but at least I was out of Hanvey house, no more nights listening to other kids crying and seeing the nightly beatings, Peace and quiet at last.

I'd swapped the mayhem of the house for the solitude of the CP block and probably sadistic care managers who liked beating young kids up.

I was taken in front of the CP kangaroo court the next morning where I was sentenced to one month in the hole.

The solitude was great at first but after a week I was going stir crazy looking out of frosted Square windows, that looked onto a kids play area, I couldn't see anything but I could hear kids playing and mums laughing.

It made me sad, I missed my brother and sisters and I kept crying.

I just wanted to go home, the month in the CP was the longest and I thought it would never end.

It was uneventful and extremely boring but apart from my introduction walloping I actually quite enjoyed my stay in there, it was bitter sweet, the screws were ok; in fact being on my own felt great, the solitude seemed to do me the world of good, I'd calmed down and accepted my fate and the fact that this was my new reality.

There would be no more family days or Christmases, no more seeing my brother or sisters.

No matter what I did from this moment onwards, my life would never be the same again.

I'd spent hours thinking and trying to imagine what my life would have been like if I'd had a normal life and parents.

But I'll never know now because this is the hand that I've been dealt.

They came for me one morning and said I'd be moving back to Hanvey, back to Richard, Paddy and Phil.

I didn't want to go , I was scared, but my ego wouldn't allow me to beg my captors or grass on Richard and the other two mugs.

I resigned myself to the fact that this evening would be one of me getting my brains kicked out, or worse still, I'd be stabbed.

A prospect that I wasn't looking forward too,

I needn't have worried because as soon as I entered hanvey I was told by nick the cry baby that Richard had been moved to church house with the older kids.

Paddy and Phil were still here, the relief I felt was overwhelming as I knew Paddy wouldn't be a problem as he was only a mug and Phil needed Richard to do is bidding , so basically the pressure was off, I hoped; unless they had formed alliances with some of the other kids.

Chapter Fourteen
Moving on in Stanford

"In three words I can sum up everything I've learned about life: it goes on."
- Robert Frost -

The dynamics and atmosphere in the house had changed beyond recognition, as it seemed the bullying culture had stopped.

This could clearly be seen on tuck night as the other kids openly ate their sweets while sitting in the tv room and around the dormitory.

I confronted Paddy in the shower, he backed down so I gave him one on the jaw for good measure leaving him curled up on the floor.

Phil was a different kettle of fish he threw his hands up straight away and said he was sorry, he said he was scared of Richard and it was the only way he could get out of being bullied himself.

He had no other choice but to join Richard and Paddy, it was a lame excuse but I understood his predicament so we called a truce.

After a week I was promoted to one of the small rooms with three others kids, one in particular joe, was from south London and the minute we met I knew I had found a kindred spirit who like me wouldn't take any shit.

We ate together, talked together and went on exercise together which sent out a message that if you fucked with one of us then you fucked with both of us, joe was a nice kid.

He wanted to run away to the new forest with his Alsatian and just live in the woods, we talked for hours imagining what it would be like to be free, away from the madness of living in here; climbing trees and swimming in the ponds with just us and our dogs, we even named them.

Mine was called Sheba and Joe's Simba, our daydreaming helped us escape the monotony and drudgery that was our existence and as the weeks turned into months any thoughts I had of going home vanished.

Until I was called into the office one morning and told that I would be receiving my assessment that afternoon, my mum and social worker would be coming up too.

The months of uncertainty would finally be over, I'd seen every one leave to go home, even Paddy and Phil had been assessed and sent home to their families and they were so much more worse than me.

I was fairly optimistic that I would be going home, I'd served my time, almost a year.

At 13 I was ready to enter civey street and get back to my beloved Camden town.

The wait felt like forever because the meeting had been rescheduled from 12.30pm to 6pm.

I was given no reason. Just a time.

When I was finally called to the dining room, opposite hanvey house I was grinning from ear to ear, my mum was sitting at the table so I ran to her and gave her a kiss and a hug.

I hadn't seen her for months she pulled me into her and said she'd missed me and couldn't wait for me to come home ,

Then my social worker, two members of staff and my keyworker came into the room, "how are you today Terry?"

"Fine" I said. "I'm looking forward to going home , and seeing my brother, sisters and friends again."

I couldn't contain myself I was smiling and cuddling up to my mum.

"Well we will have to see about that" My keyworker sniped as he pulled out a folder before starting to discuss my behaviour and school reports.

Everything seemed to be going well , everyone seemed concerned with my well-being, until my social worker said "we have found Terry a community placement at Greenacres community home in Wiltshire, we believe he still needs further support.

To return him home and to his network of friends now would be detrimental to changing his behaviour, so it's our recommendation that he be moved to Greenacres immediately."

"What's going on mum?" I asked. "I thought I was coming home?"

"It's not up to me Tel" she said, "it's their decision."

"No! NO! I want to come home!

I ain't fucking staying here"

Then I pleaded with my social worker, but she wouldn't listen she said "Terry it's for your own good."

"Fuck is it I said, I want to go home" I started crying uncontrollably, my mum started crying, then my fucking social worker put her arm around her and they both stood up and walked out.

"What the fuck is going on?"

They were gone, my last chance scuppered, these faceless bureaucrats had made a decision without taking my thoughts or feelings into account. They had mapped out my future without so much as a word from me.

I'd never even contemplated not going home today, I was crying, screaming and trying to get out of the room, my keyworker and the two officers held me back so I reached out and grabbed a knife from the wooden box on the table.

The box had three compartments one for knifes, folks and spoons, so I lashed out stabbing the officer in the arm before they all dragged me to the ground, as the bell went off and more staff came, I was then taken to the CP block again and put in a cell.

I sat there and cried until I could cry no more, then the anger came, I started kicking the door and threatening to kill everyone.

No one came, so I crawled into bed fully clothed and pulled the blue blanket over my head.

It was a week before I was allowed back into the house, joe had gone home and I was left to my own devices.

Friends come and go in these sort of places, it's funny how easy it is to let them go without a second thought.

But at least joe had gone home, my journey through the so called care system was just about to start again.

Chapter Fifteen
Christmas leave

"You can spend minutes, hours, days, weeks, or even months over-analysing a situation; trying to put the pieces together, justifying what could've, would've happened... or you can just leave the pieces on the floor and move on."

- Tupac Shakur -

It was now Christmas and I was offered the opportunity to go home for a week before my inevitable move to Greenacres was officially sanctioned, it was my last chance to see my brother, sisters and friends before I was carted off to fuck knows where.

My dad picked me up in his black cab.

"You alright son?"

"Yea dad, all good"

"Come on jump in then, everyone is waiting for us"

"Oh yeah?" I said.

As I looked out the window going down Goldhawk Road and past the big Shepherd's Bush roundabout, I noticed the bright lights of the Theatre lit up the road.

It was snowing and I could see all the Christmas lights in the shop windows, it was supposed to be a happy time but all I could feel was emptiness.

I couldn't even manage a smile I felt numb inside, the thought of moving hundreds of miles away from London and the lights, Was a bleak prospect in my mind's eye which I just couldn't shake.

The five days over Christmas seemed to fly by my sisters Tracy and Debbie were still the same, it was as if I'd never been away and my brother Steve was out most of the time down Camden town.

When I eventually went with him I was shocked to see that all my so called pals were sitting under the garages in Plender Street sniffing glue.

It was a surreal moment as in that one split second I'd lost all my respect for them and my brother.

So I jumped back on the bus and headed back home to Kilburn with only my thoughts for company.

The week was an anti-climax, disappointment; in fact I was looking forward to getting back to Stanford house.

Something in me had definitely changed I no longer felt anything for anyone.

They were just people I knew, I felt nothing, no love for them , no warmth, I had no tears left to give them.

As I got on the train to take myself back, I knew that the bond that binds us together, had been cut like an umbilical cord and tossed into the bin.

As I walked down Goldhawk Road the snow had turned to Black sludge and I could feel the wetness seeping into the bottom of my shoe, from the hole I had in it.

I had cut and put cardboard insoles into them the night before, but now they were soaking wet, I was cold, miserable and the walk along the road seemed to take forever, when I eventually got back I felt as if I'd arrived home, I couldn't wait to get back in, I'd actually missed my bed and room.

The next day we watched the great escape on the telly and as soon as we went to bed that night, back to the dormitory, everyone wanted to escape, it was a crazy idea but everyone agreed to make a break for it the next morning on the way to school.

As we walked over to the main building, all marching in two's about thirty of us, the scream went out, "ONE, TWO, THREE. . . GO!"

Then all hell broke loose everyone ran in different directions heading towards the fences and up and over, the screws were dumb struck as they watched momentarily before blowing their whistles it was organised chaos, some of the kids couldn't reach the top of the fence as the blue bands (the older kids in church house) grabbed them.

Eight had managed to get over, it was the funniest thing I'd seen for months and I cried with laughter watching it unfold.

We were all quickly put back in our houses while the captured were taken over to the CP, I don't know why I didn't just run with them?

I suppose I knew deep down that it was futile, as my dad would only bring me back.

Over the course of the day four police cars came back bringing 5 cuffed and dishevelled kids back, one had even had an epileptic fit in the middle of Shepherd's Bush roundabout a kid called John McEvilly.

Over that week we were told that one of the kids had managed to make it all the way to Gloucester on a motorbike that he'd stolen.

Two more were nicked for burglary, and one had handed himself in.

I never saw any of them again as the following day I was told to pack my belongings before a van pulled up and I was asked to go with two escorts, who would take me to Greenacres.

Chapter Sixteen
Welcome to Greenacres

"A very wise man once told me that you can't look back - you just have to put the past behind you, and find something better in your future."
- Jodi Picoult -

As we pulled through the gates of Stanford house for the last time I was sorry to be leaving as I'd gotten used to the madness, I looked back until I could see it no more.

Five minutes later we were on the motorway passing Chiswick, the journey was one of reflection and accepting the finality of my situation, there was no more ambiguity.

The maternal bond that I thought was unbreakable had been nothing more than wishful thinking on my part.

It was now time to start the next chapter of my journey, with a positive mental attitude, whilst casting aside any misguided optimism that this journey was ever going to end any other way than with me being given over to the authorities, so they could mould me into their vision of conformity.

Was this really the only option they had? To take me away from my mum, brother, sisters, friends to drive me into the middle of fucking nowhere and dump me in a community home in Wiltshire.

Carn was a little village smack bang in the middle of Swindon and Chippenham, it had a garage and a parade of shops and on the surface it looked like a poxy little shithole.

We drove about half a mile out of Carn before we came to Greenacres, it had a long driveway with trees on both sides, as we passed I noticed a little cottage, then further along there was a newish building five times the size of the little house.

We came out into the open, and I couldn't believe it, to my left was a big manor house like something out of a film, it had a large entrance, in front of the house was a football pitch, tennis court and miles of green luscious fields, it even had its own farm and next door to the manor house was a gymnasium with trampolines, wall bars, ropes hanging from the ceiling and a stage.

Further along the lane there was a massive adventure playground with ropes hanging from trees and I could see another house in the background, there were three main houses in all.

One for young kids, the other two were mixed with different ages, I was put in the big house and shown to my room on the first floor.

I looked out the window, I couldn't help wondering if I was dreaming, because I'd had a vision of locked doors, bars on the windows and screws marching up and down.

This was heaven, I could see a manicured lawn, loads of different shaped trees, this was utopia and I was standing in the middle of it.

The other kids were in school so the place was quiet, I went down to the office and was told that I could take a walk around if I liked.

I was also introduced to some of the other kids, Glen, Tom, Vince Karen, Janet , Jeff, Tina and old Reg one of the care workers.

I was also introduced to my new key worker a new age hippie looking guy called Adam who lived in a little house in the grounds.

He was softly spoken but nice with it.

My first night was eventful as no sooner had I gone to sleep, a girl climbed through my window and said I was in her bed, I told her I'd just arrived and the bedroom had been allocated to me so she better take it up with her care worker.

Tina had run away for a few days so to teach her a lesson her room was given to me, she wouldn't take no for an answer.

She pulled my covers up and got into bed with me, I spent a restless night being manhandled by her, but it was better than my first night in Stanford house.

The following morning she had disappeared again so I never mentioned her.

As I came down for breakfast that morning I felt good, even though I hadn't slept much, but at least now I was in a caring environment, with people who were here to improve our lives not break us.

That first week was a bit of a Blur as I was introduced to everyone and their mother Mr Tollor the gym teacher was a strange guy he had a Tom Selleck moustache.

He was about 5 feet of get up and go, he was only interested in the girls; watching them in their knickers and bras doing trampolining all day, he was always on my case and would never allow me into the gym when the girls were there.

Then there was old Reg an ex-army sergeant, he was always on night duty shining his torch in my face when I asleep.

He always Kept waking me up but no matter how many times I complained he just carried on.

Then there was little Craig and his missus, they were music teachers and were my favourites.

Mrs Tregenza was in charge of the farm, she was built like a brick shithouse with boiler suit and bumfluff growing from her chin, she was as strong as an ox.

The head master Mr Taylor lived in the little cottage his wife and two kids.

There was about fifty kids living on the property.

I tried going to school again but my frustration over my dyslexia kept getting the better of me, it constantly made me angry and confrontational, I was always stomping out of the classroom, which got me excluded.

I was permanently seconded to work over the farm, which was freedom to me.

Freedom to do what I wanted, freedom to get away from everyone and everything, freedom to get away from school and the problems that gave me.

Mrs Tregenza left me alone to plough the fields, make hay bales, feed the chickens, the pigs, sheep, cows and all the goats.

At Christmas I even got to kill all the chickens and turkeys by putting their necks in a metal vice before boiling and plucking them.

I was also taught to drive the tractor.

Greenacres was always a hive of activity and most of the time a happy place, we visited Stonehenge and went shopping in Swindon, the best thing I ever did there was go pot holing in Wales.

It was by far the best experience of my life especially when you consider I hated confined spaces, the day we went pot holing it was pissing down with rain we all had wet suits on as the entrance was at the edge of a stream so we had to get into the freezing cold water and climb through a little hole, that opened out in to a cave and a water fall that went down about twenty feet, we all had helmets on with a little torch on the top.

It was scary , dark and claustrophobic. I was just about to say fuck this for a game of soldiers when Richie and two of the girls Karen and Janet all started crying so the guide thought it best to let them go back.

He gave them a Mars bar each, a tin foil blanket and asked if anyone else wanted to go back to the surface.

I wanted to put my hand up but two more of the girls did and I didn't want to look like a wimp, so I bit my lip and pretended that I was eager to get down to sump one.

The others were taken out and me, Vince and Jeff continued on with our guides.

We were all soaking wet but that was the least of our problems as we now had to go over the top of this waterfall and down a rope ladder.

We all had to put a harness on and got lowered down, it was brilliant but we couldn't see for shit as the water was cascading down on us and inconveniently in our eyes, this was only sump three, sump two was a hundred foot snake-like hole that we had to crawl through, it was a really tight squeeze just to get in but no sooner as we all got in then Jeff wanted to go back, he started screaming and panicking.

I wanted to go with him but my ego wouldn't allow me to fail.

The crawl through seemed to go on forever, I kept thinking that we were going to get trapped down here and the cave was going to fill up with water, then I imagined an earthquake and being buried alive but I kept on going as I could hear Vinnie behind me saying "fuck this".

We came out into a little room that had a hole in the middle full of water, that was sump one.

That was supposedly the hardest part as we had to get in the hole and swim under water for about ten feet and come up in an even smaller room.

The first guide went with a long piece of rope that he said would be our guide.

He took a deep breath and was gone.

His light fading as he got further away.

I looked at Vinnie who was still saying "fuck this" but our guide said "it's only natural you feel like this", he gave us both a Mars bar to give us some energy, then told Vinnie that he was next.

Vinnie took a couple of deep breaths and disappeared under the water, within a second he was back breaking the surface he'd banged his head and said "I can't fucking do this!", he was shaking like a leaf and I could see the fear in his eyes.

That seemed to spur me on.

So I jumped in the water and said "no problem", I took three big breaths and dived under , pulling myself along the rope it was crazy, but I just kept going until I saw some light, then knew I'd made it.

The guide was smiling and kept saying "well done kiddo", but all I could think about was how small this room was, it was really tiny and I wondered if we would run out of air.

At least I had made it, getting back would be another story.

It was another learning experience of mind over matter, I was getting mentally stronger and today proved that.

A few weeks later I was chopping a cow's head off with a machete when a young girl, her mum and social worker walked around the corner, it was just as the head came flying off almost hitting them as it fell to the ground.

I immediately apologised, smiled and said "good afternoon".

The girl smiled back but the mum just sarcastically said "charming boy", as she pulled her daughter away and walked out of the barn, heading into the farmyard office, where they were met by Mr Tregenza.

Chapter Seventeen
Life changing moment

"I am glad that I paid so little attention to good advice; had I abided by it I might have been saved from some of my most valuable mistakes."
- Edna St. Vincent Millay -

Little did I know then, that this girl Theresa would change the course of my life for ever.

I was now 14 and getting bigger and stronger and my nightly excursions into the girls rooms had come to the attention of the night watchman who had come looking for me more than once over the last year.

The thing about community homes is we are all looking for love and the girls more than most. I spent most of my time making out with all the girls in the fields barn and bedrooms.

I was like a little rabbit and I loved it, for me it was the best thing about Greenacres, unfortunately one night as I was coming through the fire hatch between each room old Reg caught me and pulled me out onto the landing where he punched me in the stomach then in the face before he threw me head first down a flight of stairs, to horror of all the girls watching him from the banister rails, this attention seemed to bring him back on point as he quickly said I'd accidentally fallen down the stairs.

He pulled me into the office, before telling everyone to get back to their room.

When he came back he was as red as a beetroot, I thought he was going to have an heart attack. He told me off and said that would be the end of it, but only if I kept my fucking mouth shut, he then warned me to stop fucking about when he was on night duty, or next time I wouldn't be so lucky as he would throw me over the bannisters, so of course I agreed.

It was another month until Reg was on duty again but this time I'd planned a little surprise for him, I waited until he'd checked on me twice before I went out the window and down the drain pipe, I then ran over to the farmyard, broke into the office and took the padlock keys to the billy and nanny goat enclosure and let them all out together about 50 of them.

I also got a bucket load of cow shit and went to Reg's car, I smashed the driver's window and poured it all in.

I also got a tin of white paint and poured it all over the roof, the fucking prick would think twice before hitting me again.

I climbed back up the drain pipe cleaned my trainers in the sink in my bedroom, changed my clothes and hid the ones I wore in the laundry room and got back in bed and went back to sleep.

I was woken the next morning by Glen who said "someone has let all the goats out last night as there are goats everywhere, come and have a look"

I saw Mrs Tregenza, Mr Toller and Reg trying to corral them back in, it was hilarious.

I watched from the window as Reg nearly doubled in pain as the billy goat head butted him and chased after Mrs Tregenza, it took all the staff and all the other kids almost an hour to get them all back in their enclosures.

When we sat down for breakfast everyone was laughing and joking about it.

A red-faced Reg came back into the house effing and blinding that someone had wrecked his car by pouring shit and paint over it, everyone looked shocked, I just sat there eating my breakfast.

It took all my strength to keep a straight face, but I managed it, I'd gotten my own back and it felt so good because I'd done it without anyone knowing, my new tool of choice; revenge a dish served cold.

Life soon returned to normal but I managed to upset the headmaster and his wife by nicking their kids horse and riding it bare back over the field and around the grounds.

This normally mild mannered man and his adoring wife were incandescent with rage and when I brought the horse back he grabbed me and nearly shook me to death.

I'd never seen him so angry before, it was only because my keyworker Adam pulled him off me that the silly old sod didn't kill me.

I was still upset the next day, when I got up I went to the adventure playground and climbed the highest tree, I decided to crawl across from one tree to the other unfortunately, Mr Taylor and the headmaster had other ideas as they both called to me and told me to come down as I would end up killing myself.

The more they pleaded the more I wanted to do it. I was about 60 feet up and I was scared but something inside me kept saying do it, I knew it was a suicide mission but the more they called out for me to stop the more I wanted to cross it.

I climbed along the branches, then slowly reached out; I could almost touch the other branch, so I stretched out a little further then grabbed it and pulled myself across. The branch bent under my weight but I quickly pulled myself along until I was safely across.

By this time the headmaster was spitting blood calling for me to come down but I just told him to fuck off, snapped off a branch and threw it at him.

The next thing I knew the fire brigade was coming up the drive with its siren going off, there was also a police car leading it up the drive straight to me.

Adam my keyworker then called to me to come down, to which I replied "so that cunt can shake the life out of me again?

No fucking way" I said.

He then promised me that I could come to his house until I had calmed down, and that nothing would happen to me.

So knowing that I had averted another beating, I reluctantly climbed down, but not before I was given a lecture by the fire chief and the old bill for wasting their time.

I reluctantly apologised and then followed Adam to his house which was opposite the farm. I had supper with him and his wife, afterwards I played with his baby ducklings that he had in the back garden, it was great fun, until that is, it was time for me to go back and face the music.

I needn't have worried as the headmaster had found me a job in a warehouse in Carn village loading up delivery Van's and lorries.

It was great fun as I got to fly around the factory making up the orders on a battery powered pallet trolley.

The guys there were all country bumkins but a good laugh with it, at lunch times I was able to learn to drive properly as they would let me drive the vans and lorries around the yard, reversing and parking them up, it was great fun.

It didn't take me long to master it as I was driving every day; one of the mechanics taught me how to slide hammer a lorry and hot wire a car.

I spent almost 6 months working there before I was moved to another warehouse were they put me to work weighing fucking screws and putting them into little boxes.

It was the most mind numbing job imaginable and to be honest I hated every day of it, but I was on my best behaviour as I had promised Adam that I would knuckle down and stop getting into trouble.

About a week before my 15th Birthday, Adam had promised me that I could buy some jeans, trainers and a green flight jacket in Swindon or Chippenham with the money I had saved up from my job.

I was also running most morning, doing press ups, pull ups and boxing in a boxing club in a little village just outside Carn, which made me physically stronger.

I was defining my physique by trampolining and working on the horse in the gym most afternoons, which gave me muscles on muscles.

Life was good and in a couple of years I would be allowed to get a provisional license, probably do my driving test and move back to London.

Again, just when I was starting to dream again that my future was going to be ok, the shit hit the proverbial fan, as I was ordered by Craig to go to the headmaster office.

As I entered the room I saw my social worker and keyworker Adam, they all looked perplexed and all gave me a look that said it all I was in trouble.

What had I done this time?

I sat down and my social worker said she would taking back to London today with immediate effect, "why?" I asked her.

"Because your girlfriend Theresa is pregnant Terry that's why!"

Theresa was the girl who walked through the farmyard with her mum when I was cutting the cows head off.

"Oh my God" I gasped, "are you joking?"

"No I'm not joking Terry

We have to leave straight away, let's pack your stuff" she replied as she was getting up to leave the room.

"But I want to speak to Theresa"

"No you can't, she has already gone she has already been moved"

"Oh fuck off" I shouted, "why can't I see her?"

"It's school policy, she has been moved back to foster care in Cambridge"

"Are you fucking joking? I need to see her now"

"I'm sorry Terry that's not possible let's go"

To say I was flabbergasted would have been an understatement, "where will I live now?" I asked.

"Don't worry Terry, we have arranged for you to move into a shared flat in swiss cottage, a place called Dorney towers, you'll be sharing with two older boys and be back in London."

I was fifteen years old and in nine months I would be a dad, I needed to sort myself out and really quickly if I wanted to raise a child, the irony was I'd be a kid trying to raise a child and Theresa was only fourteen.

The system wouldn't allow this to come out into the open.

Chapter Eighteen
Coming back to London

"Life is ten percent what happens to you and ninety percent how you respond to it."
- Charles Swindoll -

I arrived back in London that afternoon feeling great that I was finally back but felt terrible at the fact Theresa was on her own, back in a Cambridge foster home.

I couldn't worry about that now as I had a responsibility to get myself a job and try my best to be a dad.

I signed on the dole that day with the help of a letter given to me by my social worker, this meant that my rent would now be paid and I would receive twenty three pounds a week.

The flat was on Adelaide Road, on 17th floor.

I was with my social worker when we first visited it, she had given me a key to the entrance down stairs then two more keys, one for the front door and the other for my bedroom.

The kitchen was really small just like in the series only fool's and horses, the front room was small too, it had a tv, a three-seat sofa, coffee table and a little bin.

No balcony but the view was breath-taking, I could see across London, Camden Town, Swiss Cottage and if I looked hard enough I could see Kilburn where my mum lived.

I was back in the heart of London and literally on top of the world, Regent's Park, Primrose Hill and London Zoo were just across the road.

I couldn't have asked for a better spot.

Being here was the easy bit, I now had to earn some money, which was going to be hard, Simply because I was 15 years old, dyslexic, I had no formal education, no skills and I was pot less.

Oh and I couldn't cook either, but I tried my best. My first attempt was to try to cook eggs, bacon, sausages and beans for breakfast.

Boiled potatoes, mince and carrots for tea and a loaf of bread thrown in for supper.

After spending all my money on food and milk for the week I was now skint so I popped down to the local job centre in swiss cottage and blagged a job filling skips.

It was hard work but I had no other option, my choices were limited I either starved or did labouring jobs.

I never saw the other two guys in the flat as they were always out and when they did come in they were either pissed or with their girlfriend's.

So I kept myself to myself it was a lonely existence but I was determined to do it on my own without any help from my friends, family or my fucking social worker who now had disappeared off the face of the earth.

This was because I was now classed as an adult, I was signing on the fucking dole, which now meant that she could literally wash her hands of me and absolve herself of any responsibility for my future actions.

I did what I had to do for months, but the truth was I wasn't living, I was just existing.

There had to be more to life than this surely, I was just working eating and sleeping , I was taking home one hundred and ten pounds a week, which meant after rent, travel expenses and food I could just about afford a packet of ten number 6 cigarettes and a can of coke.

I needed something else before I went crazy looking out my bedroom window every night, at a city that I couldn't even afford to go out in.

Every day I was surrounded by wealth in Hampstead Heath, Highgate and Primrose Hill. Big fancy houses, lovely restaurants, flash cars, and I couldn't even afford a packet of fags.

Then one evening I met Lee one of the others guys in the flat and his mate Chris who lived in barking.

They both seemed easy going, we had a few beers and something to eat. By the end of the night I was well and truly pissed, but so were they.

Lee mentioned that if I wanted to earn some easy money then he had something that I would definitely be interested in, but only when the time was right, well that time was definitely now as I was pot less.

I was as sick as a dog that night as it was the first serious drinking session I'd ever had and god I paid for it.

I was even late for work the next morning, my bosses Dave and his son John tried to lay down the law, but after a minute or two I told them to shove their fucking job where the sun don't shine and threw the shovel at them as I fucked off back to the flat with my hangover.

Lee was there when I got back to the flat, I told him what had happened and he just laughed and said "don't worry" gave me one hundred quid and said "I'll talk to you later when I get back".

He'd given me one weeks wages and it was only Monday, so I spent the day sorting out my room and did some shopping for the week.

I've always been organised I don't spend money that I haven't got and I was learning very quick to stretch every penny throughout the week , but my EGO and temper had gotten the better of me again so it was either the job centre or wait and see what Lee had up his sleeve ,

It was the easiest decision that I'd ever made, I would see what Lee and Chris were up to, as they seemed to have loads of money all the time and different birds coming and going at every hour and I wanted some of that.

That evening Lee asked me to pop over the pub with him, we were met by Chris who greeted me with a smile and a firm handshake.

After a couple of drinks Lee said "we have something for you but you need to think about it because if you get nicked you'll end up doing an hefty bit of bird."

"No problem!" I said "what is it?"

"Well we are armed robbers and we need someone like you, just to do what we ask; like if I said look menacing or if called upon use violence and a gun, do you think you can do that?"

"Of course mate no problem I'm definitely in"

I said "I've actually got a post office that we can do in Rowley Way"

"Is that the Langtry walk post office?" Lee asked.

"Yes" I said, "I used to be in a kids home there and every week I used to see the post master drive to the back of the post office, then open the back door, unload his car, leaving the back door open, he drives his car and parks it on the main road.

All we have to do is hide behind the bins and when he drives out we just walk in and wait for him to come back in and tie the cunt up, open the safe it's easy. In fact I could probably do it on my own"

"Ok then if you think it's a goer than we will do it next Monday, when everyone cashes their gyros, what do you reckon Chris?"

"Yes, I'll arrange the cars and drop off the guns Sunday night"

"Ok then it's a date!"

I spoke to Lee two days later, he said "ok Tel what time does the post master open up ?"

"He gets there at 7.20am the time lock on the safe comes off at 8.40am and the post office doors open at 9am.

I've looked at it twice this week, the guy is as regular as Clockwork trust me this is going to be a doddle"

"Ok, this is your job, it's your responsibility so get it right."

"No problem Lee, I'll have this cunt wrapped up before you even get in there."

"Ok let's see" said Lee.

We all stayed at the flat that night playing chess, no drinking just clear thinking, I went to bed about twelve o'clock but it took a while to get off to sleep.

After that night there would be no going back.

I would be forever looking over my shoulder wondering if today was the day they caught me, which would be inevitable.

I would be locked up for years, it didn't bear thinking about, my career trajectory was on a collision course with planet prison, but until then I would compartmentalise it as just an occupational hazard plus it was better than just existing on the dole.

I tossed and turned all night, unexpectedly I was as fresh as a Daisy when I woke up.

Chapter Nineteen

The first rung on the ladder of the criminal underworld

"When a man is denied the right to live the life he believes in, he has no choice but to become an outlaw."
- Nelson Mandela -

Lee and Chris were also awake, I tried on my jacket, balaclava, black gloves and brandished my new tool of trade my new sawn-off shotgun.

I was scared but at the same time I felt invincible, alive and stronger than I ever felt before.

Today was my initiation into the big League my day to prove to myself that my dyslexia could fuck off and do one.

I'd found my calling and it was exhilarating to think that in less an hour I would be crossing a line that many men dream of but haven't the bottle to see it through.

We had talked the night before so there was little or nothing to say this morning apart from let's go ,we all knew what we had to do ,
As we pulled up in the car I noticed an old pal walking past , he was the new caretaker of Rowley Way and a kick boxing champion to boot , so to say I was pleased when he turned the corner and started walking in the opposite direction was an understatement, my old pal Peter Crimmins the last thing I needed today was to shoot a friend.

It was 7.15am when we took our positions Chris was in the car , Lee was standing on the corner and I was behind the bins, I could feel the butterflies in my stomach but at the same time I was really calm,
Then the postmaster pulled up, I let him open up , unload and drive around the corner to where Lee was, I then casually walked into the back of the Post Office.

Pulling my balaclava over my face whilst taking the shotgun out of my jacket, it was my time to make my mark.

Then two minutes later he walked through the door so I pointed the gun at him and said "get on the fucking floor and put your hands behind your back, now!"

But he panicked and started screaming so I put him in a headlock and put him to the floor while telling him "calm down, everything is going to be ok, do you understand me?: he struggled for a bit before saying "Ok, ok".

"Right! now ! put your fucking hands behind your fucking back."

He did as I said, so I cuffed him up, then asked him where the safe keys were. He said in his pocket.

So I quickly retrieved them, just as Lee came through the door. I said keep him quiet and face down, my adrenaline was pumping and I felt great.

I went into the post office on my hands and knees as there was about 15 people queuing up outside, all waiting for their gyros.

So, I put the shotgun down beside me, opened the cage and Crept in keeping my head down.

The time lock was on the front of the safe so I waited for a bit but it seemed like an eternity.

8.40am so, I took a deep breath and removed the box off the front of the safe, it tripped the alarm, so I put the keys quickly in the lock and opened it up, bingo yes.

The safe was packed with money stamps notes and change so I opened my holdall bag and filled it to the brim, and looked over the counter.

There were old dears banging on the windows with some young mothers and a couple of unemployed guys they all looked pissed off.

I kept my head down and tried to open the cage but the door wouldn't open.

I was locked in, I'm fucked I thought, I noticed that there was a key in the parcel Hatch, I quickly turned it and the hatch went up leaving just enough room for me to push the bag and the gun through, I reached through and pulled myself out.

Lee had already gone so I tapped the post master on the shoulder and said no hard feelings mate as I walked out the back door shutting it as I left.

When I reached the corner I could see Chris and Lee in the car so I calmly walked the 50 yards or so as not to draw attention to myself. I could hear the alarm going off and police sirens coming towards me.

We had plenty of time, there was no need to panic now the hard work had already been done, all we had to do now was keep calm and drive ourselves to the other getaway car . Which was just up the road.

As I got in the car Lee was saying "hurry up bruv quickly, we have to move."

Then Chris pulled away from the kerb wheels screeching it was his turn to do his bit and within 5 minutes we were sitting in the back of a two door Capri, heading home Scott free, my first job done with no drama.

We had gotten away with £3500 pounds and an extra thousand pounds in coins and another £200 in stamps, we had arrived , I'd never seen so much cash in one place it felt surreal holding it, this was my new reality.

Chapter Twenty

My first robbery spree and the long, violent arm of the law

"To have once been a criminal is no disgrace. To remain a criminal is the disgrace."
- Malcolm X -

We went on a Robbery spree that included banks, building societies and the odd van that lasted just over a year.

I was living large, I had rented a room in Hampstead and was living like a king. Theresa had given birth to our son Tony but the distance made it impossible for me and she couldn't wait any longer ,for me to move to Cambridge, so she decided to rekindle her relationship with an old boyfriend in the process dumping me.

As much as I tried to contact her she wouldn't have anything to do with me, so that was that ,there was nothing I could do.

By this time I was entering into the club scene, going to the Camden Palace, the Electric Ballroom, the low profile and the tunnel club in Hampstead along with many other popular nightspots in and around Camden.

It was brilliant, I was having the time of my life birds, booze and cocaine.

I met a girl called Mary who said her dad worked in China but as it transpired his name was Cecil Parkinson an MP and Margaret Thatcher's right-hand man.

I never met him but he probably knew who I was, I used to meet up with Mary at the music machine in Camden Town, every night we would get drunk together, take drugs and go home.

I'd wake up in the afternoon, it was mental lifestyle but I was young and loving every minute of it. I had so many birds it was impossible to keep up with them all.

I had an au-pair called Annie in Swiss Cottage and a lap dancer in Hampstead called Angie there just wasn't enough hours in the day to keep up with my life style.

One evening I arrived home and parked my motorbike a few streets away then walked home as normal, I went up the fire escape and through the back door and for some reason I had a funny feeling that made the hairs on my neck stand up, I took the keys out of my pocket and turned the key in the lock, then

I heard it.

"Stand still!"

"Put your fucking hands up!"

"Don't fucking move"

Before I could react, there were 3 guns inches away from my head.

Someone pistol wiped me across the head, another kicked me in the bollocks, before I was man handled to the ground.

I was in a state of shock, this was the last thing I expected or fucking needed but there was also feeling of calmness that took me by surprise as up until now I had treated what I was doing as a game.

Now it was real.

I was definitely going to prison, the only questions now was for how long?

My whole world had just been turned upside down and all I could think of was I will never see my son grow up.

It was a bitter sweet moment but it was my choices that got me here in the first place, so l had to admit to myself that I was lazy, I didn't want a real job, I wanted to live the high life and that life unfortunately comes at a cost, a price that I now had to pay.

Chapter Twenty One

Prison Calling

"He who sells what isn't his, must buy it or go to prison."
- Daniel Drew -

With the possibility of years behind bars, a really daunting prospect for a young upstart of only 17 years of age, but one I had always accepted for myself and for that reason I took it in my stride.

I spent three days with the Finchley robbery squad, apparently they had arrested Chris and the slippery cunt had thrown me and Lee under the bus for the Langtry walk robbery, it was another bitter sweet moment, as one of my so called own had grassed me up, for no other reason than to save his own pathetic skin.

He had even told them where I had hid the guns at my nans flat, which was also a surprise to her, as I hadn't even told her that they were hidden in her airing cupboard, behind her water tank.

Thank God the old bill didn't go in heavy handed as my old nan was in her late 60s.

My criminal lifestyle had ramifications as my nan had now been raided and to stop them charging her, I had to put my hands up and go guilty.

It was a bitter pill to swallow but one I would gladly do again, as I had made a stupid mistake by leaving the guns round there in the first place, a mistake I would never make again.

I had been careless to trust someone I barely knew, just because he talked like me and knew people I knew, but he was not like us, he was a wrong'en, a fucking grass.

But there's no point in crying over spilt milk.

I went guilty and was promptly remanded to Ashford remand centre, where I had the opportunity to meet some of the most dangerous, sadistic cunts that God had bestowed on the human race.

Screws!

I was only inside a day when a guy had a go at Lee so I ended up knocking him out in the showers.

His pal took offence to this so while I was queuing up for dinner the next day he tried his best to let me know he was top dog there by saying that if I stepped out of line again he would personally educate me.

He then added "trust me mate you don't know who your fucking dealing with".

I took my metal tray and smashed it straight across his face, I kept whacking him until the screws dragged me off him.

He was covered in blood and looked fucked, but I had proved my point.

I was from North London and if you fuck with me then you better fight me, not try and talk me to death.

For my sins I was dragged down the block and if I thought it would be just a matter of course that I would be banged up for the night, then returned to the wing a few days later, I was truly mistaken.

Because these screws had other ideas, I was taken to a cell and unceremoniously chucked in and charged with good order and discipline and told that I would have to go in front of the governor the next morning to determine my fate.

There were 8 cells all roughly 12-ft Square with high ceilings, the walls were magnolia, hard lino floors, there was one shower cubicle on the block and a sit down toilet next to the screws office, all the cells had a piss pot and a metal bed screwed down to the floor, a jug of water and a white bowl to wash yourself in.

There was no bedding in the cell as it was given to you in the evenings, every morning you had to fold it up and leave it on a shelf opposite the screws office.

It was hard to see out of the window unless you wanted to look up into the sky, as there was a metal cage in front of it.

The cells had no TV, no books, just a bible on the window sill, it was designed to drive you mad, boredom by solitude was their weapon of choice, no one on the landing was allowed to talk and god help you if you shouted to your next door neighbour or tried to communicate with anyone else, silence was the order of the day , break it at your peril.

The next morning I was informed that I had an adjudication at nine prompt in front of the governor and true to their word I was outside his office at one minute to nine with four Burly screws waiting to go in, the atmosphere was tense, I had been accompanied from the block without so much as a word being exchanged between the officers and myself.

I was just informed that when I went into the office I had to give my name Ellis and prison number av8856.

Other than that they kept quiet until the charge was read to me.

As we entered the room I was confronted with a one eyed governor and his head of security, the two guards stood in front of me but facing me which was a display of authority and intimidation, while the other two ex-soldier screws stood behind me, they were so close I could feel their breaths on the back of my neck.

I was asked my name and number and asked if I pleaded guilty or not guilty.

"Not guilty sir" I replied.

An officer read out an incident report and I was told that there was overwhelming evidence to support the charge and to my utter amazement I was found guilty and sentenced for good order and discipline to 28 days in the segregation unit.

I tried to protest my innocence but I was quickly pushed out the door, punched and kicked, then dragged back to the block.

The beating didn't stop until I was outside my cell.

I thought it was over but I was mistaken, they threw me through the door sideways, I banged my head and legs on both sides of the door , then they all set about me telling me that if I stepped out of line in their block they would break every bone in my body.

As suddenly as they started they had gone, my right eye was swollen and my head, neck and legs felt as if I'd been ten rounds with Mike Tyson.

I never had time to contemplate the ramifications of my situation as they were back outside my door, so I quickly stood up and backed into the corner and waited for the door to open and the onslaught to begin.

Instead of a beating , a little prick came in while the other three stood in the doorway, he plonked down a bucket, a bar of white Windsor soap, scrubbing brush, a cloth and a rubber kneeing pad,
he then informed that I had to scrub every inch of the cell daily and failure to do so would end badly for me.

He then gestured to the bucket so I took it dipped the brush in the warm water and soaped the brush, I knelt on the rubber knee pad and started to scrub the floor it took me about forty minutes, then the door was opened so I could empty the bucket and put it back in the wash room.

I was told I had to make my bed pack up and place it back on the shelving.

It had to be folded squarely, blanket sheet, second blanket sheet, fire blanket then pillow.

I did it to perfection then stood back while they inspected it , I was then asked if I thought it was done properly, to which I replied "yes sir", he then kicked it across the floor and said it was shit, "do it fucking again".

I did it again making sure it was perfect but he kicked it again, then all four of them started beating me again, but this time I managed to fight my way past them and into my cell and rolled under my bed.

A big Irish, white-shirted screw tried to kick me but missed, unfortunately for him, his shin made contact with the metal bed strut which must have hurt as he went ape shit, effing and blinding and calling me all the cunts under the sun.

I stayed there until they were gone, fucking hell this wasn't even my first full day down the block, but nevertheless I had a black eye, I was battered and bruised all over.

The block was cold, I never had any bedding to keep me warm and the only place to have a shit was in a piss pot in my cell. This was my life, the days seemed to drag like I'd never known before, I was always hungry, cold and dying for a fag.

I counted down each day - at this point I had 27 days to go.

You quickly learn in prison that in order to do the time you map out routine and break your day up so the time doesn't seem as long.

The days started at 7 o'clock and the first task each day was to put my bedding out, seconds was slop out (which was the delightful job of emptying your piss pot), then breakfast, then scrub the floor.

    12.30: dinner

    2.30: exercise 1 hour

    4.30: tea then take your bedding back in.

After that you were banged up until the next morning.

This was the hardest part of the day because there was no TV, no padmate to speak to so you are alone with nothing but a bible and your own thoughts to occupy the next 14 hours.

The kicking's stopped as soon as I adhered to their regime, but every time someone new came on the spur the same thing would happen to them, I would see stroppy young kids coming down the block like myself full of testosterone and eager to show they were Tough Guys, but the minute they came out of the governor's office the reality of their situation would hit home.

They soon realised that they were no longer legends in their own heads but scared terrified young kids.

It was all a game to the screws who believed in what they were doing as they seemed to enjoy their sadistic behaviour, it came at the expense of the kids they were brutalising on a daily basis.

The month went by slowly, when it did end I was glad to see the back of it.

Unfortunately for me though, I managed to get in another fight a week later where I broke some guys jaw and was given another 28 day down the block on for it to be extended for another 56 days.

Thankfully the screws knew me now so I was excluded from the initiation ceremony and the beating.

As the days turned into months the anger was replaced by monotony and a renewed determination to keep out of trouble.

I filled my days by doing a thousand press ups, burpees and sit ups.

Chapter Twenty Two

A time to reflect

"The way we experience the world around us is a direct reflection of the world within us."
- Gabrielle Bernstein -

I was sentenced to four years and considering my first 3 months were to be spent down the block, where a day felt like a week and a week felt like a month; my total sentence felt much larger than it actually was.

After I was sentenced I was transferred to Chelmsford where I stayed for four months until I was moved to Aylesbury Young offenders prison.

Aylesbury was an old Victorian prison the windows were seven feet off the ground , the cells were dark and dank and within twenty minutes of arriving I'd trayed a geezer on the hot plate for no other reason than the way he slammed down the food on my plate , he was trying to let me know that he was in charge but my reaction was one from months of frustration which he unfortunately was the catalyst.

I was banged up on the wing with no association for 2 weeks which was supposed to teach me a lesson, but I was lucky enough that the wing TV was just opposite my cell, so I just watched it through the crack in my door.

Aylesbury was a volatile place filled with young men from London, Birmingham and the surrounding areas that were all thrown together.

Which was a recipe for disaster.

Three months into my stay there, me and one of my pals had a run in with two big black guys from Birmingham over a game of pool.

My pal wouldn't back down so I offered to help him, unfortunately for us though one of the guys was built like a brick shithouse, so my pal opened him up.

I did the other guy, who was a proper mouthy cunt, with a knockout punch to the jaw.

Because my pal took a razor blade to the other guy cutting him, firstly down the face and then straight across the chest, he was nicked by the old bill which meant he could face additional charges.

It was a crazy situation, I can remember was him running down the landing screaming and covered in blood, as his brother was laid out unconscious on the floor next to the pool table.

Luckily for me the brothers were shipped out to another prison and my pal was moved back to London. I was given 28 days down the block, I didn't mind as I was allowed plenty of books from the library.

The rest of my stay was uneventful and before I knew it I was going home.

I'd done two long years behind the door, my leaving was bitter sweet as I would be leaving good friends behind, Randy, Harry and the Leary, all pals from Camden town and all armed robbers.

The night before I left we all played music out the window, Phil Collins a bit of reggae, it was the best night of my stay by far.
In the morning my door was opened before anyone else's, so I took the opportunity to say my goodbyes through the crack in the doors, then I made my way down to reception.

Just one small bag and my guitar which I donated to the prison, I then I signed my papers , then left the building through the front gates.

Chapter Twenty Three

Freedom - A fresh start

"You have brains in your head. You have feet in your shoes. You can steer yourself any direction you choose."
- Dr. Seuss -

Just smelling the fresh air felt so good. I'd been dreaming of this moment for two long years.

I promised myself that on this first day of freedom I would walk to the top of the hill and touch that tree that had been my view out of my cell window for so long. I was going to play my guitar, then sit on the green grass, smoke a fag and cleanse myself of the stench of Aylesbury forever.

But instead I walked into the first sweet shop I came to and bought myself 20 Bensons and Hedges, a Mars bar and a can of coke. This was my celebration.

I then walked to Aylesbury train station, where I jumped on the train back to London. It felt great seeing all the pretty faces and listening to normal conversations. My first stop on reaching London was to see my probation officer in Arlington Road Camden Town.

I rang the intercom and was buzzed in by the reception girl who kept smiling at me from the minute I walked in, maybe she could feel the animalistic nature of the Beast just waiting to be unleashed after my little stint in prison. So I gave her a smile back and sat down and waited.

After about 10 minutes the reception girl came from behind the counter and went through the door to the toilets, she looked beautiful I couldn't take my eyes of her, she was a pretty little thing who had such a beautiful smile.

My gaze seemed to awaken something in her, as no sooner had she opened the door than she beckoned me to follow her into the ladies toilets. So I did as she asked and as I entered she put her finger up to my lips and told me not to speak. She then quickly locked the door and pulled up her dress, then pushed me to the wall and straddled me standing up.

It felt so good after so long, we kissed and caressed each other until she started shuddering with pleasure as we came together, then she put her finger to my lips again and said shush as she tidied herself up. She unlocked the door and walked out without saying a word, not even a thank you very much she just went back to continue her duties behind the glass partition.

I stayed there for a minute or so, so I could catch my breath. I couldn't believe what had just happened, but I wasn't complaining, in fact it felt great to back in London, my beautiful Camden Town and me all grown up, a man and not a boy any more.

After speaking to my probation officer I learnt that the girls working on the reception desk were all doing job experience after being released from a woman's prison.

She also informed me that I would be living in a hostel in the old police station in 90 West End Lane, West Hampstead next door to the railway pub.

I was only there a couple of months when I met an India girl called Natalie, who was a part time model and worked at a picture framing place in Kilburn, she was going out with the owner who was a millionaire and drove an Aston Martin.

But after meeting her a few times and spending a few nights together she decided that money wasn't everything and 6 months later we were married.

I got myself a job and was living an honest life working as a scaffolder, it was hard work but it kept me fit.

We had son called Kyle, unfortunately the marriage didn't last long as she had decided that having more kids at that time would be detrimental to her enjoying her life.

I only found this out after coming home from work one day to be told by her mum that she was in hospital recovering from having a termination that she didn't even discuss with me, I decided that any trust or feelings I had for her were now null and void. I packed my gear and left that night, but we did have a son who I'm remarkably proud of.

Chapter Twenty Four

Kelly

"Every strike brings me closer to the next home run."
- Babe Ruth -

It was exactly 3 minutes after leaving Natalie that I met my long-time girlfriend Kelly and the mother of my three daughters Charlene, Terri and Chloe.

It was a simple but honest meeting of two people who needed each other at that moment in time. I was walking down the road with my belongings when Kelly came up beside me and asked me where I was going, as she had wrongly assumed I was going on holiday with my bags packed.

It was an endearing and honest mistake, but she had a way about her that I liked straight away.

She also had a little twinkle in her eye, so I told her that I'd just separated from my wife and was now temporarily homeless. She seemed taken back but Kelly being the kind hearted person she was, offered me a place to stay in her hostel, emphasising with a smile that there was no strings attached.

Not being one to look a gift horse in the mouth I immediately took her up on her offer, plus she was a cracking little bird who had a beautiful smile and I fancied her the minute she opened her mouth. We eventually tied the knot that night and the rest is history as they say.

We squatted for a while until the Council gave us a place. When she was pregnant with a second child Terri, I managed to get myself into a bit of trouble whilst out having a Christmas drink with some friends.

I was walking along the street when I was pulled up by two plain clothed old Bill who I wrongly assumed were trying it on with me, so I ended up knocking one of them out and the other over the bonnet of a car on his arse, then stupidly continued to walk home.

Two minutes later a police van pulled up beside me and before I knew it six plod were beating the shit out of me before I was handcuffed and taken to West Hampstead police station, where I head butted the desk sergeant after he slapped me in the face.

For this indiscretion I was subsequently given a year in prison for assaulting a member of the Constabulary.

It was on this sentence that I met Stevie Kent, a 50 year old guy who was known as the king of the jump ups. He taught me everything he knew about sign ups, jump ups and anything else he knew, by the time I returned to civvy street I was his new prodigy and I took to it like a duck to water .

Chapter Twenty Five

Jump ups - a new revenue stream

"Some people steal to stay alive, and some steal to feel alive. Simple as that."
- V.E Schwab, A Darker Shade of Magic -

How a jump up works is really simple. We would follow vans and lorries as they came off the motorway into London, as they made their deliveries we would bolt-cropper the locks and empty them of their cargo.

It really was that simple and London being London it was like the streets were paved with gold, we took everything.

Computers, clothes, cigarettes and booze the list was endless and the money just came rolling in.

It was like taking candy from a baby, I loved the job so much that I got up at 6 o'clock each morning to catch the lorries coming off the motorway at Brent cross.

There was me, John, Jerry, Tommy and Ronnie. They were so good at their jobs and we made a great team.

I managed to buy a house in Camden town, a Shogun Jeep, a Volvo 850 and a convertible Saab.

Kelly had a Previa people carrier and a Ford Jeep, we were living large, we took the kids to Disneyland stayed in a 5-star omni hotel in Sunset Boulevard and I was back and forth to Spain. Life was good.

Out of the blue one day the filth were all over us. We had nicked a computer lorry and Jeremy my good pal had decided to use a new buyer so had arranged to meet them at Chalk Farm train station.

One of the buyers had pulled out twenty grand and was flashing it about and soppy bollocks Jeremy had unfortunately taken the bait , but thank God I was watching from a distance and told Jeremy to move the meet up the road to Swiss Cottage where I had a better vantage point as I thought they were old bill.

No sooner had I arrived at swiss cottage that I saw what was quite clearly plod everywhere; two walking up and down the street, a man and woman with jackets on that I recognised, there was about 10 to 15 of them, all plain-clothes.

I gave Jeremy the signal that they were old bill, but he just wouldn't listen as he kept saying "I've seen the money they're ok Tel".

But I shouted down the phone telling him to get the fuck out of there, he still wouldn't listen, he just kept talking bollocks so I said "you're on your own then mate, I'm off".

As I drove past him I saw them all flop on him, he was handcuffed and placed face down on the ground.

I drove straight to mine and grabbed some money my passport and was just about to open the front door when two car loads of coppers pulled up and ran into my block cutting my exit off, I ducked down and made my way to the downstairs toilet window as the plod started banging on my next door neighbours door, who just so happened to be an ex old bill, luckily for me he was out.

They were now looking in my window and after about ten minutes they calmed down a bit as my other neighbour came out and said he saw my other neighbour leave in their car twenty minutes earlier and thinking my neighbour was me, they jumped back in their cars and disappeared.

I took the opportunity to just walk out, jumped on an underground train, to Hampstead were I met Kelly, telling her what happened and that I thought it best if I fucked off to Spain until things blew over.

She understood, we said our goodbyes had a cuddle, and I reassured her that everything would be fine.

Chapter Twenty Six
Escape to the Continent
"Every moment is a fresh beginning."
- T.S. Elliot -

I called a pal and asked him to book me a train ticket to Dover and a ferry ticket to France.

He booked it in his name with me as the reference name to pick it up on his behalf, I used to do this all the time so I knew that this procedure would throw any one off my tracks, especially the old bill as they would have expected me to book a ticket in my name, which is exactly what I did next.

I booked a flight to Amsterdam for Schiphol Airport from Heathrow which I hoped would set off alarm bells, with the filth waiting for me at Heathrow Airport I went to Charing Cross and jumped on the train to Dover.

From there I got on the ferry to Calais, hired a car and drove to Lloret de Mar where I changed cars again before heading up to Marbella, Malaga and Fuengirola where I rented a Villa in Benalmadena between Winn's bar and Chequers bar.

It didn't take me long to settle in as I told the locals I'd just gotten divorced and had come to Spain to get away from it all, I met a girl call Julie who worked in Chequers bar and whose dad owned the car hire place.

In Winn's bar I also chatted up the barmaid, a tall Mediterranean girl called Catherine, I would spend the weekends with her and the rest of the week with Julie , an arrangement that suited me well.

I had been introduced to a guy in Marbella through a pal of mine in London, I had planned to start bringing in my own puff and earning some money, and within a month or so I started bringing in puff from Morocco, bringing it into a little place in coin just outside Fuengirola, the puff would be landed by a rib (speedboat) on the beach.

I would pick it up in the dead of night, I would then take it to a little place in coin, count it, vacuum seal it, then repack it and drive it up to Valencia or Alicante , it was a 340 mile journey or 680 miles all round.

A journey through the A roads, it would normally take me about 15 hours for the round trip, it was exhausting but dangerously exhilarating as every trip was different.

My day used to start about 4amI would drive to coin pick up about 300 kilos then drive to Benalmadena, via the hill restaurants as it had a petrol station (service station) there.

We would all fill our cars up, my car had Valencia number plates, my two pal plates consisted of one Malaga and the other English.

The reason for this was because the Guardia civil and the national police (national civil police force of Spain CNP) were proper bastards they had motorbikes, vans, cars and were very resourceful, they could set up a rolling road block in seconds , so we had to be one step ahead of them and on point.

The front driver would drive ahead about five kilometres with Malaga plates and the back driver would have English plates.

If there was a road block he would phone me and let me know,
I would turn off immediately.

If the police set up a rolling road block then I would pretend to pull over which would be the signal for the back driver with the
English plates, to speed up and draw them away.

Normally because he had English plates the police would wrongly assume he had drugs on him and speed after him giving me the opportunity to get away to fight another day.

It was a tried and tested method and it worked on a number of occasions, a situation that left me sweating and emotionally spent.

The drive was monotonous especially after doing it 12 or more times over that first year, we started using vans and sometimes lorries driving up tons of puff, it was by far the best experience of my life up to this point.

I just loved doing it, As it was like being in the movies, but with us the good guy and the Guardia civil the baddies.

When I wasn't working I spent my days on the nudist beach with either Julie or Catherine or going out on my jet skis.

I was living the high life; eating in the best restaurants in Puerto Banus and I lived in eStark 92, just outside Fuengirola, most nights I would come out of there about 5am.

The guys and myself were putting our lives on the line most weeks,
so we used it as an excuse to party like crazy at the weekends, estark 92 was probably the best place to unwind, the hostesses came from all over the world and were out of this world tall Brazilians, Swedish and Russians.

Some nights I would end up with two or maybe three girls in one bed just sniffing and drinking champagne, it was wonderfully surreal, I was a boy from Camden who had done what most people could only dream about.

I saw myself as a pioneer, not one of those people who sat on their fat arses dreaming about sourcing it, I was buying it from the source instead of getting it off some mug on the back streets of London.

I was an explorer who was changing the way we did things, I wanted it all and I would do whatever it took to get it, but I never hurt anyone in the process.

I wasn't a wannabe gangster like some of the mugs who I met in Spain, who talk a good game and who are Legends in their own heads.

I never carried a gun because I always worked with proper people, if you don't rip people off or disrespect them, then you will never get any trouble, you will have a prosperous and happy life instead of being killed or being put on a life support machine in hospital.

A scenario I'd seen played out a million times over there, some people forget that the whole idea of this job is to keep off the radar, the less heat you bring to yourself, the more prosperous you'll become, so why draw unnecessary attention to yourself by needing to be someone you ain't.

My life had changed beyond recognition.

But like most things in life there is always a price to be paid.

Chapter Twenty Seven

A price to be paid

"Understand there is a price to be paid for achieving anything of significance. You must be willing to pay the price."

- John Wooden -

My relationship with Kelly was not good, partly because of the distance and secondly because of the womanising , she obviously understood what the criminal life style was like, it was common knowledge that everyone had two separate lives, the wife and kids stayed at home and the tarts stayed in the clubs and the back ground "never the Twain shall meet", which meant out of sight out of mind, as long as you always came home, it was an unwritten rule, or so I convinced myself.

Every run we did was like our last because you never knew if the nation police or Guardia civil would take you out.

We would drive up keeping to the speed limit and drive respectfully and adhere to the Spanish highway code but on the way back we would race like demons.

A few times we were pulled over and given the equivalent of a 100 pound fines.

One particular night it was pissing down with rain, I could barely see out the windows because in Spain they don't have lights on the sides of the road it's like a black desert.

The lorry drivers drive like lunatics and the Spanish like they're all at Lamont (Le mans race) it was like taking your life in your hands every time we drove back in the evenings.

I remember driving up so many times and trying my best to keep my mind clear, subconsciously I used to start singing and these words would always come out loud and clear, road block, la la la road block, it used to drive me insane but I just couldn't stop it.
As I said it was a long drive and on the way home to Benalmadena I nearly fell asleep a couple of times, the hours that we were driving were galling, to keep ourselves awake we used to have a bet with each other, who would get back the quickest, first prize being 200 quid.

This one night we had set off late as our pick-up driver had been delayed by 3 hours, so we parked up and waited, as my pal in England updated us every hour to the progress of our transport people, when he eventually arrived it was dark and pissing down with rain so we quickly unloaded our cargo and regrouped at the service station.

We had a bite to eat, a coffee each and stocked up with cokes, sweets and a sandwich, then we all started our cars and off we went.

Chris steamed ahead and me and Jamie took it easy, but it was so dark that I lost sight of them both after about twenty minutes, I put the music on full blast and just tried my best to stay awake.

I arrived back about 2am and tried to call the others, but their phones were off, so I assumed they had gotten back and gone to sleep.

I parked my car outside the car hire place and posted the keys through the letter box and told myself that we'd had another successful day, job done, I had two beers then went to bed and crashed out.

I woke at 2pm to Chris banging on the door, as he said he'd been to Jamie's place but his car wasn't there, which was strange as he was a creature of habit, and always called Chris to let him know that he'd gotten back all right, they had known each other for years, so when he hadn't called last night Chris was worried, but put it down to the long day and night we just had.

However, this morning when he went round Jamie still wasn't there, he wrongly assumed he was with me.

Spain is a big country and we were not natives so there was nothing we could do apart from wait and see if he returned home, I wondered if he'd been nicked for speeding or had broken down.

We just didn't know, so we waited in the London bar in Fuengirola, we heard nothing for over a week, until his girlfriend called Chris and said that Jamie had been involved in a car accident, his car had rolled over a ravine killing him.

It was the last thing we had expected but something we all knew was possible as the roads were treacherous, especially at night but even more so when it was raining.

I was sad at the fact that we had lost a friend but it was also a sign that it was time for me to go home, so I packed my bag and told the guys I was off.

Julie was heartbroken as I'd promised her a lifetime with me, but I just had to get out of dodge as it was only a matter of time before the heat would be on us.

I had a few close shaves over those couple of years, I'd been In Alicante when the guy who I'd arranged to meet met me at my hotel instead of our original meeting place, which had spooked me so I collected the three hundred and fifty grand he had brought me and left straight away, and instead of heading off the next day in my car, I actually left my hotel in the middle of the night and jumped on a coach, a coach that took me all fucking night to get to Malaga.

I booked into a hotel and slept like a baby, subsequently missing my two pals, who in return thought I'd been taken by the old bill, so had shut down the whole operation in their panic.

But when I explained that the driver had come to my hotel and hotted me up they realised it was the only course of action left open to me.

The other time I was nearly nicked was when I was in a hotel in Marbella.

I had four hundred thousand pounds on me and was waiting until the morning to drop it off when one of my pals knocked on my door in the middle of the night and fired off a fire extinguisher at me, as he and two of his pals had decided to get pissed, and had forgotten that I had all the money in my room.

Unfortunately the manager of the hotel didn't see the funny side of it and had called the police while telling us all to get out of his hotel, with the police on route and my pals all pissed, I had to think fast, I picked up my rucksack full of money and quickly went out the exit, leaving my pals there to sort themselves out.

I walked along the beach and under an underpass which took me into the hills outside Marbella I walked for about hour, when I came to a road that I knew, I put the money in a water drain under the road, then made my way to the guy's house that I was supposed to drop the money off too in the first place.

After I explained my situation to him, he sympathised with me, then I borrowed his car so I could go back and pick the money up.

We spent a couple of hours counting the money then got pissed and went out for dinner, a weekend that I will never forget, but again job done, it's what I do.

Chapter Twenty Eight
Back to Blighty

"It is in the character of growth that we should learn from both pleasant and unpleasant experiences."
- Nelson Mandela -

The only flight out that night was to Newcastle so I booked a ticket and arrived at midnight in England.

I jumped on a night coach and arrived at Heathrow at 7am that morning, what a fucking journey that was, but at least I was home.

I spent a couple of weeks at home with the kids before I was contacted by one of my pals who had set a meeting with a Dutch guy, who he said needed to be picked up at Heathrow Airport then properly entertained as he had a proposition that would change all our lives.

All I knew at this stage was that my pal had been nicked in Spain for thirty grands worth of diamonds and was now in a Spanish prison.

He'd made a new contact in there and because he was basically their hostage he was able to do a deal that would take us to the next level in our criminal endeavours.

Which meant I had to pull out all the stops tonight, I'd called a pal who owed me a favour; he also happened to own a prestigious wine bar and restaurant down at king's cross, he would afford us a bit of five star treatment.

I also arranged for an escort girl to meet him in his hotel suite in swiss cottage and we also laid on a driver and bodyguard to look after him during his stay.

He was collected from Heathrow airport and taken back to the hotel so he could freshen up, then he would be brought to me and my co-conspirator Ray at the wine bar.

Ray was my money man he had access to storage space and a warehouse bang in the middle of king's cross and we had worked together before in Spain.

He was also my distribution partner with the puff, like me he was curious to what our European friend would be proposing this evening.

Before we could ruminate on it I received a call from my driver that our passenger was five minutes away, I told the concierge and bar manager to lay it on thick as we were entertaining a very important client this evening.

I had a Savile Row suit on that I'd had specially made, with gold cufflinks and a nice discreet gold Rolex watch.

Ray as always looked immaculate the guy just oozed confidence, class and respectability - he was my secret weapon in persuading our European friend that we had money, influence and were well connected.

Our visitor came into the bar as if he owned it, he was wearing a full length leather jacket and a massive diamond embezzled Rolex watch that stood out like a Belisha beacon and a smile that lit up the whole place, the guy was immaculate, manicured finger nails, teeth as white as snow and a fantastic sun tan to boot with a softly spoken Dutch accent.

I introduced myself and we exchanged pleasantries.

"I'm Terry and this is Raymondo"

"Ah I'm Axel nice to finally meet you Terry, I've heard so much about you"

"Like wise, sit down please"

As soon as we sat down a waiter came over and offered us the wine list.

Axel chose one red and one white.

We ordered our food - I ordered halibut rockets and runner beans, Axel had a large T-bone steak and Ray settled for the swordfish.

When everything was cleared away we ordered a Brandy each and three cigars.

Then after a bit more small talk Axel said he was looking for a distribution network in England that could handle large quantities of weed, he said roughly 28 tonnes to start with, 7 tonnes tomorrow and after that he would incrementally top us up as and when we needed it.

I think he was expecting us to be flustered but I kept my composure, inwardly I was perplexed by the amount, I wanted it , but I'd never sold weed before and nor had ray.

Before ray could say anything I said "no problem, we can move that in a couple of weeks or so"

Ray kicked me under the table, but I said "we have people all over England who can take large amounts so realistically I'd say send it down tomorrow, or we can arrange for one of our guys to pick it up and bring it to us , is that ok?"

Axel went quiet for a few seconds then got on his phone and spoke to his people, two minutes later he put his phone down and said "your man will have to pick it up in Scotland tomorrow evening, is that ok?"

"No problem, we can facilitate that".

He wrote down the address and gave it to me.

We discussed the price, it would come to us at £1100 which gave us a realistic profit margin of £200 a kilo for a quick sale, which was about five million six hundred thousand for the whole parcel.

Their cut was 30 million 800 thousand.

Ridiculous money but when you consider it only cost them about 50 dollars a kilo at source, then you get some idea why drug trafficking is so lucrative.

But I wasn't complaining, I had just committed us to either a world of shit or one of those moments in your life that you look back on and say I can't believe we just did that, but we did and we did it easier than I ever imagined, we actually even shocked ourselves at the ease of the whole deal.

By the end of the evening Axel was in high spirits and wanted us to all go out, we made our excuses that we had to organise Ourselves and the team.

I told him not to worry as I arranged a car for him and a beautiful young lady who would continue the party on our behalf, he graciously accepted the trade off as one of my guys helped him into his car.

When I returned to the table Ray was pulling his hair out,
he said "what the fuck have you done? you can't fuck with these people Tel they will fucking kill us if we can't deliver on this"

Adding that he couldn't sell weed as he wasn't a fucking weed dealer.

I told him not to be so pessimistic as I had it covered, "it ain't a problem trust me"

"Trust you? Are you fucking kidding me?"

"Don't worry ray, I'm seeing some good pals tomorrow who will be able to help us"

This calmed him a little "Ok let's talk tomorrow".

We then ordered cabs, thanked the manager and staff for making the evening a success and went on our way.

I had a restless night but I'd made a few calls before I went to bed to some trusted guys I knew who were more than capable, at least I hoped they were and I arranged to meet them in the Mornington arms in Camden.

Chapter Twenty Nine

The Weed Deal

"I say luck is when an opportunity comes along and you're prepared for it."
- Denzel Washington -

The guys I had arranged to meet were two mixed race guys, big T and little Warren.

Big T was a good friend of mine so I met him first, I said "I have a move that will make us both rich" adding "I have an unlimited supply of weed at a discount price if you can move two tonnes a week, can you help me?"

"What's the price and what does it smoke like?"

"It's cheap £1400 you'll easily get £1600 or £1650 no problem, there's room for everyone as long as you don't get greedy, we need to turn this over quickly so get it out cheap."

"Ok" he said "I can move all you have"

"What do you mean everything at that price?"

"Yes" he said "but don't give it to anyone else just me"

"I've already promised Warren a shot at it"

"Fuck off no!"

"I've already promised him brother"

"Ok just him then Tel, No one else please"

"Ok brother" I said "deal".

"Ok Tel"

"What can you move a week?"

"A couple of ton"

"Are you sure brother?"

"Yer no problem in fact I'll probably do more , just give it to me and let's just earn some money Tel!"

"That's all I wanted to hear brother"

"Ok later"

That went better than I could ever have wished for and I still had Warren who was fashionably late, but he like Big T had the weed game on lockdown, I told him the same as Big T and his eyes lit up like pound signs, he could do likewise when it came to quantity so job done.

I called Ray and said I've placed all the furniture as promised and he said he would believe it when it was done.

I spent the day sorting out the pick-up from Scotland and a slaughter house down here in London which took me most of the day.

I also picked a select team of men to work with, men I'd grown up with, who I could trust with my life, the first thing I did was order a money counting machine, then I opened up a safe deposit box in the old bank in Finchley Road, we would use this as our holding place as it was safe and secure.

Two days later my pal pulled the lorry into the warehouse, the weed was all boxed up so we spent two hours unloading it, six of us, it was hard work but enjoyable, as we all knew the money would come rolling in.

This was our dream job.

We unpacked each box, weighed each kilo and to my dismay I noticed that they were all underweight , some were coming back at 900 grams and 950 grams.

This was a fucking disaster as now I had to call my pal in Spain and arrange for the suppliers to come and see our problem.

A day later and to my surprise I was contacted by two different groups, one triad and the other the Italian mafia, their consiglieres were Roberto and Mario both nice enough guys.

I liked them straight away and mark and Peter who were both Thai; yes I knew their names weren't real, but these were the names they wanted to use, and I liked both of them as well.

I told them my problem and then arranged for them all to be blind folded and put in the back of a van and brought to our slaughter house which they all agreed to.

It was like something out of a gangster movie but this was real life and happening right in front of me, it took all our strength to stop ourselves from laughing out loud, as the guys brought them through one at a time, we then explained our predicament and asked them to pick any box in the room and weigh it.

First the Thai's then the Italian's 900 then an 850 it was plain to see the problem so I suggested we take the weights of all the kilos and add it all up and then subtract it from the overall price which would benefit everyone, they all agreed so we all shook hands on it and the job was afoot again.

We had re-established ourselves as honest and sensible, but most importantly a team who were flexible.

And true to our word we managed to get rid of the weed and cash it out within one month.

The operation was slick but extremely boring, we would pick up cars and drop them off at strategically chosen locations around London, it was endless and thankless but counting money was even worse, it was fucking tedious, we rented out a flat in Belsize Park with just me and two others knowing it's whereabouts.

The money was collected then brought to the flat than put through the machine, then wrapped with an elastic band.

We had mountains of money and it took 6 or 7 hours sometimes and by the end of the 28 tonnes I was glad it was over.

We took the money in suitcases and handed over two million pounds at any one time, as this was the safest way to do it.

We would take the money to the Finchley Road deposits then we will get a phone call that a driver would be outside at a certain time, it worked like clockwork, we were smashing it.

I was the king of the manor, big T, Warren and my guys were rolling in money, everyone one was happy and I was eventually singled out to fly to Cambodia on behalf of the Thai's, which I said I'd gladly do it.

The job was to teach the Thai's to weigh and pack the weed properly so we didn't have to make the same mistakes again with the weights,
an easy enough job I thought.

A month after we'd sold everything I was contacted and told that arrangements had been made for me to fly to Cambodia.

Chapter Thirty

Half the world away - my Cambodia adventure

"If you think adventure is dangerous, try routine. It's lethal!"

- Paulo Coelho -

The taxi came for me at 5.30am to take me to Heathrow airport, I was feeling anxious simply because it was now my sole responsibility to check the weights and quality of the weed the Thai's were now going to send us and any fuck ups would be mine and mine alone.

This was in itself a daunting prospect, but in my case it was further compounded by the fact, I knew fuck all about weed so it was another case of me winging it for the greater good.

When I landed in Thailand the first thing that hit me was the heat, it was dry and it took my breath away, the second was the traffic it was crazy.

First of all the traffic jam and then the manic drive by my taxi driver to get me to my hotel, which was the holiday inn, the second I walked in I found my saving grace - I entered the foyer and the air conditioning hit me like slap in the face, it was beautiful to finally breathe fresh cold air again.

I quickly booked in, collected my keys and headed up to my room. I took a well-deserved shower as I'd been travelling for the last 24 hours and stank to high heaven.

I took a 10 hour sleep and woke up the next morning to my mobile going off; it was my Thai connection his name was Harvey, he said he would pick me up at 2pm and put the phone down.

I took the opportunity to shower again and change into some summer clothing, then went down to the reception.

Harvey arrived at 2pm sharp, he was about 35 years old well dressed and smiled a lot, his English was prefect, he said there had been a delay in getting the go down ready which was Thai slang for a warehouse.

He told me not to worry as he had arranged for me to stay in Thailand for an extra week until we could fly to Cambodia, I pretended to be perplexed but Inwardly I didn't give a toss as I was looking forward to seeing Bangkok's Patpong red-light district and taking in the sights.

Harvey had other ideas he said we were going to the fishbowl first and then dinner then that evening, he had also booked us into a karaoke booth in one of the top gambling hotels.

I accepted as he gestured to me to follow him out of the hotel , where we were met by a black Toyota Land Cruiser and two Thai bodyguards Thomas and Gavin.

Again, they were nice guys, very friendly but I could also see they were very capable guys.

Both had side arms in shoulder holsters which I could clearly see.

We drove through the traffic for about forty minutes before we came to a building that had private parking and security guards who waved us through, we parked just opposite the main entrance where my guys got out, opened my door and invited me to follow.

As we went through the double doors there was an explosion of noise, men were sitting in rows and pointing at girls who were behind a massive sheet of glass, every girl had a number and was wearing a bikini, five rows of girls about hundred or more of them, it was like a cattle market.

You picked a girl and she went up to a room while you were taken to a changing room where you could take a shower and change into a white robe.

I was taken to a room and asked to wait.

Five minutes later a beautiful Thai woman came out, she took off her robe to reveal her naked body, she then took my robe off and asked me to lay face down on a rubber mattress, which I did.

She took a sponge and dipped it in hot soapy water and sponged my whole body with it, she then used her body to massage me.

God it was the most beautiful sexual experience I'd ever had without actually having sex, it was so relaxing until she asked me to lay on my back which was awkward as I was standing to attention, but she just reached down and picked up a condom and placed it on me.

She then went to work again and after about ten minutes I couldn't hold back any longer, she smiled and said "good?".

I smiled and said "yes! definitely good!"

It was like the film Emanuel I couldn't stop smiling.

She then took me to the shower where we showered and then returned to the bed.

I'd gone to Thailand and arrived in heaven.

After couple of hours I dressed and went back to lobby where the others were waiting I thanked Harvey for his hospitality and we moved on to a restaurant in town which was another amazing experience as I was shown live seafood, still swimming about in fish tanks, all kinds of fish, crabs ,lobsters crayfish and every assortment of fish.

I was asked to pick what I wanted.

It was brought to my table and cooked live in front of me. It tasted and looked fantastic I was starting to fall in love with Thailand.

Afterwards Harvey suggested we go to the karaoke hotel which was on the 17th floor of a high glass hotel with gambling and lots of drinks, woman and show girls on stage.

We placed bets and I just rolled with the flow, basically having a bonding session with Harvey that would hopefully cement our working relationship, so I stayed sober just drinking coke while he drank spirits and enjoyed himself.

At midnight we were escorted to a booth that was our karaoke room Harvey loved it, singing Frank Sinatra, Tom Jones and even a bit of Gene Pitney.

I even joined in singing Elvis and Please Release Me by Engelbert Humperdinck, Harvey, Thomas and Gavin seemed to be having the time of their lives.

The lights went on and a woman came in followed by ten girls.

I was asked to choose one or even two to keep me company back at my hotel, I tried to decline but they insisted I take a girl so I reluctantly picked one and spent a restless night enjoying the hospitality of my new best friends.

The week seemed to fly past, I was receiving 5-star treatment and to be honest I was loving all the attention but like all good things they had to come to an end.

Harvey came to my room on the last night and told me to pack my gear, in the morning we would be flying to Cambodia, he gave me two tickets then said he'd meet me again before he disappeared out of the door.

I booked a cab to the airport and was surprised that my flying companions were Mario, his wife and a 12-year old boy.

They welcomed me on to the plane.

It was a bumpy ride and for the first time on this trip I was afraid that the plane wouldn't reach its destination as it was only a small charter aircraft, which held about forty people. The seats were cramped and there was no drinks trolley or food being served.

I'd gone from 5-star treatment to third world economy class and if I thought taking off was bad then I was mortified by the landing, the plane hit the tarmac and bounced off about four feet before landing again, my guts turned over and for a second I thought the plane was going to roll over. It came to a shuddering stop and my head hit the seat in front.

Fuck this for a laugh I thought as I looked at Mario who was laughing and joking that it could have been worse, his wife's face was white and the boy didn't seem at all concerned.

It took me a few minutes to regain my composure then the door to my left opened and to my astonishment Harvey, Thomas and Gavin were standing on the tarmac.

Mario said his goodbyes and said he'd see me back in London.

Then headed into the terminal.

I was taken around the airport to a waiting car transporter that took me to a hotel where Harvey said I had to wait until I was picked up in a day or so, he also asked me not to use a mobile or landline as Interpol and the American's were all listening in and an English voice would set of some alarm Bells, especially my London accent; so no phone calls.

It was a long three day wait until I was contacted again by Harvey who said "we would be off tomorrow morning bright and early", so basically four days sitting in my room bored shirtless not a good start to my covert mission into the jungle.

To be honest I felt like telling them all to fuck themselves, but erred on the side of caution, as I could easily just disappear into the jungle and never to be seen again.

When they eventually picked me up I was more than ready to get moving I'd been here in Thailand and now here in Cambodia for 11 days and achieved fuck all.

As we drove off I asked Harvey how long it would take us to reach the Go down (warehouse) he said "if we get through the checkpoints and nothing goes wrong than maybe 3 or 4 days".

I was under the impression that the Go down was somewhere near the airport but now I'd just been informed it was hundreds of miles away and hidden in the fucking jungle and to compound my misery it was so hot and sticky that the mosquitoes were out in force driving me insane, I'd been targeted relentlessly by them since I'd arrived.

Luckily Thomas had seen my discomfort and had managed to buy some mosquito repellent which seemed to do the trick.

The Thai's are very religious people and every 50 or so miles Harvey, Thomas and Gavin would stop at a monastery and pray to the buddha and at times the four Faced buddha.

I even found myself praying too, that I would make it home safe to Kelly and the kids.

The scenery was breath-taking and after I'd calmed down a bit I was starting to appreciate the beauty of this country and the people.

The poverty was evident and everywhere we stopped I saw the disparity between the haves, the have nots and the have fuck all's.

The further we travelled the worse it was, what disturbed me the most was that every so often we came to a road block guarded by the commonest Khmer rouge, they were mean looking fuckers who never smiled, my bodyguards were nonchalant but I could feel their contempt for having to bail down every time we stopped, it was uncomfortable to watch.

After day three we came to a turning that took us into the jungle and along a dirt road, this road was rough going but only lasted for about an hour, before we came to locked black metal double gates.

We all got out and stretched our legs, Harvey was on the phone and seemed agitated that the gate was unmanned, out of nowhere a guy came out of the jungle carrying a Kalashnikov rifle slung over his shoulder he spoke to Harvey then quickly opened the gate .

We drove through the forest and came out into a clearing, bang in the middle of the clearing stood a wooden warehouse about 15 feet high, 40 feet long and 15 feet deep all around us were boxes of weed packed in plastic bags, there was also A vacuum seal machine and scales.

I took a bag and weighted it exactly 1000 grams then I checked another box 1000 grams one kilo.

It seemed they had sorted out their own problems with the weights and all I had to do now was test the quality, it was definitely good as I was as high as a kite after only half a joint.

I couldn't talk so I gave a thumbs up, meaning everything was looking good.

Harvey was happy, I had supposedly done my job. Or so I thought.

It wasn't until we got to a little village that night and I had come down from my high that Harvey said we had to go back tomorrow and pack a new delivery, about 7 tonnes he said that it was destined for Ireland and then over to Scotland, before being taken down to London for my team to sell, I had apparently tested someone else's consignment destined for fuck knows where.

I had to laugh as Harvey said we had to pack all the gear ourselves starting from tomorrow morning which meant, me, Harvey, Thomas and Gavin would have to weigh and vacuum seal every kilo.

A mammoth task at the best of times but in this heat it would be a nightmare.

When we got back to our ramshackle hotel I went and had a shower, just as I finished I spotted something out of the corner of my eye, it was the biggest cockroach I'd ever seen and I shit you not, I jumped a mile. I ran back into the shower grabbed the hose and used it as a gun to push the cockroaches round the room and back into the toilet where I flushed it down a hole in the floor.

I was sweating, when Harvey came in and I told him what had just happened but all he did was laugh.

He called Thomas and Gavin who burst out laughing as well, in hindsight it was only a cockroach but to me it was monster fucking bug, I saw the funny side of it and laughed along with them.

I then dressed so We could all go out to dinner and have some drinks which seemed to work a treat as it calmed my nerves.

We arrived back at the hotel about 11pm and to my surprise Harvey had arranged a welcoming committee five Thai girls, I tried my best to decline again but Harvey wouldn't have it.

As he shut my door and wished me good night, I felt obligated to spend the night with a stranger, I told her not to worry, then asked her just go to sleep as I was knackered but passed the idea off as some sort of heroic display of chivalry to save face.

The following morning I was taken to the warehouse where I spent 9 hours packing and showing them how to package and weigh the weed .

It felt good to be finally doing what I had come here to do in the first place, I kept telling myself that after this last shipment, I'd have enough money to move to somewhere warm and retire, a lie every career criminal tells themselves.

It actually took another 4 days making boxes up and filling them with 20 kilos in each box before I could leave, taping and marking the boxes seemed to take forever.

It was repetitive work but I didn't mind as I would be on my way home soon.

I didn't mind the long hours because as soon as the job was done I would be rewarded with my freedom.

Even though the whole experience was enjoyable I was missing Camden town and the cold weather and my kids.

The journey back was just as laborious but at least the end game was me getting on a plane and getting out of there.

When we finally got back to my hotel, I was told that I had to hurry up and get my passport from the hotel staff as the king of Cambodia had taken a stand against foreigners and drug traffickers which meant I had get out of Cambodia pronto.

Harvey and the boys dropped me at the airport, we all hugged and said our goodbyes, it was plain to see the authorities were clamping down as there were armed soldiers everywhere, I wasn't too worried as I had my ticket and I was booked on the next flight out anyway.

When I passed through passport control I was asked why my passport hadn't been stamped coming in. I said I thought it had been.

I remembered Harvey had taken me around the airport, we hadn't gone through passport control, I couldn't tell him that, so I did the only thing I could do... I blamed them and when this apparently didn't work I figured the next best thing was a bribe.

I took out all my American money, three thousand five hundred dollars and offered it to him to get me on my plane, he seemed annoyed that I had offered him money and started shouting at me in Thai, which brought in another guard who seemed angry as well.

After a few minutes he again asked me how I'd got into the country, I said "I arrived by plane at this airport two weeks ago and I've been sight-seeing ever since".

I then showed him my arrival ticket which seemed to calm him down, he said I had to wait to be questioned, so I said I had to get a connecting flight and If I miss that my ticket would be invalid, so for that reason I needed to get on my plane and now.

I took the opportunity again to offer him all my money, this time he took it all before gesturing for me to follow him, we walked through the terminal and through the customs hall, onto the tarmac where he escorted me back onto the plane but before saying don't come back.

I hadn't had time to think about the consequences of not getting on the plane or of the real reality of coming here and possibly being detained in a Cambodian prison, as the plane took off I shuddered at the thought of not seeing my kids again or London.

I'd been blinkered by greed, money and the dream of a better life, I got in this game to make my kids' lives better, to give them a better life, a home, an education and a future , a future away from the game and one that that I never had for myself.

But this life was corrupting me I was drinking, taking cocaine and womanising everything I hated, I was now becoming.

I had promised myself that I would be the best dad and provider. However, the more money I got, the further I was being dragged into the Abyss.

But at least I had averted catastrophe and was free to fight another day, I had done my job and in six or seven weeks I'd have several tonnes of weed to sell, I felt like a criminal James bond who had completed his mission.

I shouldn't have been feeling sorry for myself I was better than that bollocks.

When I landed back in Thailand I was skint, hungry and completely mentally exhausted.

I had to get back to England so I called Ray and explained my predicament he seemed concerned at first, but once I finished he started laughing at my plight.

Adding I better nick a boat and try and make my own way back to England that way, he then said he was skint.

"Stop fucking about" I said "I need to get the fuck out of here"

"Ok I'm only joking, I'll book you on the next flight call me back in one hour"

"Ok lovely Ray"

I walked around the airport trying to kill time but my mind kept taking me back to the Bangkok Hilton (prison) I'd heard stories of drug traffickers spending years there for a couple of ounces of gear,
so if I was implicated in the importation of seven tonnes of weed they would have thrown the fucking keys away.

I'd had a lucky escape, theoretically this would definitely have to be my last adventure over here.

Ray was true to his word he booked me a first class ticket on a virgin Atlantic airways, but the flight wasn't for another 24 hour as this was the only slot he could get me .

I waited and waited and slept like a baby in the Virgin Atlantic first class lounge, when I eventually got on the flight I was offered caviar, slippers and even a dressing gown.

I drank champagne and watched all the new film releases on my private telescreen at my seat, it was brilliant to finally get back to civilisation.

Chapter Thirty One

Family time and a well-deserved break

"Other things may change us, but we start and end with family."
- Anthony Brandt -

The flight was endless but landing at Heathrow was euphoric, as a present to myself and the family when I got back I decided to take them to Disneyland for a couple of weeks.

I booked us all first class tickets and we stayed in the omni 5-star hotel on sunset Boulevard it was exactly what I needed especially after the last few months working non-stop.

I definitely needed time for me to have some quality time with the kids, seeing their smiling faces as I sat on the plan was priceless, they were over the moon and Kelly was made up too.

When we landed in Miami it was humid heat, hot but the kids loved it.

I rented a people carrier and drove up to Florida singing songs and eating burgers and chips as we stopped at all the rest stops.

The hotel was fantastic, the people were great, we swam in the pool every day and visited Disneyworld and all the different theme parks, Didcot, SeaWorld, Water world, we saw the dolphins, the killer whales, we ate candy floss, steaks, it was a happy time for everyone; the best few weeks of my life, it was so much fun that I extended our holidays for an extra week so the kids could enjoy it all and more.

We drove to the Everglades to watch the alligators being feed, the kids had their pictures taken with snakes and baby alligators.

At Disneyworld we went on every ride, the theme park rides were fantastic, the girls absolutely loved every second of it, the jaws boat ride scared the living daylights out of them though.

We queued forever to get on Space Mountain and sat through a re-enactment of back to the future, the rollercoaster rides were epic and hearing the kids laugh and seeing them larking about was worth all the drama that I'd gone through over the last couple of months.

It was at times like this that I justified my criminality and lifestyle, the reality was that this holiday was just a sticking plaster on a gaping wound that I had inflicted upon them, my only saving grace was they were so young to comprehend what their dad really was.

Chapter Thirty Two
The First Irish Connection

"The lawyer with the briefcase can steal more money than the man with the gun."
- Mario Puzo, The Godfather -

I received a phone call one morning from Ireland, that my container had arrived in cork so I quickly booked a flight over.

When I arrived the Irish were pissed off as the only thing in the boxes were red Chinese bricks and brick dust.

Our consignment of weed had been switched or stolen.

So I called Harvey and explained the situation, he said it was not possible so I told him I had no reason to lie over a couple of fucking tonnes of weed, plus the Irish can confirm my story.

Harvey wasn't impressed so I asked if he could send over one of his people from London to check the boxes as they came out of the container, as we had only taken six boxes off so far, the rest were packed into the forty foot container.

Harvey agreed and the next day Kevin another Thai bodyguard arrived.

He checked all the boxes and by the time he finished we had about 7 tons of bricks on the floor.

The only reason they believed me was because the bricks were made in Cambodia, Harvey called back and said he would get to the bottom of it and could I talk to the Irish and apologise for him.

I tried but they were having none of it, all paddy kept repeating was that they had done their job and wanted paying.

I tried my best to calm him down but he came to my hotel that night and said he couldn't work with the Thai's again as they were too unprofessional.

So the deal was off which basically meant our transport into Europe and technically England was gone.

No matter what I or Harvey said or offered them they said no, they had washed their hands of the whole sorry situation.

I spoke to Harvey two days later and he couldn't apologise enough but the damage had been done, I'd arranged the warehouse and transport into Ireland

and even paid the fucking Irish their money because they had done their job.

But he wasn't concerned with all that.

He only wanted to know if I could arrange another door into England, which I couldn't at the moment.

He then said the people who had switched the weed for the bricks had been caught and taken care of, so it would never happen again, he kept repeating himself asking if I could arrange transport so I said no again before walking over to the docks and throwing my phone in the sea.

I'd had enough, It was game over.

We had done so much work on this and now I'd ended up losing my money and the door into the country and not just that I'd lost all our fucking gear.

Chapter Thirty Three

Going Dutch

"It is our choices that show what we truly are, far more than our abilities."

- J. K. Rowling -

It was time to evaluate my situation and go back to what we were good at selling A's and Charlie(COCAINE) I knew the game inside out as I'd been selling kilos of it for years on and off plus A's(ecstasy) was the new kid on the block, so I booked a flight to Amsterdam via Schiphol Airport.

I phoned a couple of pals Sergio and George, Sergio was Albanian and George was Yugoslavian they were both ex-military and dangerous guys, I'd met them in Madrid a couple of years back when we were smuggling cigarettes through Spain and France, really nice guys.

I'd also arranged to meet big Ron an ecstasy dealer who was a larger than life character all 30 stone of him, I'd met him in Amsterdam through a friend of mine when I was coming over and buying Charlie, fags and anything else I could get my hands on.

Ron's claim to fame was he had fired a rocket launcher through a competitors window one night blowing up the house, he'd spent a number of years in prison because of it and subsequently built a reputation as someone not to fuck with, however I liked him and every time I stayed in Amsterdam he borrowed me one of his houses in Utrecht and the use of his speed boat.

I took the boat out every day when I was there, at night we would go to the red light district as he owned a number of high class brothels, all the rooms had Jacuzzis and some even had heart shaped beds, satin sheets, mirrored ceilings, even dungeons and every time I visited he didn't disappoint.

I would always object and he would always insist so we would drink all night and do COCAINE and I'd end up going back on my word, it was a seedy world but one that was a necessity if you wanted to do business with these guys in Amsterdam.

It was like a test, if you did cocaine, slept with all the girls and partied all night then you were accepted as one of them, but if you declined you were looked upon as old bill (police) and someone who couldn't be trusted.

Add drink, drugs and woman into the equation then it was the accepted face of crime and our way of life, that unfortunately went with the territory.

I met Ron outside the van Gogh Museum with his two bodyguards, two burly looking guys and as mean as you like.

He looked pleased to see me and we booked a table in a local restaurant so we could discuss business.

I wanted 350000 ecstasy tablets at the right price which at that time was about 90p.

Ron wanted a pound and my transport guy wanted £15000, the pills were making five quid wholesale in London so I pretended to be offended by his extortionate prices and accepted reluctantly.

We had dinner and spent the evening doing what the nouveau Riche do, we spent money like water, we bought champagne, birds and cocaine.

I waited at Ron's place for 3 days until he called and said my order had been completed and it would be ready at my earliest convenience, so I called my transport guy and said I'd brought him some clogs and I would be posting them over to him.

He replied "so they should be here on Thursday?"

"Yes" I agreed,

"What time?" I asked.

"Probably afternoon delivery" he said,

"Ok bye".

It was now Tuesday and he would be at our arranged pick up point on Thursday at 2pm.

Amsterdam can be a lonely place when you're waiting for things to happen, I found myself walking round the red light district looking in all the windows and wondering what sort of life these girls had to put up with.

Thousands of men walking by and leering at them and using them like pieces of meat, old men, young boys, ugly, fat and obnoxious creatures all drunk and off their faces.

Seeing this made me philosophical as I walked through the Alleyways through the black section, the Chinese, the old, the fat, the transvestites section, God Amsterdam was a den of inequity where money, violence and drugs equals power.

I remember years ago when I first came to Amsterdam I was as hungry as fuck for excitement, I slept with hundreds if not thousands of women over the years, I used these same windows, morning, noon and night.

I was like a kid in a candy store.

But lately I was starting to get bored of it all, in fact I didn't enjoy it anymore as I wasn't doing it for me, I was doing it to be accepted, Harvey, Ron, Sergio, George and everyone I knew had no respect for women, life or people. Money had made everything accessible and cheap.

My alarm went off at 6am, I had rented a car and had arranged to drop it off to one of Ron's guys who would fill the boot up with my pills and park it in the underground carpark next to the Victoria Hotel opposite Amsterdam's Central Station, leaving the keys in the petrol cap compartment.

We had done this so many times over the years it was second nature to us, I picked the car up and headed up to the Dutch and French border checkpoint where I had arranged to meet my guy on the Dutch side.

It was an open border so it was an easy drop off point, I knew the lorry he was using, so all I had to do was pull up, open the back and load him up.

I sat back in my car and waited, watching until I saw him come back and get in the cab of the lorry and drive off.

My job had been done, I drove to Amsterdam so I could drop my hire car off, I unwound with a few beers, a joint and whatever the night had in store for me.

The next day I met up with Sergio and George as they had sorted out ten kilos of cocaine that I'd ordered the previous week.

Chapter Thirty Four

Dutch Tragedy

"Death is the wish of some, the relief of many, and the end of all."

- Lucius Annaeus Seneca -

We went to Sergio's place as he had put it in his safe, his apartment block was just outside Amsterdam.

I tested it by washing it in bicarbonate soda and heating it on a spoon it came back about 84 percent which was good, I arranged for the money to be dropped off in London to one of Sergio's connections who called back straight away to confirm that he had received the monies.

I called a cab and took the gear to another hotel where my transport guy was staying, we did the swap quickly in the staircase as there was no cameras there, and I left through the exit door.

I worked like this for over two years back and forth meeting up with Sergio and George who I had the pleasure of calling my friends; we had so many good times eating at the best restaurants and going to the best clubs.

One night when I was at big Ron's watching TV I received a call that Sergio had been shot and killed and George had been shot in the back and had been paralysed, they had been on a meet, apparently buying some cocaine when a Serbian group burst in and robbed them.

Sergio was killed instantly with a bullet to the head.

It was the worst kind of news, I was shocked, I wanted revenge for my friends, I wanted to find and kill every last one of those Serbian bastards.

I couldn't even call their families, friends or even George, as I didn't know their families like that, plus we had only ever exchanged numbers , so I couldn't even go to the funeral, when I tried to contact George his phone was off he just disappeared into thin air and to this day I've never heard from him.

The killing had shaken me so I decided to give Amsterdam a miss as the Russians, Albanians and Serbians had started moving in on the drug and prostitution trade they were ruthless bastards who didn't value life at all, they would kill you for the price of a tin of beans.

I decided to head home again but got side tracked, a pal wanted me to sort something out for him in France in Ostend.

Chapter Thirty Five

Oh la la - Side-tracked in France and a return home

"Every dream has a process and a price tag. Those who embrace the process and pay the price, live the dream. Those who don't, just dream."
- Jeremy Riddle -

He had a warehouse and wanted to start bringing cigarettes back in to England.

It was a lot safer then drugs so I agreed to help, I called my pal Raymondo who arranged the transport for me and another pal to send up the cigarettes from Luxembourg, it was an easy bit of graft and to be honest I'd had enough of all the bollocks dealing with gangsters.

The cigarette game was easy and the people in it were business men and family men who saw it as a way to earn lots of money but without the risk, my job was to unload the cigarettes and put them in new unmarked boxes then repack them and put them on another lorry heading back to England.

I also had to get back to blighty and arrange a drop off point and establish a distribution network where my team would unload the lorry, pick up and load individual vans, then take them to their drop off points, pick up the money and get it back to my pals, easy.

The job also gave me the opportunity to work from home which would be great as I could get the sea cat from Dover to Calais then drive up to Ostend or I could take the ferry to Ostend from Folkestone which took 3 hours.

We had arranged for two hundred cartons a month which was approximately one million cigarettes, every carton was worth about £550 which gave us a return of £90000 profit plus a pound a sleeve for the transport which came to £10000 so we came away with £80000 divided by two teams my side was left £40000 takeaway the extras, vans, cars, petrol ,wages, hotels and the farm which left £30000 of which I got about six thousand a month, it wasn't much but it paid the bills and it beat working a normal 9 to 5.

Everyone earned money and everyone enjoyed the work.

It worked like Clockwork I would slip over to Ostend open up the warehouse to unload the lorry, take the cigarette sleeves out and put them into plain boxes.

Our driver would pick them up and return them to the farm where they would be unloaded, we would pick up our punters vans, drive them back to the farm, fill them up and return them.

This went on for just over a year, we were just coasting along.

Chapter Thirty Six

Reunited with Lady Justice

"For to be free is not merely to cast off one's chains, but to live in a way that respects and enhances the freedom of others.
- Nelson Mandela -

Out of the blue one day I got back early and decided to go to the farm to help out the boys, I met them at the supermarket carpark I gave my pal my car and I took a Luton because he couldn't drive it.

He took off, I tried to keep up but lost him for a bit.

I caught back up with him eventually, he was about ten cars in front of me when I saw him pull across the main road, through the electric gates and into the farm yard, I started to indicate...

Out of nowhere a police land rover smashed through the electric gates, all I could see were guns pointed at my pal as another land rover came through the hedgerow, then another van, the whole farm came alive with armed police, they swarmed in everywhere nicking the lorry driver and my two pals.

There was nothing I could do, so I drove back to London's King's Cross and headed to our warehouse but when I got there the police were putting my pal in a police van handcuffed, he looked shocked and bewildered, he knew the risks, we all did - it was all part of the game.

I drove to mine but noticed a police van parked in the car park with two police cars, the fuckers were waiting for me to walk in at my new girlfriend's house in Hendon, me and Kelly had split up 5 months before.

I phoned my house phone and left a voicemail saying "I am on my way to Luton, just popping over to Amsterdam to do some business , but don't worry love I've got my passport, see you in a week or so love you"

My answer machine was one of those ones that you can hear the person leaving the message, so if anyone was hiding in the house they would hear every word.

It only took a second, until I saw them all come out 3 plain clothed officers, they jumped into their cars and headed towards the M1 at Brent cross, the uniforms came out sheepishly and walked back to the cars and vans in the car park, they looked sick.

I drove to the Marriott hotel in swiss cottage, booked a room and ordered some room service a large steak dinner, a bottle of chardonnay and got totally pissed which took the edge off the day that I was having.

I called my girlfriend sunshine that evening and over the next couple of weeks contemplated my next move whilst I stayed in the hotel.

The outcome was that I had decided to call my solicitor who made contact with HM customs and excise at customs house, he arranged for me to go in for an interview.

I met my solicitor at the entrance of Customs House, it was different from going into a police station as they offered us tea and a room to sit in.

We were given a dossier of all the questions they wanted to ask me which gave us an opportunity to see the evidence.

We could clearly see from the questions that it was not a lot, in fact they had nothing on me, apparently they were waiting on finger print evidence from the fag boxes/cartons.

Unfortunately for them that would not implicate me as I had worn gloves, so basically they were pissing in the wind , however they still charged me and asked me the questions, like why had I gone to Ostend on 17 separate occasions and why had I not surrendered earlier.

I told them I had a girlfriend in Ostend who was married so I couldn't possibly give her name and the reason I hadn't surrendered myself was basically because I'd been ill and had been staying round at my sister's so was unaware they wanted to speak to me, the whole interview lasted about 90minutes before they bailed me to court.

On the day the case was to be heard the charges were dropped for a lack of evidence.

My pals on the farm were also both found not guilty as they too had pleaded ignorance in as far has they had been hired for one day to unload a lorry, their defence was that they had been hired through a courier company that was legit and that because the boxes were unmarked, how could they have known that they contained cigarettes.

Unfortunately, Raymondo had received a fax from the transport company, the only bit of evidence they found at his house.

That one piece of paper made him an accessory after the fact.

He was sentenced to one year in prison with six months off for good behaviour, he was out on tag within 5 months.

Unfortunately though he never recovered from his stint in prison and on his release he moved over to Antwerp and brought himself a little block of flats and was living off the rents.

I only saw Raymondo once whilst he was in prison and that was in Wandsworth.

This was simply because he had changed, he'd lost his bottle, he told me he loved the life of being a villain and all the money.

But, in reality was he wasn't cut out for this life and had decided to move abroad.

I wished him and his girlfriend well and promised to visit them both when I was next in Brussels.

I actually visited them twice but alas he eventually sold up again and brought a hotel in one of the Caribbean islands.

It went Pete Tong (wrong) after a couple of years and the last thing I heard he'd had a double heart bypass, was skint and was living in a council flat in Folkestone.

I really do miss him, he will always have a very special place in my heart, I have so many fond memories of the restaurants and bars we used to frequent in Hampstead and Highgate and the laughs we had, he was a lot older than me and I always saw him as my mentor, he taught me a lot.

Chapter Thirty Seven

Rubbing shoulders with A-Lister's

"Celebrity gives us delusion of self-importance."
- Al Goldstein -

After the cigarette saga I took a few months off and concentrated on my new relationship with my girlfriend sunshine who was Sadie frost's sister.

Sadie was at the time married to Jude Law the actor who starred in Enemy At The Gates and A I .. artificial intelligence and her best friend was Kate moss.

I met sunshine through a good pal of mine called James who I'd become partners with, in a small courier company in Camden town,
Sunshine was a nice girl who liked to party quite a lot, she introduced me into the Primrose Hill set.

They liked nothing more than to self-indulge and party excessively, so I fit in straight away.

It was also around this time that I'd started working for the Colombians who were based in Elephant and Castle.

They were controlled by a woman who had taken a shine to my pal, he had been working with them for a while now but only doing a couple of kilos a week.

With me he was now able to take it to the next level, I was able to share all my contacts with him, it was a great relationship as the two of us had grown up together so the trust was there from the beginning.

We bought a couple of Peugeot street fighter bikes and slowly built up a network of suppliers, buyers and everything that came in to the country through her was given to us, over a
Hundred kilos a month sometimes.

Within weeks we were supplying all over London and further afield the money was coming in hand over fist, it got to the stage where we were working 7 days a week, just to keep up with the demand and at times there just wasn't enough hours in a day.

The faster we got it, the more our customers wanted it.

We were burning the candle at both ends partying, sniffing and smoking but we didn't care.

I was working all day. At night, I'd be invited over to Sadie and Jude's house, it was crazy I'd have Kate moss sitting on my knee laughing while drinking champagne and joking it was surreal.

I can't even remember a time when I was normal when I was around them; the drugs and drinking were breathtakingly legendary.

However, Jude was the opposite he was really shy and quiet I never once saw him take drugs, he wasn't what I expected at all, but nevertheless I liked him as he was all about family which was great for my kids as Jude liked to go ice skating, so we would all go over to Queensway ice rink every time he invite us all over.

He was the polar opposite to Sadie who liked nothing more than to be seen in the bars and restaurants around Primrose Hill, with Noel and Liam Gallagher and all the models, singers and actors, she thrived on it and it was great being part of that, as I managed to acquire lots of new customers.

Sunshine's dad was Dave Vaughan a renowned artist and painter who apparently painted all the Beatles Rolls-Royces'.

He was a really nice fella, a down to earth Northerner, he loved a good drink and came over to ours every time he visited London with whatever girlfriend he was with at that time.

What surprised me the most was Sadie employed her sisters to clean her house, she never passed any of her wealth along to help them out even though she was worth millions, she was one tight arse cow.

My pal tony owned the Queen's pub in Primrose Hill, so when we went out they were guaranteed their privacy and a lovely bit of Thai food from the restaurant in his pub.

Everyone who was anyone at that time was drinking in Camden town; Amy Winehouse was my favourite, it was a mecca for the celebrities at this time.

No more so than Primrose Hill and the Haverstock Arms, I met the Oasis brothers Liam and Noel, who loved to party especially Liam.

I used to drink with Sean Pertwee and Rhys Ifans who was in Notting Hill, really nice guys.

Sean Pertwee even invited us to his wedding the after party that he had in Portland Square was incredible, the DJ Goldie, Kate moss, Jude Law and Sadie, Robbie Carlyle, Jonny Lee Miller and many more.

It was a great night but the winner was the toilets, they witnessed most of the action, Kate Moss and Goldie were very friendly with each other.

There was enough cocaine used and cocktails drank to sink a battleship that night.

It's probably why no one was allowed to take a camera in, photos were forbidden and the security was tight regarding that, no press were allowed in either.

Everyone just let their hair down and did as they pleased. Cocaine could be seen shining like a Belisha beacon on certain celebrities noses, but I couldn't possibly say whose.

My drug use at this time was recreational but the lifestyle I was now leading dictated that I used more than the average joe.

It was definitely the summer of love and excess.

It was also at this time that Sadie Frost became the most paranoid person I'd ever met, no matter where or what she did the press were always there, it was a fucking nightmare and she didn't take this lightly.

She blamed every one of her friends, mum and even her sisters.

Eventually we stopped going near her because she was basically searching for a mole and that was the last thing I needed, to be around her in that state of mind.

She even suspected her ex-husband Gary Kemp from Spandau Ballet, who I found to be a nice guy, he used to pick up his kids at weekends and take them out. I liked him because he wasn't pretentious he was basically one of us, but with the added advantage he was a talented songwriter.

It did eventually transpire that an International hacking scandal by The Mirror Group and the News of the World would be credited for bugging Sadie's phones.

By the time this was discovered she had alienated everybody in her circle apart from the leeches.

I did feel sorry for her because she was eventually proved to be right and if I'm honest she was actually good company, very articulate and she also had one of the sexiest voices I've ever heard, especially when she wanted to be heard.

I was focusing on expanding my network as the Columbian's were upping their game, because at first we received maybe six to ten kilos every three or four days, now they were sending us batches of tens and twenties which had to be cashed in after every sale as they said money had to be returned to Columbia immediately.

It meant a little more work for us having to count the money every night and then taking it over to them, but that was the price we had to pay for fame and success.

I was doing my house up, I'd had new roof put on, a fitted kitchen and fitted bedrooms.

Sunshine had just bought a house, the house we were now living in, it was a beautiful four bedroom semi-detached house in Hendon with a massive back garden and a driveway for four cars.

Everything was going well so we decided to go to Spain for a couple of weeks as I wanted to buy a little place by the sea just outside Fuengirola.

We had discussed the possibility of me packing up the drug game and renting out both our homes so we could retire to a beautiful Villa by the sea I'd worked hard for years so maybe it was time to jump ship and think of settling down.

We looked at a number of places and eventually settled on a place in Mijas it was love at first sight 3 bedroom gated property just two hundred and seventy five thousand pounds, it would be the perfect end to my illustrious criminal life.

We arrived back in London, rejuvenated, suntanned and reenergised, I recruited a couple of pals to do my job and in another month London would be a distant memory.

Chapter Thirty Eight

A costly mistake

"Learn from the mistakes of others. You can't live long enough to make them all yourself."
- Eleanor Roosevelt -

It's funny I've met a lot of people in my life but none I could ever call my real friends, they have all just been business acquaintances.

Most of the guys I grew up with are either dead , dying or drug addicts so leaving wouldn't be hard, however the kids are another story, because they were the reason I came back to England in the first place they are the light where there has always been darkness in my life.

It was a month until we were moving so until then I reluctantly went back to work.

I arranged to meet Tony a pal I'd been working with in Tufnell park, as he has a good network so I'd decided to team up with him to have one more last massive push to get enough money for the villa and a few years in front.

Tony had been in the game, like me for years, so he was easy to work with, he had his punters and I collected the money.

It was working beautifully, we were sitting in his front room and a news flash came on the tv, all we could see was that a plane had smashed into one of the twin towers in New York it was crazy.

We watched perplexed and focused on the carnage in front of us, then another plane hit the other tower, which got our attention this was definitely a terrorist attack.

I watched it for most of the day whilst arranging for one of my guys to pick up ten kilos in the morning from outside Highbury train station.

It was a long day watching the towers collapse and the news bulletins repeatedly playing it over and over again, thousands dead and missing; police, firefighters and civilians, there would definitely be repercussion for this attack and god only knows how bad it would get.

The next day my Columbian connection called me and said he was on his way with the gear.

Then two minutes later my other pal said his mate was coming down from Manchester and would his two kilos be there?

"Yes" I said.

Then my other pal cancelled his four and Steve and Brian cancelled theirs, so I quickly called my Columbian friend and said "I only need two kilos today as everyone has cancelled because of the twin towers"

He said he couldn't turn round to lower what he had brought with him so I would have to take the ten.

"You better otherwise you will be wasting your time coming to me"

He reluctantly agreed and I apologised for shouting at him, he was now on the underground and on his way,

As he put down the phone my guy called me and explained he'd been watching the television all night and had been drinking, sniffing and smoking shit, so was in no condition to meet the Columbian at Highbury.

"Don't worry it's only two bits, I'll pick it up"

I quickly dressed and called a taxi to take me to Brent Cross station.

When I got to Highbury my guy wasn't there so I called him "ten minutes" he said then put the phone down.

I called my punter who said he would pick me up as his buyer was running late.

"How late?"

"About 30 minutes"

"Fucking hell mate"

"There's nothing I can do Tel, sorry mate"

The Columbian came out the station smiling then handed me a hessian shoulder bag with the 2 kilos in it.

I thanked him and said I'll call him later.

My pal pulled up and I jumped in his Mercedes and we drove to an apartment block down Pentonville Road, Kings Cross and he disappeared into the block.

While I impatiently waited in the car, as I looked behind me I noticed two traffic wardens and a postman walking towards me.

As I looked up three police cars pulled up and before I knew it the traffic wardens and postman were smashing in the windows, it was mayhem they were all over me screaming at me to put my hands up.

They dragged me out the car, I wasn't too worried as my pal was in the block of flats with the Charlie.

To my utter dismay he walked out of the door still carrying the hessian bag on his shoulder, which still had the 2 kilos in, his fucking mate had never turned up.

We were caught bang to rights and dopey bollocks had brought it right to them.

I had also had 20 kilos of weed dropped off to me that morning , which my girlfriend had put in the spare room because I was in such a rush, I only hoped my pal had picked it up as we arranged.

My world had just crumbled and there was nothing I could do about it, to compound my misery my girlfriend Sunshine had been arrested for 20 kilos of weed, as my soppy pal was late getting to mine, he had seen the old bill going in so had driven past.

It really couldn't get any worse.

As I sat in that cell contemplating my demise, I couldn't help but blame myself for my own stupidly, I'd done the job I paid others to do and now I had to pay the fucking Piper.

The filth had their ace card and they played it straight away, Terry we have arrested sunshine and she is going to get a custodial sentence unless you own this.

"Fuck off, I hardly know her and to be honest mate she could do with a holiday, I don't give a fuck , see you later"

I was then returned to my cell.

It was the only way I could play it, as I knew that if they thought I didn't gave a toss then they had to come back with a better offer, that would hopefully see her walk and me do the bird.

I didn't want to go guilty, because basically I hadn't been caught with anything, my pal had and so had sunshine with the weed.

It was one of those shit situations but I had to put my hands up, it's just something I'll have to accept for now.

I suppose it was a fair cop.

Chapter Thirty Nine

Back at Her Majesty's Pleasure

"When the prison doors are opened, the real dragon will fly out."
- Ho Chi Minh -

Over those first few months we went to court a few times, Sunshine was being supported by her family, who had graciously checked her into the Priory clinic at a cost of twenty grand.

A cost that I had to pay for under the proviso she didn't see me ever again.

I had pleaded guilty which meant she was excused of any involvement in my crimes and reluctantly all charges were dropped against her.

I on the other hand received 6 years which wasn't so bad as it was my first offence for drugs.

I had to do four years which would fly by but not before everything I owned was confiscated and seized by the proceeds of crime act, my money, house and my cars were all taken.

I literally left with the clothes on my back which made me bitter and resentful.

I'd lost so much, Kelly had got married and eventually Sunshine did too, my dreams of living in the sun with Sunshine in Spain was now just a footnote in history.

I could have laid down and just died but that wasn't my style, so I went to the library and started teaching myself to read and write, I also took out yoga books and every night I practiced yoga, meditation and mindfulness because I couldn't let hate consume me.

I felt let down by everyone, people I'd helped out over the years just disappeared, not one person sent me even a tenner, I was too proud to ask for anything anyway, only Kelly and my dad helped me through.

So I knuckled down and did what I had to do to survive intact.

I have always been a strong person, so a couple of years behind the door would be a breeze for me.

I would bide my time and see if I could think of a plan to get back all that I had lost.

By the time I reached my D cat I had been in prison 3 years, I had done a number of rehabilitation programs and courses and none of them had even touched the sides, in fact the stupidity of it all amused me.

I have seen men do every drug addiction recovery program, thinking skills, anger management courses, physical activity, diplomas, degrees, open university courses, even go out to the local colleges and still they leave prison and go back at it.

Unfortunately it's all about the perception of change, bums on seats evidenced by a piece of paper that says you took up the challenge to change, it's really all bollocks, age has so much to do with change not prison, they can claim what they want but the reality is prison in this country doesn't work.

How do I know this? because I was seen as a model prisoner, I'd done all the courses, I'd worked my ticket and given them exactly what they wanted to hear and see, which was compliance and the perception of change.

But it was this sentence I had started to think about ways to circumnavigate security procedures, I read books that educated me on how companies look after their valuables and books about people who had committed audacious heists. As they say knowledge is power.

I was in HMP Stamford Hill, a D cat prison selling drugs, drinking and smoking marijuana.

I'd even managed to pull a bird who was going there from a woman's prison, she was doing a physical education course and guess who was helping her? yes me.

We had been writing to each other, she is a well-known Essex bad girl called Tracy Mackness a very close friend of Linda Calvey.

We have also been going out on town visits together and meeting up at my pals flat in Maidstone, you couldn't make this shit up.

After nearly four years in prison she's like a breath of fresh air, I feel like a teenager again and she's a smart cookie she'd done a pig husbandry course and wanted to breed saddle back pigs.

She'd also managed to persuade her pal to give us a bit of land on the m25 to raise some pigs, it was her dream not mine but I decided to back her 100 percent, she brought a van and had it signed up with the giggly pig (the company name) and she rented a butcher shop.

She started making 35 different flavoured sausages, we started selling them at the Ally Pally farmers market and Romford and fuck me we sold out every week but it was hard work, especially feeding the pigs and trying to put them in their pens, in the winter it was wet and cold work.

I was covered in shit most days and I hated every day of it, but I stuck it out until I thought she could do without me.

There were good times, don't get me wrong, I enjoyed seeing the little piglets running around in the fields but disliked going to the abattoir with them immensely it just wasn't in my nature.

Chapter Forty

A little payback

"The human heart in its perversity finds it hard to escape hatred and revenge."
- Moses Luzzatto -

I remember one day after I'd been out of prison for a while Sunshine called me out of the blue and asked to meet her.

I arranged to meet her in the Stag pub in fleet road, I also arranged for Tracy to pick me up around the same time.

Sunshine turned up all done up and started telling me she had made a mistake by leaving me and getting married, she even started crying.

I didn't give a shit she had lost any right to my affections when she betrayed me, I paid all the bills, the mortgage payments, she had also lived of what I had earnt over those years but the second she and I were nicked she threw me under the bus.

So when Tracy turned up in her Mercedes Sports car, wearing a little mini skirt looking fucking fantastic, actually she looked a million dollars. I walked over to the car as sunshine was in mid-sentence and kissed Tracy and got in the car.

Payback's a bitch, as we pulled away Tracy asked me who I was talking to when she pulled up, I said some crack head asking me for some spare change, we drove to the Three Masons in Hampstead for dinner.

As much as I liked Tracy after about six months of killing myself getting up early and working at the farmers markets I decided to call time on our relationship.

We did it by mutual consent as she knew I was restless, I wanted to get back in the game, but not with her as she had gone straight, we have still remained friends even to this day.

Chapter Forty One

Back in the game and spiralling into the depths

"Every man has his secret sorrows which the world knows not; and often times we call a man cold when he is only sad."

- Henry Wadsworth Longfellow -

It didn't take me long to start something else I invested some money into a pill making machine and started making speed Balls the ecstasy tablets, which only lasted a couple of months as it soon became apparent that the bottom had fallen out of the game, MDMA had gone from twelve hundred quid wholesale to three thousand pounds, which knocked any profit margins out the window, as it was cheaper to buy them from Amsterdam than make them here in London, which put paid to that business venture.

I then tried the Charlie game again but everyone and their mother was in the game now, plus all the Charlie I looked at was either repressed or totally shit.

If we managed to buy a good bit we would repress it ourselves and farm it out but again it was slow going and eventually the arse fell out of it too and I ended up on skid row again.

I was managing to nick a couple of hundred quid a day.

Out of the blue I was then ordered to live in a hostel by my probation officer who said I'd be better of living there then in my private rented flat, the reason for her heavy-handed approach was I simply I couldn't prove where I got the three hundred and fifty quid a week to rent the flat from.

I had refused to sign on the dole, so she made me sign on, it was a fucking nightmare living there, as there were crack heads and prostitutes coming and going at all hours of the night.

One night when I came in, one of the guys who I had known from prison asked me to pop in and as I was a bit pissed I agreed, which turned out to be one of the biggest mistakes of my life as he offered me a crack pipe and like a cunt I accepted it.

Unfortunately it was the best hit I'd ever had and before the night ended I'd brought 6 rocks off him and returned to my room, for the next 12 months I went on a bender that would see me go to the depths of despair and become everything I despised in a human being.

I would go out all day and earn money and at night I'd sit in my room like a hermit doing crack, then to come down I'd smoke weed and then do heroin (chasing the Dragon) on tinfoil it was so good that I just couldn't get out of it.

I was spending two hundred pounds a night, I'd also drink a bottle of vodka or rum and smoke 40 cigarettes every night.

I'd sit in a dark room and listen to every noise, thinking it was the old bill trying to sneak up on me, my hearing was super enhanced, I could hear everything. I was so paranoid I had knifes everywhere and at times I wouldn't even breath for fear someone would hear me.

I'd piss in my sink because I didn't want to be seen by my house mates, I'd clean my crack bottle and smoke the dust.

When I ran out of crack or dust, I'd comb the floor, bed and carpet for the crumbs, crumbs that fell off my pipe.

When I couldn't afford crack I'd start buying more and more heroin, eventually it was only heroin I was buying, it tasted foul but the more I had the better it tasted, I found myself in the middle of the night calling low life dealers, then walking round the streets like a cunt.

Waiting on street corners like a seasoned muggy druggie, it was like a cancer that I just couldn't stop, I was ashamed of myself and embarrassed that I had fallen so far.

Day after day I hated myself and as the weeks and months went by I could see no light at the end of the tunnel.

I would beat myself up, I was at rock bottom and no matter how hard I tried, I just couldn't stop it.

There were no nightmares or walking through flowered covered fields, just an escapism from me and my fucking life.

It was retribution for all the misery I had caused everyone, I'd sold every conceivable drug and probably made many victims and addicts along the way, I've definitely destroyed families and lives and now I was paying the Piper.

I had turned into a loser, it was only by the grace of God I was still able to maintain my appearance, I always had clean clothes and shaved every day.

I ate properly too, so to the outside world and everyone one in it I was still the same old me.

I had to believe in some way that by me falling in to this world I'd now become more empathetic to the plight of those I'd always looked down on.

I would say I was definitely better placed to understand their need to escape into an alternative reality because for the first time in my life I had experienced escapism through the use of heroin, it had helped me break free from the nightmares that had plagued me for years, dreams of childhood trauma, beatings and being abandoned and thrown out like the trash.

I now knew why most drug addicts were prepared to sacrifice their appearance, to beg, borrow and steal so they can retreat into their own world, a world that isn't cruel, dark and violent.

It's a world that hasn't abused them physically, sexually and emotionally maybe they have found their utopia and society are the real denigrates who are the ones who haven't found the door that's been able to free them from their earthly shackles.

All I knew now, is that this life comes at a cost to everyone and everything you hold dear and love.

It makes you selfish, heartless and thoughtless, I've never been one to wallow in self-pity but taking drugs had made me contemptible, I promised to take the kids out but constantly let them down, I forgot their birthdays and on some occasions I could hear them knocking on my door and I just ignored them because I didn't want them to see me on one.

It was at these times I prayed that God would kill me and take me away from all this shit.

But thank God he never listened.

One day Terri, Charlene and Chloe were outside my hostel and seeing them made me more ashamed then I'd ever felt before, I tried to ease my conscience by giving them some money and promising to pop round that evening.

I'd spent just over a year trying to escape my reality, by going deeper and deeper into the recesses of my mind trying to find the answers to why I was on this mission of self-destruction and still the answers alluded me.

It told me that my drug induced psychosis was drug dependent and not the medicine I believed I needed.

Knowing this was an important first step in my fight to gain control of my sanity, the first realisation that I had to stop feeding it.

This realization that I was achieving nothing but repeating misery was the kick up the arse that I needed psychologically.

I slept that night better than I'd slept for ages knowing that tomorrow morning my fight back to normalcy would begin.

I needed to get this shit out of my system.

The only way I could help myself was to let my body take control, it needed rest, good food, and exercise.

Chapter Forty Two
The Road to Recovery

"Our greatest glory consists not in never failing, but in rising up every time we fall."
- Oliver Goldsmith -

I started the day by firstly getting rid of all my used lighters empty bottles and gauze.

I cleaned the room from top to bottom, washed my bedding, curtains and even painted the walls with some spare paint I found in one of the kitchen cupboards.

I shaved showered, went out and bought myself some trainers, shorts and running tops.

It was now time to stop ruminating and start fighting for what was left of my sanity.

I'd made so many bad decisions whilst infecting myself with the filth in my system over the last year.

I'd been on a few bits of work and managed to take home about forty grand but it had nearly cost me my life.

We had taken down a score and when we got back to my pals place he was still pumped full of adrenaline and decided to re-enact a scene from a fucking Al Pacino film by pulling his gun out and pointing it at my head, forgetting that the gun still had one bullet left in the chamber he pulled the trigger but the gun jammed, it was only by the grace of God that I didn't end up on a concrete slab in the mortuary.

My other mate quickly grabbed the gun out of his hand, it was only because of his quick thinking and foresight that my other pal never got the opportunity to pull the trigger again, he's the reason I'm still here and why we are still friends to this day.

Another time a guy pulled a Uzi submachine gun out on me and pointed it at my chest and stomach, saying that I had taken a liberty by going through his front door one night to collect a debt whilst his wife and kids were in the house.

He had apparently left them and escaped out the back door and jumped over the wall.

I explained to him that the guy who had come round to his house was in fact working for me, but he had over stepped the mark by kicking in his front door as I'd give strict instructions to only take it out on him and not any of the family especially not in front of any woman and children.

He pointed the gun at my stomach again and said it didn't matter what I had to say because he was going to kill me.

So I just said "fucking do it then, because whatever happens you soppy looking cunt you're a fucking dead man any way".

He then went all red in the face and just backed away.

I couldn't understand why until I looked behind me, a police car was driving towards us along the road, what a stroke of luck, I couldn't believe it.

I just walked towards them, went home picked up a little sawn-off shotgun that I had, called a pal and borrowed his black cab. I sorted out my problem, with no dramas.

I'll just say he's still alive.

It was moments like this that played in my mind like a record player over and over again, I'd wake up in the middle of the night soaking wet with sweat. I'd see myself being buried in a coffin with my kids crying at my grave.
I'd have dreams about waking up buried and trying to get out of my grave, I dreamt of being buried alive, it's been a recurring nightmare that had plagued me for years night after night.

I dreamt of suffocating then slowly running out of air.

It's funny how your mind plays tricks on you, I've been stabbed in leg, chest and have had 150 stitches in my arm.

I've been beaten and battered by grown men since I was a kid but that's nothing compared to the dreams that have tortured me nightly throughout my life.

Nothing physical has ever made me scream out loud, like the way I scream in my nightmares and the only medicine that's been able to stop those nightmares was heroin, the same drug that almost destroyed me.

After one year of madness I stopped cold Turkey, day one was a lot easier than I ever imagined, I went for a run over Hampstead heath. I did the boxers run or half of it anyway, it wasn't a pretty sight,
I was coughing and spluttering everywhere.

I lost count of how many times I stopped before I reached the top of the hill, on the way back I was sick everywhere.

I walked to the top of kite hill and looked out across London, I made a covenant with myself that I'd beat this shit and get fitter and stronger then I'd even been before.

I have always been mentally strong and resilient so I was under no illusion that I couldn't beat this, it would be just a matter of time.

I eventually got home I showered and cooked myself some spaghetti Bolognese and slept like a baby.

By week two I was getting round the boxing run and my breathing was so much better, I even started doing pull ups, dips and press ups, muscle memory from all those years of training was now paying dividends.

By week twelve I was smashing it, I'd even joined a gym in Hampstead next to the royal free hospital called the armoury,
I was boxing and doing circuit training with the other fitness instructors and beating them.

After six months I was as fit as a fiddle and healthier then I'd ever been in my life.

I was 6ft 1in and 17 stone of solid muscle and I felt invincible.

My relationship with the kids was back to normal, I was visiting them most days and my year of madness was but a distant memory.

It was now time to get back in the saddle, I had been in contact with a couple of old pals who like me were fearless and smart with it, one was ex-army pal called Dez and the other two both solid characters, one was from Angel in

Highbury and Islington called Mickey and the other a Kilburn boy called the tall fella, simply because he was 6ft 4in and very capable, in fact these guys were all capable especially Dez.

Chapter Forty Three
Getting the team together

"A journey of a thousand miles starts with a single step."
- Lao Tzu -

We had all worked together before so there was no question about them all being staunch (trustworthy) we all met up and agreed that the plan was to earn enough money to go our separate ways, I wanted to go back to Spain.

Dez was a family man who had settled down, he had just bought himself a nice little four bedroom detached house, the tall fella had also brought himself a lovely big house in the country with the wife and kids.

Little T was living with his girlfriend and I had met a lovely girl in Hampstead and had moved in with her.

We all had our specialities, the tall fella was a confidence trickster, Mickey was procurement he could get anything guns, cars, vans and even uniforms and proper ID's.

Dez brought military discipline and planning which was key if we wanted to be successful in what I wanted to do.

We had all become disillusioned with the drug game and were looking for a new revenue stream, that would challenge us and make us stand out from your normal run of the mill armed robber, I came to this conclusion after sitting in prison talking with lots of armed robbers, who had either been shot or crippled by the old bill.

A few were notorious and quite a few I spoke to were not so notorious, but never the less they all had one thing in common; guns, violence and hit and miss robberies.

For example if you rob a bank, security van or jewellery shop, you are basically going in blind, its hit and miss if you get the prize because so much can go wrong.

There could be a silent panic alarm button.

A passer-by could see you going in with your balaclava on and guns blazing, he then calls the police.

Remote security monitoring was becoming more popular, this is where footage is viewed around the clock at a secret off-site location, they can then trigger police response alarms.

There are so many variables, like a passing police car, plainclothes officers, beat coppers, fast response robbery squads, all cruising the area.

The prisons are full of guys who have taken a fifty fifty chance and because they used guns they all received life sentences, IPP's or twenty five stretches.

Long sentences for taking money and a gamble; when you consider that there is also a shoot to kill policy by the flying squad to deter armed robbers, then you have to wonder why men still take that gamble.

I've met loads of guys in prison who are testament to that policy, they have seen their friends and accomplices killed, some have been crippled themselves and many more paralysed.

My dad was an armed robber, him and his crew shot and killed a security guard, it was an accident, but that's always going to be the case if you carry a gun, accidental deaths are part and parcel of the game or being shot by the police.

Once you're known by the filth for carrying a gun its basically open session on you, a kind of fight fire with fire mentality that is a vote winner with overzealous members of the public that believe capital punishment is the answer to all of the country's crime problems.

We wanted to be different, but professional at the same time and of course we wanted to widen the odds in our favour of ever getting caught and getting away with the prize every time.

It was only by sheer luck that I'm not one of those guys sitting in prison, paralysed or dead, as I was once asked to get back a couple of kilos of Charlie (cocaine) by a team from a south London gangster.

Some mugs in Dagenham had stolen gear from one of their punters, they wanted to make an example of them and get their gear back.

I drove over there for them with a snub nosed revolver in my waistband, whilst my pal had a machete tucked into his trousers, we were smartly dressed. The plan was simple, to just knock on the door, retrieve the coke and leave them with a memento of our visit.

However when we arrived I decided to drive by, I also asked my driver to park two streets over so we could casually walk there.

From the minute I got out the car I had a strange feeling that something wasn't right, so as we neared the house I decided to walk past, then about ten houses down, we slowly turned into a little block of flats, I put the gun on the top of a shed roof, along with my pals machete.

We both cut across the back gardens and came out behind our target house in the next street, where we noticed an armed response vehicle, as we passed the hotel car park, there were three car loads of old bill, they were all waiting for us to come from the other direction, from the London side, but we had come the back way in and luckily for us we did.

It wasn't over yet, we had to run the gauntlet of police, we casually walked passed them into a shop nearby, we were fucked but luckily for us a black cab just pulled up and the driver came into the shop, I asked if he could drop us at the nearest train station but he just said he wasn't working, adding that he had just finished for the evening.

"No problem mate".

We were definitely fucked now, as we had to walk back past all the old bill.

If this was a set up then the likelihood was they'd have photos of us, it was a nightmare situation, but just as we started walking back the cab driver came out behind.

"Come on guys I'll drop you at the nearest station"

"Thanks mate" I said as we both got in the cab. To say I was relieved was an understatement, as we drove past we could see that the police were agitated and were itching to take out anyone who knocked on that door tonight, we left the gun and the machete where it was.

Two days later we were told that the guys in the house, the two wankers that had stolen the coke in the first place, had been so scared of reprisals, that they had called the police and told them that a contract had been put out on them, hence the armed response team at the back of their property, it had been a close shave and one I will chalk up to divine intervention and a very lucky escape.

Chapter Forty Four
Inspiration

"Imagination is more important than knowledge."
- Albert Einstein -

After this and all the war stories I'd heard in prison I wanted to level the playing field and believe it or not, my inspiration came one night when I was sitting in my cell watching the Ocean's 11 movie.

It dawned on me the answer to the perfect caper was simply to become one of the enemy, a fast response robbery squad with our own ID's, uniforms, equipment, cars , vans and a dog ,the full shebang.

No guns, no violence or casualties it would be the perfect crime, we would use the police uniforms to gain entry.

As I knew from my own experience with the police, when they came into my house, that regardless of my own capabilities I would always be compliant and never fight them in front of my family.

If we applied the same principles to most security guards, who were either ex- army or police they would do the same, because they all had respect for authority and wouldn't question a search warrant or a warrant card.

With that in mind over a couple of months I had been testing that theory by just walking in to places and pretending to be a metropolitan police officer, flashing my warrant card and saying that we had received information that a gang of thieves had targeted the area for computer technology and software and we believed that they would be potential targets if their security wasn't improved.

I would then ask the head of security to show me around the building so I could better optimise their procedures and implement changes where and when necessary.

This was a simple roux and worked like a dream every time and in quite a few places they actually took me to their strong rooms where they kept the most expensive software, computer chips and motherboards. It was so much fun, it appealed to my natural ability to entertain and I actually started enjoying it.

I remember one guy made me a cup of coffee and even showed me where he hid the strong room keys, so if anyone did over power him, they wouldn't be able to gain entry to the safe.

Unfortunately for him, he was one of our first victims, a place we robbed with keys left behind the water system in the security room, he wasn't on duty at the time, but I can only imagine that he never mentioned his security lapses and that he in part had facilitated in our endeavour some weeks previously, making us in the process a small fortune.

We did this on numerous occasions because getting the right information was paramount to us, it saved time and effort trying to locate the mainframe server room's.

It was like taking candy from a baby, we were also starting to get noticed by certain underworld figures who wanted money or merchandise returned without too much fuss.

We were fast becoming the go to firm when something couldn't be breached, we were able to circumnavigate certain security procedures and my research whilst inside was starting to pay dividends.

Convincing joe public was easy and on a couple of occasions we even convinced the real feds, I remember we were sitting in the car with our police caps on and this geezer came out of one of the houses and knocked on the window and asked us how we were doing, he produced his warrant card and said he was in the job and could he help.
I leant forward and said we had someone under surveillance and were just making sure that he definitely lived there.

He asked where we were from so I told him Kentish town police station, he even offered us coffee, we declined but thanked him anyway.

He shook my hand and left with a smile on his face .

Our confidence was growing and we were working non-stop over this period unfortunately I can't mention what we did as our clients anonymity is still a close guarded secret, but we were now at the top of our game.

Chapter Forty Five

The Fixers

"Behind every successful fortune there is a crime."
- Mario Puzo, The Godfather -

Due to our successes a well-known associate of ours had been contacted by a consortium of villains, they wanted us to fly over to Antwerp and retrieve a consignment that was in a bonded warehouse on a trading estate, somewhere in Europe, he said we would be paid handsomely, half upfront for all our expenses and the remainder on completion.

But only if we retrieved his merchandise.

For us it was a no brainer, we accepted it straight away and was told it was a carousel fraud, also called missing trader intra-community value-added tax (VAT) fraud, fraudsters import goods VAT-free from other countries, then sell the goods to domestic buyers, charging them VAT. The sellers then disappear without paying the tax to the government.

We were tasked with stealing the consignment we didn't ask questions, all we knew was that we had to get into a warehouse, cuff three security guards, get the case number from the computer, grab a forklift, load it up, drive to France and drop it off.

We then had to call back to London so they could release our funds , it was as simple as that.

We had been sent a photo of the premises, the opening times, also the number of employees who worked there, who the key holder was, we were even sent his registration number and home address.

Dez, the tall fella and Mickey flew over to Antwerp and I took the ferry to Ostend and hired a high-top van and drove up to Antwerp.

I took the time to drive to the warehouse and give it the once over, it was smaller than I had imagined there were 12 units side by side and ours was right in the corner protected by trees and four lorries; it would be easy.

In Europe most of the security carry guns, so I was worried we might have to go in hard and hurt them, but I needn't have worried because there was only one security guard and five people working in there and no guns.

Three in the office, one man and two women, a guy on the forklift and a floor manager along with the guard sitting in a security box outside, which made six.

I watched it for a couple of hours and noticed that it wasn't a busy estate in fact it was really quiet, so far this looked pretty straight forward, but I'd let Dez take a look and get his opinion over the next couple of days.

When I arrived at the farmhouse we had rented for the week the boys were there getting ready to go out to the local restaurant, we were roughly twenty miles from the job, there were quite a few tourists in the town so we wouldn't stand out like sore thumbs, we had a lovely meal mussels in white wine sauce and steak and chips all round.

I told the team what I thought and how we should approach it but to be on the safe side me and Dez would look at it properly in the morning, to figure out the best approach.

Mickey had brought some number plates, which I would put on the van in morning once we were out of town.

We had four blue boiler suites, caps and black work boots and gloves, the tall fella drove to France to pick up the keys to the slaughter where we were going to leave the gear, he would also make sure there were no cameras that would see us going in or out of there.

We needed to minimise all the risks and it was only by doing these simple things that we would get back to England without too much drama, especially if the shout went out (the alarm raised).

Me and Dez were both sitting in the back of the van when two uniformed guards came out of our warehouse, both had guns in their holsters, fuck I hadn't seen them the day before, what had changed?

I don't know.

We watched them leave then go in and out of all the other units then get in a little security patrol vehicle, it was 8am and we were lucky to have noticed these guys, we stayed there all day and at 6.30pm they came back again.

But this time we watched them go into all the units, before they left.

This was good news for us, as we could now hit the warehouse in the morning after they left, knowing that they wouldn't be back until the evening.

Sometimes regular patrols make it easier for criminals as it allows for a window of opportunity.

But to be on the safe side we decided to add another day to our schedule to make sure they stuck to the script and thank God they did, we spent the night going through the plan, Mickey would drive into the unit as soon as the guards pulled away, I would take the warehouse security guard out of the game, Micky would grab the forklift driver and I'd take the floor manager, Dez and the tall fella would secure the guy and girls in the office and get the case number.

I would find the pallets and load it onto the van.

On paper it was a done deal, but nothing ever runs smoothly in this game, there are always things that are out of your control that you just can't foresee or factor in.

We had covered all the bases and tomorrow was our D day.

Everyone was up at 5am, showered, shaved and ready to go by 6.30am.

We all met at the van; Dez and the tall fella in the back with Mickey driving and me in the passenger seat.

We pulled over about twenty minutes outside of town, I quickly jumped out and changed the number plates.

From this moment on there would be no turning back, we were now all in our boiler suites, caps on and had our cuffs at the ready, just as we arrived the security guards were just pulling in, we waited and then waited some more but for some reason that hadn't come out.

I took the opportunity to get my clip board out and the little parcel we had wrapped up and walked along the other side of the road, as I passed one of the units I saw that the two Scotland yards (security) were having a cup of tea and a chat with two office birds, it was just one of those things.

As I walked back, they both came out and headed towards their patrol Jeep, got in and sped off, my heart was beating and my mouth was dry ,the adrenaline was kicking in.

We drove up to the security guards box I quickly jumped out and pushed him back to the wall, then I gave him a little tap on the jaw and said put your arms behind your back, I picked him up from the floor and walked him into the warehouse.

Once in there I placed him face down and then called out to the floor manager while Mickey had the forklift driver cuffed and facedown,

I approached the floor manager who was about 6ft 2in and quite well built but surprisingly he understood why we were there and turned round and tried to run but I quickly took him to the ground and cuffed him, so far it had taken us about three minutes to do our part by over powering them, Dez and the tall fella were busy too sorting out their end.

I pulled the shutters down so no one could see us or walk in, the place was now secure.

We took our three captors into one of the store rooms and placed them all face down, Mickey's job was to look after them.

The tall fella and Dez joined us within a minute with three, so now Mickey had six people to guard, all face down on the floor.

Dez had the case number so I asked the floor manager where our pallets were located, he said he would show me, so the tall fella and Dez took him, whilst I jumped in the forklift.

And true to his word the floor manager showed us three pallets, fuck we had stupidly assumed that there was only two pallets to load up, now we would have to take one of the vans that belonged to the company we were robbing to France, fuck we never had any spare plates either.

I quickly loaded up a van and told Mickey to leave straight away, we would stay in the warehouse for as long as we could, just long enough for him to get half way to the slaughter, unload the gear then dump the van.

After he pulled out I loaded up our van and told the tall fella to go, we would stay behind for another hour, to give him enough time to get to where he was going.

Me and Dez made sure everyone was ok we even gave them all a glass of water and told them not to worry, I also took another set of van keys to one of the Van's outside.

We ended up waiting 45 minutes, before we locked them all in the store room by parking the forklift against the door, we then locked everything up and got into one of the firm's vans.

I drove back to our hotel, Mickey and the tall fella had their passports on them so would make their own way back to England as arranged, I dropped Dez of at the airport, then drove to France to pick up my hire van which the tall fella had left parked up.

I quickly changed the plates over again and drove to Ostend where I parked the van up after having it washed and cleaned at a service station, I took all the boiler suites and binned them, wiped the inside of the van down, then posted the keys through the letter box.

As I got on the ferry I couldn't stop smiling to myself, we hadn't planned for the extra pallet, which meant we had to nick two vans that had the company name on, it couldn't have gone any worse for us, even if we had planned it that way.

We were lucky that we had plenty of time before the scream went up, everyone was safely back in England, which was good, I on the other hand still had another 3 hours on the ferry to go and probably another 2 hours after that back to London.

It was going to be a long night, but at least we had done the job and were still free.

I'm afraid to say that is all that really matters to us , we had arranged to meet up in London at the New Inn, a lovely pub and restaurant in St. John's wood to celebrate our safe return, we also had to carve up a few quid.

We had a bit of dinner and a burn-out -piss- up , which was just what we all needed after the last five days.

Our fixer called me a couple of days later and said that all the employees were released at 6.30pm that evening when the security patrol eventually came back.

The staff and security guard had all come through their ordeal unscathed and the police were now looking for a gang of ruthless bastards (his words), he also added that the theft didn't make the news or the mainstream papers, so all in all a sweet little job, he said his people were extremely happy.

I took the next couple of weeks off and decided to fly to Spain and soak up a bit of sun and ended up on one of the nudist beaches, just outside Benalmadena with my girlfriend.

It was a relaxing time, we spent every night in a different restaurant and sunbathed every day. In the afternoon I swam out to a rock about a hundred yards off shore, climbed out and sunbathed naked on it, it felt brilliant, the sea was calm, deep blue and the sun was shining.

It was so relaxing until my girlfriend called for me to return to the beach, so I smiled at her and stood tall in all my glory and dived in.

But as I broke the surface, it felt as if someone had slapped me on the arm, as I looked around and into the water, all I could see were jelly fish everywhere.

I'd been stung and it didn't feel good, so Instead of swimming back to shore I panicked like an idiot and headed towards the rocks and as I pulled myself out a spiny sea urchin stuck in my knee.

The shock made me slip and I lost my footing smashing my toe against the rock as I fell.

By the time I got back to my girlfriend I could barely walk, my toe had swollen up, the sting on my arm was about two foot long and it was hurting like fuck, so I went to the beach hut and said I think I've been stung.

The girl took one look at it and came from behind the bar with a bottle of vinegar and some ibuprofen, which only added to my embarrassment as my dick had shrunk to an all-time low and had retreated up my arse.

My girlfriend was in hysterics laughing as I limped back up the beach towards her, saying that's what you get for showing off.

To take my mind of the pain I slept until the sun went down. When I eventually woke it took me forty minutes to walk a couple of hundred feet back to my car.

The pain was severe so we drove to a chemist and brought some painkillers and a bottle of vodka, I spent the night drowning my sorrows.

It took three days before I could even get out of bed, but the break had done me the world of good as I looked tanned and healthy when I stepped off the plane back in England. I was ready and eager to get back to work.

That Monday morning the tall fella and Dez called round and said that we had been offered another job down near the coast, it
was mostly money and some jewellery worth over two hundred and fifty grand.

The target was a guy who by all accounts was a proper handful and wouldn't part with his ill-gotten gains without a fight, so we needed to take him out hard, fast and quickly.

The information we had was that he had a floor safe buried in the front room located in the left side alcove under a book cabinet.

The key to the safe was hidden in his garage in a metal snap on red tool box.

The back story was that our client had been partners in a company with his pal who swindled him out of half a million pounds, so this was payback.

It was a five minute job and we would walk away with a hundred and twenty five grand in cash.

The only problem was that we would be going in blind, we knew that he lived on his own but he also had a girlfriend that stayed with him at weekends.

We couldn't get a photo of the house or plot up on it to do any reconnaissance, as we would stand out like sore thumbs, as it was a little village in the middle of nowhere and these places normally have nosey neighbours and this guy was no fool and could have a go.

We could take our guns and just go in but the potential for something going wrong and the police being called was extremely high.

So we had to go in as police officers as this would definitely be the best option.

We got a map of the area and planned our routes in and out.

We also needed a backup car plotted just in case anything did go wrong.

We picked Friday as it was forecast to rain heavy, which normally means no one on the street plus people are less likely to have a clear look at you as they would be too busy under their umbrellas and the house windows would be steamed up.

Fog or rainy winter mornings are the best options for doing a bit of graft.

We called Mickey and said we needed the police van again. Mickey had a guy who he could hire a real ex- police van and ambulance from.

Vehicles that were now hired out and used on film sets, they also had security patrol cars and a Securicor van.

We used the ambulance loads of times because no one ever takes notice of them, also a black taxi, but for now the police van was our best bet.

We always fill up with petrol in London before we do any jobs no matter how far the journey was, we also take full jerry cans.

We do this because every service station has cameras and normally if the old bill know which direction you came or left from, then they will forensically check every petrol station CCTV.

Also we never used the toilets or the shops, again for the same reason, the ideal scenario was in and out without a trace, keep the old bill guessing.

We normally go to Dez's place and change into our uniforms, as his gaff is off the beaten track, he also has a garage for the van and an eye for detail.

Every bit of our uniforms were meticulously cleaned and chosen by Dez from the cuffs, radios, vests, police caps and boots.

We looked like a commando unit sharp and crisp which was effective when going into places, especially as we were not carrying or using guns, CS gas, tasers or cosh's.

We were just using our voices, intellect, brazen good luck and professionalism.

We rehearsed and went over every job.

Nothing was left to chance apart from the unforeseeable moments like when we were in Antwerp.

We learnt from every mistake and we were definitely getting better and more comfortable, there was no more hesitation, we were for all intent and purpose real police officers.

We would read them their rights (memorandum), handcuff them, most thought they were hardened criminals, but they soon realised that we were the real deal and as they pondered on the fact they had just been done by fake filth.

I suppose for some of them it must have been a relief, as we found drugs, porn and incriminating evidence on quite a few of our raids which we photographed and left behind, hence the reason none of them ever went to the old bill and reported us, as most, if not all of them were corrupt.

That Friday was cold, windy and pissing down with rain and as we pulled into the street it was still dark so we parked right outside the house, so if he looked out the window all he would see was a police van.

I got out with Dez right behind me.

The tall fella stood at the gate while Mickey stayed at the wheel, Knock! knock! knock! it took a minute before a light came on in the hallway.

I stood tall as the door opened and he stood there in his pyjamas slippers and a bowl of cereal in his hand, he looked confused as I said "we have a warrant for your arrest , and a warrant to search the house" and with that I cuffed him.

All he kept saying was "what's all this about".

I took him in the kitchen and said "an allegation of rape has been made against you sir"

"What do you mean?"

"Look let's calm down sir, have you got any drugs or guns on the premises?"

"No I fucking ain't"

"Have you got a safe sir?"

"Why!"

"I think you know why sir!"

"I don't, I don't know anything honestly"

My Job was to confuse him and distract his attention as Dez located the key and the tall fella cleared a path to the safe.

When they had finished Dez gave me the sign for the all clear, so I laid the guy face down on the floor and tied his legs and dragged him into the front room.

I then whispered in his ear "if you make a sound or got free I'll come back and cut off your ears" I tapped him on the back and said "goodbye, it's been emotional".

The journey back was uneventful but when we came back into London a police car and van full of police was parked up as there was a traffic jam on the motorway.

It was just our luck to pull up right alongside them, eight coppers in their van and three old Bill in the car.

I told Mickey to keep calm and just keep driving, Dez was pretending to do some paper work and the tall fella was faking sleep, I looked over and gave them a salute, I nodded and two even saluted back, it was another one of those moments if we had reacted differently we would have been fucked.
We had bags of money, jewellery and we were literally 6 feet away from them.

As we pulled past there was a sigh of relief from the tall fella, Micky started laughing and Dez just smiled at me.

I laughed aloud like Mickey and the tall fella said "fuck this Tel I'm taking a train next time" we all laughed at the absurdity of what had just happened.

We had kept our cool and that's all you can ask of the men you trust and would give your life for.

The bond we had all forged over this period had cemented us into a cohesive group that was working better than any team I'd worked with before, the chemistry was right, it had all the perfect ingredients for success.

We all had a feeling that nothing was impossible for us, all we needed now was a job that would take us to the next level, because the 200 and 300 grand jobs were not going to take us out of this life,
we needed a once in a lifetime job that would set us up for life, but they were few and far between and only ever happened in films.

The computer chip game had seen the arse fall out of it over the last couple of years, those million and five million pound jobs had been done and the insurance companies only allowed shipments of between £300.000 or £350.000 now, so by the time you carved it up, we were only coming away with 60 or 70 thousand between four of us, which was less than twenty grand each,
the money was good but again those jobs, were few and far between.

We all had money now and plenty of it, I had an expensive car, clothes and life was brilliant but that elusive job was yet to materialize and I was starting to wonder if it ever would.

The camaraderie we had between us all was different from anything I'd ever experienced before, yes we were friends and sometimes we socialised together but the majority of the time we all lead totally separate lives, we only came together to earn money.

You could say it was a purely a professional relationship that we had , which is why I believed that it worked so well, we all had respect for each other and knew our roles.

I could communicate with all of them, without even talking to them, Dez in particular seemed to have a sixth sense because wherever I needed him to be, he was there.

The tall fella on the other hand was always where he wasn't supposed to be and Mickey was Mickey, dependable, reliable and fearless.

Chapter Forty Six

A Career Job - The Beginning

"If you don't take risks, you'll have a wasted soul."
- Drew Barrymore -

It was about a month until I spoke to all of them again, the reason being I'd been summoned by my guy, the fixer who had given me the carousel job In Antwerp, so I had arranged to meet him in Pond street, opposite Hampstead heath in a little cafe that had tables outside so we could sit quietly without being overheard, called Polly's.

The old lady and her husband who owned it were like an institution, I'd known them for years, so I knew that it was a safe place to meet.

My guy the fixer was fashionably late but when he did turn up he looked a million dollars, he was wearing a discreet Rolex watch, a gentleman's cap, a multi coloured cravat and full length overcoat.

The guy had style, he personified the old archetype villain, good manners, respectful, he had a nice suntan and a husky voice like Ray Winstone.

We had coffee, cakes then did the normal small talk, before he gave me the information

"I have been contacted by a consultant in Ireland who is involved with some influential bankers from America whose associates are part of a consortium of investors that have invested heavily in construction that has taken off in Ireland.

However some of these individuals have circumnavigated banking procedures such as due diligence(KYC) and certain Bos (banking officials) were involved in prime mortgages.

Because of certain irregularities and oversights, sensitive information regarding all their transfers and transactions can be evidenced, which would eventually lead back to them and their American counterparts.

So they have put together a package that they feel should adequately pay for your services and the return of certain sensitive information that is being held at a data protection facility in London.

Details can be discussed if you accept the job"

He also added "This is a high risk heist"

The figure he had just shown me should alleviate any pain that the job would throw up, he said "I can't stress enough to you Terry that this job is a priority and sensitivity is paramount as the information held on these computer chips can't fall into the hands of the FBI or ever see the light of day, the consequences of that happening would be catastrophic not just to my people but the banking industry in general"

"Ok, but how can I give you a yes or no without seeing the details?"

My fixer said "all I can say Tel is that the job is extremely well protected and has state of the art security, at any one time there are between 8 to 10 security guards on duty, 6 cleaners and maybe 4 technicians.

There is also an independent security company who had a live feed into the data centre room.

To top it off there is only one way in as the building backs onto a canal, oh and there are three police stations within a mile radius however there is some good news, no one is armed"

"Have you offered this job to anyone else?"

"No, but three other teams have attempted to retrieve this information but have all failed, that's why they are now offering you and your team one and half bar (£1.5 million cash) into an account of your choosing"

"Ok, what happened with the other jobs?"

"Well last October (20th, 2006) EasyJet's primary data centre was robbed by a team with valid swipe cards but failed to get the information, then two weeks later, several routers cards were stolen from a Level 3 facility interrupting services but again they were challenged so had to pull away.

More recently there was an armed raid into a C1 host data centre in Chicago, that was in October this year 6 weeks ago, that team cut through an exterior wall and assaulted employees, no one was seriously hurt, but again they failed to secure the data, that's why the security has been stepped up, especially at this data centre in London"

"That's why no one else will take this on" I said, "especially now after three fuck ups!

Why ask me and my guys to take on the impossible?"

"Because you and your team are the only ones I know who are capable of pulling off something like this without hurting everyone or drawing too much attention to it, as it needs to look like just another opportunist robbery, my backs up against the wall on this one Tel, it has to be done soon and done properly"

"I really don't know mate, on the surface this job sounds impossible, even if we were to use guns, which we won't be using , it just sounds fucking crazy.

Are there any panic buttons in the building?"

"Yes!"

"How many?"

"I'm not sure at the moment"

"Do you have any idea where they might be?"

"We believe they are In the security guards monitoring room on the ground floor. Also Terry, the whole place has a sophisticated keypad entry system, with biometric and card access on all the interior and exterior doors throughout the building.

Terry the place is like Fort Knox!"

"Ok" I said "I'll talk to my boys and get back to you later, but If we do this, I will need a couple of weeks to put it together"

"Of course, Terry"

"I'll also need some money upfront for vehicles and miscellaneous, about thirty grand."

"No problem mate, I can arrange that"

"Ok let's see if we can do something to help your situation.

Listen next time we meet, let's do it at the Old Viaduct, over Hampstead heath, at the red archers bridge, do you know it?"

"Yes!" he said "I'll meet you there"

"Wednesday 2pm, I'll ring you to confirm first, bring the money and all the details of the data centre and anything else that might be relevant to us"

"Ok"

My head was racing after I left him, my team was good but doing this job in the middle of London with 10 or more security guards and three police stations within a mile radius and let's not forget panic buttons, CCTV, biometric hand scanners and a keypad door entry system, also an independent security firm monitoring the data room, this job couldn't be any harder, especially if we also had to add in the technicians and cleaners.

This job would need a lot of ingenuity.

I called Dez immediately and asked him to get the tall fella and Mickey to arrange a meeting as soon as possible,
at the New Inn pub, St. John's wood.

I wasn't drinking when the boys walked in for obvious reasons, we all ordered coffees and then sat in the corner.

I then explained to them what had just been offered to me by the fixer, the tall fella said we would have to be pissed or crazy to do this job.

"It's fucking impossible, especially with no guns Tel, we only need one guard to panic and press a panic button, then we are all in the shit doing years behind bars, I really don't know Tel.

"Mickey what do you reckon?" I asked

"I'm with you Tel, whatever you decide mate it's your call"

"Dez, what do you think mate?"

"I think you're fucking crazy Tel but you already know that don't you!" he laughed as he said this.

"Look. They are going to wire us 1.5 million pounds straight into our accounts, as soon as we hand over the motherboards, that's three hundred and seventy grand each for one nights work, we would be crazy not to do this, or at least take a look at it.

We can always say no but I reckon we should at least have a proper look at it, before we make any rash decisions.

Let's just say yes for now and get all the details, if everyone's in an agreement then let's at least try it"

"Ok" said Mickey.

"I'm definitely in" said Dez.

"I still think it's a suicide mission" said the tall fella "but of course I'm in. Yes you cunts."

"Ok then, as soon as I get the details we will dedicate ourselves to this full time, Me and Dez can spend a couple of weeks looking at it to see if there are any weaknesses or flaws in their procedures.

In the meantime Mickey, can you get us a British Telecom van from your pal at the auctions?

Dez you talk to your pal Frankie and see if he wants a bit of work for the night, we can put him on wages if you want, also order some new police uniforms.

I'll talk to Frankie, when and if we decide to do this or even use him, I'm going to meet my guy the fixer over Hampstead tomorrow and get everything off him, afterwards Dez can we meet at your place, say about 6pm, so we can go over it?"

"Yes no problem Tel"

"Tall fella, can you get the police van and a car?"

"Yes no problem Tel, Do you want a dog as well while I'm at it?" there was a hint of sarcasm in his voice.

"You know mate, that's not a bad idea, can you get an Alsatian?"

"I was only joking Tel, no!"

"It's a brilliant idea brother, can you borrow an Alsatian or not?"

"I think so yes"

"Get it then, the bigger the better."

"It won't be a problem Tel, trust me"

"Ok then, I'll see you tomorrow Dez, Mickey call me when you get that van, and let's all meet up tomorrow night ok?"

"Yes"

"Yes"

"Yes"

"Ok, later guys."

Chapter Forty Seven

Verizon - The Job

"The biggest risk for us on any job is if the people that work there actually do their jobs properly."
- Terry Ellis -

I called my fixer to say I had a preliminary yes from my team, however it still wasn't a hundred percent as we needed all the details and preferably some schematics of the layout of the building, especially if we were even going to consider taking on this job.

I told him that he had to understand that doing this job wasn't like on the tv where you cut a few wires and redirect the cameras, because that's all made up bollocks for the films.

This is real life and the consequences for me and my guys would be 15 years or more in prison if we got caught.

Because of that I needed a bit of latitude in as far as getting all the relevant information was concerned before I agreed to do the job, so it was imperative that he get back to his people straight away to get me the information that I needed.

He agreed and said, "I'll See you tomorrow 2pm"

"No problem mate"

The ball was now in his court, his Irish and American counterparts, had failed on three separate occasions to acquire the data that they so desperately needed.

I saw no reason why they wouldn't give me what I wanted or I would just have to pull the plug on the whole thing.

I wrapped up warm today, as it was a cold November afternoon, I made my way to towards Hampstead heath.

I normally like to arrive early to Scope the place out, also to see if anyone is following me, being surveillance conscious is part and parcel of the game, so as I walked up fleet street and onto pond street, I was able to look at the reflections in the windows, to see if anyone was following me on foot.

My pal Johnny was on the flower stall, so I stood with him for ten minutes chatting and making sure that it looked to all and sundry that this was just a normal day out for me.

I popped into the little cafe on the corner and bought us both a coffee, then when I was ready, I started walking up, past Hampstead over ground station then up the tree lined path towards the ponds.

It took me twenty minutes to make my way through the woods, until I was certain that there were no prying eyes on me, I got myself into a good position to see if my fixer was being tailed.

But like me he seemed to materialise out of nowhere, as I watched him walk to the middle of the red Arches bridge.

There were only two dog walkers and an old couple, but nothing untoward, so I made my way towards him.

He greeted me with a nod as we both lent on the wall looking out over the pond.

He said it wasn't easy but he had managed to locate the floor plans to the Verizon data centre and the exact room where the mother boards were being held.

He then handed me two envelopes one with 30 grand in, the other with all the information, he said the job needs to be completed by 11 December as an audit had been scheduled that would expose his clients to a world of shit from the financial stability board.

Which would expose them and their banks to the subprime mortgage market fiasco, which in turn will probably lead to a run on British banks, helping prompt the biggest depression since the 1930s and probably years of austerity.

"No pressure son" he said, as he laughed and walked off adding "keep in touch".

That night when I arrived at Dez's.

I still couldn't believe I had actually put our name and reputation to this job, it could all end so badly, especially if we fucked it up, but it could also be the deposit we all needed to get out of this life, so I had to look upon it as calculated decision, but a decision that we all had to make together as one firm this evening.

I put the two envelopes on the table as everyone pulled up chairs and sat down, it was now time to see if this was all pie in the sky or something we could do.

The first and most important bit of the jigsaw puzzle was security and their procedures.

We had to be hundred and ten percent on this, as there would be no second chances or going back with this one.

Background:

The target is a Global telecoms and IT firm called Verizon business in King's Cross, St. Pancreas way.

It boasts of its "state of the art" security.

The company, whose customers include JP Morgan, is one the biggest telecommunications firms in the US, on its website, Verizon states that the security at its data centre includes, around the clock uniformed guard service with interior and exterior closed circuit television surveillance and electronic access at all entrances, including biometric hand scanners and electronic keypad systems and panic buttons.

They also have a dedicated five man team monitoring the surveillance screens at all times and another six men team patrolling the hundred or so rooms set over three floors.

The room that we needed to get into also has a separate independent security company monitoring it, with a live stream
making it impossible, unless we were able to disconnect it.

So if we are going to even attempt this we needed to look at every angle, we had two weeks to come up with a plan that everyone was happy with.

The canal was a potential way in, the roof also had a number of access points , but was heavily protected by steel doors, an alarm system and was also camered up.

Every door was reinforced with steel and opened outwards making it impossible to ram, all the exit doors only opened from the inside and again were all camered up.

From looking at the schematics it seemed that they had catered for every eventuality, right down to the location, as they were right bang in the middle of three police stations; Kentish Town, Highbury and Islington and Albany Street.

"Ok guys any ideas?"

The tall fella said "can we get jobs as security guards because that's the only way we can get in there before the alarm goes up?"

"I meant Any sensible ideas, dopey bollocks. Dez what have you got mate?"

"I'll need to get up on the roof and have a look first. We also need to get a close up look, without drawing too much attention to ourselves, which is going to be hard.

As there is no parking along its right flank, the front is also heavily manned and the whole perimeter is camered up"

"Micky what have you got brother?"

"I've got a brand new British Telecom van"

"Brilliant, that's going to get us right to the front door, if we drill a couple of holes in the sides we can watch it without getting out.

Micky if you drive me and Dez down tomorrow morning we can start surveillance, we need to know how many people and security guards are in there throughout the night, I'll do the day shift first and Dez you do the nights, Mickey you park up the van and come back five hours later, we can do five hour shifts, that's ten hours a day.

Tall fella you get the Van and cars ready, also talk to your pal with the dog as well, I'll give you a list of things we might need over the next week or so ok?"

"Ok mate"

"Is Everyone happy?"

"Yes"

"Ok"

"I'll be here tomorrow 5am Mickey, you ok with that?"

"Yes of course Tel"

"Dez we will pick you up in Camden town, chalk farm outside Nando's say 5.30am? We can then change over there"

"Ok let's get this party started"

Dez called me this morning and said he'd taken a look at the Verizon building late last night and it was one monster of a building the size of two football pitches and more, the back entrance was definitely a no no as there was only one blind spot which he had managed to take advantage of.

It had allowed him to get up to the roof undetected, apparently he went up an Ariel mast, he had also taken a rope, tied it off and had abseiled down the side of the building to the second floor, but was unable to gain entry as the windows were all sealed shut and the glass was bullet proof, he said he also tried the fire escape doors but had triggered the alarm which brought the guards there within seconds, the police were also there within four minutes, the response time was fast, as he had just managed to slip through their net by swimming across the canal with all his gear and clothes on, so nothing was left behind.

So the roof and back was definitely out of the question, we couldn't go through the left flank wall either as it was made of reinforced concrete, which now only left the front door which had an airlock door, a biometric keypad entry system and a swipe card.

There were also cameras everywhere along the front and a police patrol came past as regular as clockwork, every twenty minutes or so, the front of the building was lit up like a Belisha beacon.

The job was looking ominous and we hadn't even managed to do one full day of surveillance yet.

By day two I was starting to think about pulling the plug as me and Dez had decided to stay in the van together, and after almost ten hours of pissing in a bottle and eating cold sandwiches we were none the wiser to how we were going to get in without setting off the alarm system and alerting one of the guards into pressing his panic button.

The more we looked the more we realized that there was no easy way in, then just as we were about to call it a day two technicians buzzed the entry system.

We saw two security guards came from around the back, out of the monitoring room and speaking to them through the intercom, they were asking them to show their ID's through the window, after about 4 minutes they let them in, the same thing happened with the cleaning ladies and two more technical staff.

In the daytime they just buzzed you in whilst sitting behind their desks, but in the evenings the security was stepped up.

The day time was out of the question as there was too many people going in and out, so to do it then would definitely have been suicidal.

We were back to Square one and fast running out of options, by the weekend when we arranged to meet up again, I was going to call it a day. But something happened that would put it all into perspective, I was at a pals place in west Hampstead when a police van pulled up and four uniformed officers got out and sealed off the street, a guy had gotten on to the library roof and was threatening to jump off, everyone was looking up, which gave me an idea, that was so simple if it worked, it could get us in with just enough time to overpower the guards before they realized what was going on.

We still had the problem of the live feed from the independent security company monitoring the motherboards room.

Maybe we would have to take a calculated gamble to get round that one.

I called Dez and met up with him in Hampstead at the top of kite hill, where we sat on a bench so we could look out across London, we discussed the issues that had been so problematic to us and by the time we met up again that evening with Mickey and the tall fella we had a plan of sorts, a plan that we both thought was realistic and surmountable if we had the bottle and enough bodies on the job to do it.

We needed Frankie and an additional four men, all working together so they could take the motherboards out with battery powered electric drills, then carrying the motherboards to the van, if we were going to pull this off we all had to work as one unit, there was approximately 80 motherboards which meant each man carrying two chequered washing bags full.

That including us, would make 10 men with two bags each,
ten men doing the impossible.

We had come up with what we thought was a workable scenario, tonight we would set that plan in motion with the tall fella, Mickey, Frankie, Dez, myself, and four other guys that we knew from south London, who were fast, efficient and knew their way round a mother board terminal.

We would pay them up front, which meant they would be happy with twenty grand for one hours work, our job would be to secure the building so they could just walk in off the street, we would cuff all the security guards, the cleaners and technicians, all 16 of them.

Their risk was basically negligible at best , unlike Frankie who would be a pivotal figure, so we would up his wages to the same as ours, equal shares.

And the Alsatian would be rewarded with chicken and steak for a month of Sundays, God willing.

When I eventually made it to Dez's, Micky, Frankie and the tall fella were there, we called the south London boys first and arranged a meeting with them, me and the tall fella for that weekend, as they were his pals so we could discuss their part in it and of course their money.

"Ok guys" I said "me and Dez have been over the Verizon job with a fine tooth comb literally a million times and it's been a difficult week in as far as finding a way in or any flaws in their system. But we have, we have decided to use a ruse to gain entry and in the second phase of the job regarding the private security company and their live feed, we have decided to blag it a 50 / 50 gamble"

I explained the whole job and how it was going to work right down to shutting the doors on the way out and to my surprise everyone was in agreement, Dez in particular was chomping at the bit as he had planned it down to the last second.

Dez is ex-army, so timing was everything to him especially if we wanted to get out without getting our collars felt, he was a perfectionist like me, the job should take us approximately one hour,
to secure the premises, disable the live feed and retrieve the motherboards.

We went through it again and again and decided that Thursday the sixth of December was going to be our judgement day,
it was my birthday on the 9th, so with luck it would be a double celebration, if we pulled it off.

On Sunday me and the tall fella popped over south London, we gave the boys an outline of the job minus the address as we didn't want any hiccups regarding someone talking out of school on their side.

All we said was that we would do all the work and they would be called in, they argued the toss, we offered them ten grand, but they stubbornly asked for twenty as we predicted.

We protested, then reluctantly relented and then shook hands, everyone was happy.

The Time and the meeting place was set it was now time to meet Buster the Alsatian who didn't disappoint, he was as big as a barn door and his bark was menacingly loud, the guy who owned him was a good friend of the tall fella, we had promised him that he would return him unharmed and in one piece with no dramas, also with some remuneration money for himself, which now meant everything was ready, the south London boys, the van, cars and the dog.

Dez called me Monday morning and asked me pop over to his that evening as he had a surprise for me.

When I turned up the house was deserted no lights or anyone in, then he called and said he was running a little bit late but I should hang about, It was another forty minutes until he turned up, he had a blue Mercedes Jeep full of black holdall bags and was smiling from ear to ear.

"What you been up to mate?" I said.

"Wait and see. Now Help me carry this stuff in"

As we walked in I asked where his wife and kids were.

He said they were away for a week "I've sent them on a little vacation to the country, I'm driving back down there tonight,
but I'll see you and the guys back here in morning as arranged, so don't worry"

We put all the duffle bags on the table, then Dez opened one up and said take a look at these babies, he took out a flak jacket, a police vest, cap, a pair of boots, a belt , cuffs and police radio. The full kit and caboodle, it was all real police issue uniforms and all brand new.

He even had a police fluorescent dog handlers jacket.

Five brand new kits in all.

We both tried them on and they fitted perfectly, the police caps were the bollocks, the boots made me another two inches taller and with the vest , cuffs and Radio hanging from my police belt, we looked every bit like a fast response robbery squad.

Everything was almost ready, first we would all have to meet up again on Wednesday to go over the plans for the last time before doing a dry run past Verizon, so we could get the timing just right, we then repacked the bags away again, before putting them in a cupboard under the stairs.

Tuesday was ritual day for all of us, it's a time we put aside for our wives, kids or girlfriends.

It's normally a day before a job (robbery) before we commit ourselves to the possibility of years behind the door in the big house (prison).

Dez took his wife and kids to the country, the tall fella went home to his wife and kids, Mickey went to his girlfriend's and Frankie stayed in with his family.

I took my kids to London zoo, we had dinner in the cafeteria, I bought them teddy bears, it was cold but they loved it. In the evening I booked a table in a restaurant in Camden town called the Caravas for me and my girlfriend.

The day is our way of saying goodbye without actually saying it. You cuddle your kids as if it's the last time you'll ever see them again, treat them extra special for the first time in months, you also make them feel loved, wanted and cherished, treating them as if they are the last people on earth, you promise them that at the weekend you are going to buy them the iPhone and bike they've always wanted.

We do this because they are our little princesses, our angels, we convince ourselves that the reason we are doing this final job is for them, so we can retire and sail off into the sunset and have a wonderful life, but the reality is this is our day of atonement to put everything right with them before we leave.

We do the same thing with our girlfriends and wives, it's our way of letting go whilst at the same time letting them see we are worth loving and worth waiting for, the reality is we only do this to ease our consciences, yes we are good dads and yes we love our kids and wives, but do we love them more than we love money and living this life, the answer has to be a resounding no.

I suppose, we love the life it's in our blood.

I have done this so many times over the years, that I now see it as creating good karma for myself before a job, whilst giving myself an excuse for doing bad.

The final countdown to the Verizon robbery has begun, in less than 24 hours we will be knocking at the door of our destiny.

One more dress rehearsal, check the vans and cars, make sure that the south London boys are on point, then go over the plan one more time, before going home and having an early night.

We all got dressed in our uniforms and if I'm honest we looked fucking impressive.

Everyone looked the part fit and healthy Dez an ex-para, the tall fella 6.4, me 6.2 in my new boots, Mickey was tidy and looked official, confident, Frankie was big and imposing, we looked like the robbery squad.

So phase one completed.

We then took it all back off and folded it and put it away.

Next, we picked up the van and two cars, we dropped one car off at the drop-off point, close to some wasteland where we had arranged for the van and car to be burnt out.

We then drove to the job, as we drove past Verizon, Dez went through it with everyone step 1, step 2, step 3, step 4, and so on, everyone was on point and focused.

It was good to see everyone so committed I felt like a proud father seeing his kids graduate into the big league, I was looking at four real men; men that I would trust with my life, we had gone through so much over the years and now we were going to conquer our very own criminal mount Everest.

So whatever happens after today, we would either be forgotten in the annals of time or celebrated in criminal folk law.

Tomorrow the 6th of December 2007 was D-day, we had arranged to meet up at Dez's house, at 1pm sharp, the robbery was scheduled for 9pm that night and we were to be out of there by 10pm.

The traffic at that time would be minimal, but Camden town would be busy with party-goers and drunks, so hopefully, the police would be preoccupied with them.

"See you tomorrow guys and don't be late and remember; no drinking, no clubbing and no drugs, have an early night and bring your A-game"

The 6th of December was just like any other day, I'd slept like a baby last night, and even stayed up until about 11.30pm watching tv and thinking about today and how it would turn out, I knew the Verizon building inside out now, even though I'd never even set foot in the place.

I'd photographed every inch of the outside and gone through every conceivable scenario of what would or could go wrong, I'd even walked the escape route three times, if anything went wrong, I would have to swim across the canal, run along Camley street to Agar Grove, cut through Camden square which would bring me out onto Camden road, where I'd melt into the traffic, I hoped.

So many things go through your mind that it's almost impossible to think of anything else apart from the job, my girlfriend had tried to talk to me this morning and last night but I was away with the fairies.

To be honest when she did eventually go to work this morning, I was glad to see the back of her, not because I didn't like her but because I needed time on my own to focus on the job at hand without any mundane conversations or distractions.

I tried watching the morning news to try and take my mind of it but it didn't help either.

Amy Winehouse was nominated for six Grammy Awards, unfortunately the rest of the news was the normal frivolous bollocks, so I quickly turned it off again and took a walk along Queen's Crescent market.

It's funny I've lived in Camden town and Hampstead all my life and have never really appreciated it, but this morning everyone and everything looked so much more familiar, it felt like I was looking at it for the very last time.

The blue sea chip shop that I'd used a million times as a kid, the pubs I'd drank in as a man, the Sir Robert Peel, the butcher shop that my pal Freddie Bishop used to own and even the corner sweet shop where I'd got my cigarettes, lottery tickets and morning papers from Brian Cole's shop on the corner.

This mental torture always happens before a job, it's the minds way of showing you subliminally what you are giving up, especially if you continued on this path of self-destruction and criminality, the heart and mind conspire against your better judgement and sensibility.

It has a sentimental effect on you which in turn starts to makes you question your thought process, yourself and your chosen life trajectory.

It's the hardest part of the job, the internal fight between good and evil, between myself and my subconscious.

Be it right or wrong, the stronger part of my personality always wins out over the good in me.

Unfortunately for me it's the side that controls and dominates my better judgement, turning off the hidden me, the part that's constantly pleading with my subconscious to stop putting myself in harm's way and all these dangerous situations, that I seem to put myself in.

I've learnt over the years to ignore the voices in my head, it's taken me years to fully understand why my mind does this to me, it's probably why the armed robber is a dying breed, it's simply because to get past your own subconscious hurdles of your own conscience is by far the hardest battle that we as criminals will ever have to face.

It's the reason why there are people who would fantasise about the perfect robbery but will never get out of their armchairs for the fear of getting caught and doing years in prison, it's why films, especially robbery films have captured the imagination of those people who would dare to dream.

As I walked back past St. Dominic church in Malden road , I took the opportunity to walk in and ask God to protect my family and see his way clear to looking favourably on myself, Dez, Mickey, Frankie and the tall fella.

As a criminal we feel that life has dealt us a bad hand, so to rectify that and our own failings we blame government ,society and the rich; this in some small part helps us absolve ourselves of the creative way we go about earning our livelihoods.

Rightly or wrongly, only destiny knows the truth.

But for now we are the good guys and the police, Verizon and their security guards are the bad apples who want to put us away.

It was nearly 12pm, time for me to make my way up to Dez's house, I'd left my range rover outside Hampstead heath over ground station opposite the old Magdala pub, where Ruth Ellis had apparently shot dead her boyfriend David Blakely back in 1955, I hoped today wasn't going to be another Ellis moment in history, as she was the last woman to be hanged.

I was the first to arrive at Dez's house, and as I pulled along his driveway I could see him sitting in his conservatory at the back of the house, having coffee while watching TV .

I went in the side gate and deliberately made a noise, as I didn't want to startle him, he greeted me with a smile and offered me coffee and a cake.

He'd also laid on a banquet of cakes, sandwiches and cold drinks for all the boys for when they arrived.

We now had eight hours left before kick-off.

Eight hours to gee each other up and convince ourselves that we were invincible, which in some respect we were.

We had done this so many times, that we had a self-belief that in whatever we did was ordained by God, especially with Dez's regular army training sessions.

His disciplined ideology about team work and rehearsing every aspect of the jobs that we did. It only reinforced in all of us that we were capable of achieving anything, especially if we worked as one cohesive unit.

The tall fella had confidence the likes I'd never seen before from his job as a distraction artist, he could sell sand to the Arabs and charm the pants off superman, he was really that good at his game.

Mickey had a self-awareness and an assurance that belied his years.

Frankie was just big enough to convince any wannabe security guard to think twice before becoming a hero.

And me I was probably the glue that brought us together and made everyone believe we were the best, I was also fearless and had a self-belief that I could do anything if I put my mind to it.

Together me and Dez were like gelignite and dynamite, explosive!

When we went through a door on a job, we took no prisoners, we worked fast and efficiently and at times I thought he could read my mind, that was how in sync we were.

The others were just as capable in their own right, but they had that pack mentality, where Dez and myself were lone wolfs, we could act independently of each other, we really didn't need anyone.

I suppose that comes from years of being independent, especially in my case, I had grown up fast as a kid, going in and out of children's homes.

I don't know much about Dez's upbringing , because he never talked about it, he was a lot like me.

He was independent and self-assured and extremely intelligent, his business acumen was second to none, which always surprised me.

I wondered many times why he ever got into this game in the first place, I suppose it's a bit like being in the Foreign Legion, we leave our past and histories at the gates and accept each other from our lived experiences that we forge together as men through the same common goal, money, greed and an opportunity to create a better life for ourselves and our families.

As soon as I sat down the door bell went, but before I even got to the front door I could hear the tall fella, Mickey and Frankie laughing and joking which is normally a good sign, the calm before the storm.

When I opened it, the tall fella said evening all and was met with a round of hello's from each man in the room.

Each firm needs a comedian like him, as good humour is paramount in uniting a team, it's the best ingredient for success, bravado, sarcasm and a bit of witticism helps keep the morale up.

We all went through to the garden and made small talk, Dez then asked me "do you really reckon we can do this Tel?"

"Yes of course mate" I said, we then talked about his kids, we discussed the tree house he'd just built them in the garden, "it is the size of my front room" said Mickey.

"Mine too" said Frankie.

I chatted with the tall fella and asked how he felt, he was honest and said "it's not going to be easy Tel , but I reckon we will do it"

This constant reinforcement with the guys is what gets us to the front door of most jobs, because encouragement is key to our success.

The tall fellas confidence and eternal optimism was infectious and came out loud and clear as Dez and the rest of them raised their cups in mock celebration.

As we raised a glass and said "here's to success"

The jocularity and banter over the next couple of hours saw us through as always, but the time was fast approaching 7pm, two more hours and we would be knocking at the door of Verizon.

The butterflies in my stomach were getting restless and my thoughts had turned to my kids again.

My three daughters, my innocent little baby girls, who had no idea what their dad was doing today, what he did for a living or who he really was.

I had to stop thinking like this so I shook my head and put the kids to one side as it was time to get into character and bring the real me to the surface, that mean calculated bastard who was prepared to do anything to get this job done, it was time to psych myself up and concentrate on getting in and then out with the prize in one piece with all my boys liberties intact.

It was now time to get into our police uniforms and pump each other up, we all went into Dez's dining room together.

Dez passed over all our bags, I put mine on the dining table and took my clothes off, then bit by bit I transformed myself into the head of a fast response police unit and into an officer, who would take no shit or attitude from any fucking wannabe security guards.

The minute I saw everyone else in their uniforms I knew we would get in and out without any trouble, I could feel the confidence from everyone in the room failure tonight was not an option, the talking was definitely over, it was time to rock and roll.

In ten minutes we would be on our way, the dog was already in the back of the van. Buster was now the tall fellas responsibility, he had to do his bit as he was the official dog handler.

Frankie would man the front desk when we eventually mopped all the guards up.

It was my job to do most of the talking, I would knock on the door and show my ID and as soon as I was through the door I would orchestrate everything like a conductor of an Orchestra.

"Ok guys it's time... Frankie, Mickey you take the cars, Frankie drop your car off at the changeover point and then get in with Mickey and follow us.

Me, Dez and the tall fella are in the van with the dog, ok, let's go, this is it guys, it's do or die time, good luck and let's not break any legs or noses.

Ok Mickey, let's do a coms check first.

Can you hear me in the car over."

"Bravo foxtrot T (yes T)"

"Frankie do you copy, over."

"Bravo foxtrot T (yes T)"

"Tall fella how's the dog, over"

"Fucking vicious you cunt over."

"Dez you on, over"

"Bravo T (yes T)"

"Ok all coms working, let's keep the chatter to a minimum, until we reach tango1 (Target Verizon)"

"Lima Charlie (loud and clear)"

"Roger(message received)"

We drove to Chase side and turned down a little dirt road where Frankie parked up the first car, he then jumped in with Mickey, this was our safe place to burn the van and car out without anyone seeing them once we'd completed mission Verizon.

It was now quiet time as we drove down to Camden town, the journey would take forty minutes to drive, everyone seemed preoccupied with their thoughts, they were probably going over the job in their own heads.

Dez was in the front with me, we didn't say much, we just kept it real as the time for talking was over, we had all brought ourselves to this one moment in time on our own terms.

No one had been forced, or persuaded to come along, everyone was here of their own volition, they were not here because they were skint, desperate or owed money.

They were here because they wanted to be part of something special, to challenge themselves and prove that they were the best at their game, anyone could hold a gun to someone's head and threaten their way in to a bank, building society or even a security van, those jobs only take two or three minutes and basically anyone could do them, especially if they were desperate enough.

But to plan something as audacious as the Verizon job and then carry it out and make your mark, well that was a different kettle of fish entirely.

It's something few men will ever get the opportunity to do in their whole lives, to actually have an adrenalin rush that nothing can ever equal or compare too, imagine the most euphoric high that no drug can duplicate or replicate.

To be part of this and be doing it with my friends and guys I would lay down my life for, well that's heroic and something very special.

It's something that should be celebrated from the roof tops and shouted across the roofs of London, but because we are criminals we can't do that, we are bound by an invisible underworld oath of silence, to never talk about our exploits or share them with friends , family or anyone ever, unless we have done a long sentence for that job.

My life as a criminal was a bit like Christopher Columbus, in my case I was exploring the frontiers of criminality and pushing the boundaries of crime, in what can only be described as the holy grail of criminal immortality.

It's what we as criminals aspire to do, leave our mark.

To do the ultimate job to the detriment of our freedom and families.
It's probably why I'm sitting in this van this evening and why I'm driving into the abyss, it's because of the danger and the excitement of the explorer in all of us, I suppose it's an inherent hereditary need to conquer our fears, to climb the proverbial mountain and ascend to the top of the mountain; we all have it in us, it was just that our chosen discipline was crime.

As we approached the gate house in Highgate village the five south London boys joined our convoy as prearranged in their car, we were now ten handed as we drove over the crest of the hill and down towards parliament hill fields, straight through to Kentish town road, until we were level with Kentish town police station.

We were right under their noses dressed as police officers driving past their command centre, it was surreal.

Kentish town was alive with people all going about their business, but none the wiser as we passed a police car and two plod on the street I looked over.

I couldn't help myself, I saluted them and smiled as Dez laughed.

We were now three minutes away from Verizon.

At the bottom of Kentish town road at the traffic lights, once across these lights we would be on St. Pancras Way and right on schedule, over these lights then across Camden road, past the Constitution Pub and down fire engine hill.

The South London boys pulled over onto our right and parked up.

As we were about to pull over onto the pavement a police car came up behind us, their Siren went on.

Fuck what had we done wrong?

Was it a set-up?

Everyone was on their radio's at once talking and asking questions.

"What's happening?" the tall fella shouted.

Mickey said "should we abort?"

"No, No. Everyone just shut the fuck up and be quiet it's only a fucking police car and he's just pulled past us and he's now heading up the road towards kings cross.

It's ok. It is fine, everyone just calm down we are going to drive around the block and come back again, nothing's changed ok.

The job is still live, now get ready"

I displayed the kind of calmness a leader has to in the face of adversity, the reality was that I had shit myself and believed we had a rat but if I had shown an ounce of trepidation the job would have been done for. This is what I do, I hold the jobs together and pull us through adversity.

We drove down royal college street, which was ironic, as one-two-one Royal College Street used to be my old home as a kid and just up on the right used to be that bit of waste ground where the bus was and where I got my head split open as a kid with that brick.

Theoretically I was now back to Square one, back where it had all started all those years ago as a kid, but would I end up with a bloody nose again tonight, like all those years ago?

As we mounted the curb and drove the 15 foot to the front doors of Verizon, Mickey and Frankie pulled in beside us, blocking off anyone's view from the main road that might be looking.

The south London boys were still parked up so we still had a full complement, we had lost vital time as we were now 12 minutes behind schedule.

Time we had to make up.

So I got on the coms to everyone and said "get ready everyone... GO,GO,GO, NOW!"

I opened my door and quickly let the tall fella out of the Van's side door with the dog.

Dez was right behind me; Frankie and Mickey brought up the rear, as I looked through the window into the lobby I could see a tall black guy about 6 foot 3 and built like a brick shit house.

He was the head of security, beside him were two more black security guards and a woman security officer also about 6ft.

I buzzed the intercom and said "open the door!"

"What's going on?" came the reply.

"We have had a report that someone is up on the roof" I held my police ID up to the camera and the tall fella stepped forward with the dog, we looked for all intent and purpose the real deal but still they were fucking hesitating.

I banged on the Window which seemed to knock them out of their trance-like state, as the big guy stepped forward and took out his biometrics key card and swiped it, swiping me in.

Bingo the game was afoot we were in.

I calmly held the door open for Dez, who did likewise for the others while I continued to walk in.

I walked straight into the control room and saw three guards sitting behind the camera monitors.

I quickly said "have you got a camera positioned on the roof?"

"Yes, but only one on the fire escape door"

"Have any of you been up on the roof in the last hour?"

"No! None of us"

"Ok, I need to get up on the roof now" I pointed to the head of security and ordered "you take me now!

But before I go I want you three to stand up and stand against the wall."

"Why?" one of them said "what's going on?"

"The report that we have, is of a person on the roof, he is apparently dressed as a security guard, you say none of you have been up on the roof. So for my protection and my officers protection, I'm going to have to handcuff you all, until I have established who you are.

We have to search the whole building, is that clear enough?

Now get up, turn around and face the wall, cuff them now"

I then took the head of security and the woman security officer and walked them into the stairwell of the building with Dez, I said "I'm going to cuff you here because I didn't want to do it in front of your men, it's for our protection that we need to cuff everyone, are you ok with that sir, madam?"

He looked confused but quickly turned around so I could cuff him and then the woman, I cuffed them both to the metal stair Rail.

I then walked back into the lobby and told Mickey to bring everyone into the stairwell, which he quickly did.

We could see from the monitors that there were three more security guards on the second floor, that we needed to get to, there were also two more guards on the third floor.

I turned to one of the guards and told him to get on the Radio and call the three guards on second floor down to the reception desk.

Which again he did, this left only two more to contain on the third floor.

Once we managed to mop up the three guards who were now coming down, we could see from the monitors that they were waiting for the lift on the second floor.

So me, Dez and the tall fella waited for them to come down, Frankie waited at the front desk, Mickey guarded the stairwell.

Everyone was in position, I took a deep breath and as soon as the lift door opened I quickly explained why we were here, they like the other guards looked perplexed but they all reluctantly complied, but not before I had to threaten them all with the dog, which thankfully did the trick.

The tall fella took them back to the stairwell, Dez took all their biometric key cards off them and handed them out to the team, he then called the South London boys over and let them all in while Mickey and myself went up to the third floor.

He went down one corridor and I took the other, they were long and all camered up, the cameras were spaced out every twenty foot, so I pulled my police cap down and Mickey did likewise this place was definitely hiding something it was spotlessly clean, all brilliant white I could actually smell how clean it was, there wasn't a speck of dust in sight.

As I turned the corner I almost bumped into the guard, but this time I didn't fuck around with him, as I was on my own, so I just whacked him up against the wall and took him to the floor as quick as I could and cuffed him.

He was shaken up a bit, but unharmed.

I called over the coms to Mickey, who told me that he had his guy in cuffs too, " brilliant mate", we then took both of them down stairs, so they could join their pals, it was going well so far but it had taken us 14 minutes to finish stage one.

Next I called Dez, "are you in position brother"

"Yes mate"

"Ok I'm on the front desk mate cut the live feed now"

It took less than twenty seconds for the independent security company who were monitoring the live feed to call.

I paused then picked up the phone and said "Verizon security here, how can I assist you?"

The guy on the other end said "our link has just gone down, it's dead"

"It's ok, there's been a surge in the mainframe computer system which I'm afraid to say has knocked out all our monitors, but not to worry as our technicians are now dealing with it as we speak.

They have just assured me that we should be back on line and up and running with in the next forty minutes or so, I'll call you back as soon as it's done sir"

It took him a second or more to respond before he said "ok, keep me up dated"

"Will do sir of course, bye for now"

"Bye"

"Dez It's all clear brother GO! GO! GO!"

I was sweating now as this was the fifty/fifty gamble that we had factored into the job.

We still weren't out of the woods yet because the guy might still have been bluffing me, he might have already called the police, we wouldn't know either until they either pulled up in force or came through the front door.

This for me was the worst part of this job as we had no control over it.

We were relying on faceless security guards sitting behind a desk looking at a blank screen to play the game, but I couldn't dwell on it , as I was worried about Dez, because he now had to remove all the motherboards and store them in anti-static bags, he also had to disconnect every motherboard while being really careful not to let the electric drills touch them.

Then remove all the mounting screws in the main frame computer cases, disconnect the CPU memory hard drives, the optical drives, video cards, sound cards, the expansion cards and other ports, a mammoth task at the best of times but under pressure, well that was another story, but Dez was more than capable.

While we were waiting I took Mickey and did a sweep of the building, on the second floor we found two technicians, who were working away at a terminal oblivious to what was going on, so we cuffed them both, on the third floor we came across four cleaners, so again we cuffed them and took them down to the stairwell lobby area, with all the other guards and tech guys.

We tried to allay any fears they might have by constantly telling them that the search of the building was almost complete, we even gave some of them a glass of water.

This seemed to help, the uniforms would reassure them that nothing was going to happen to them, we now had 16 bodies being guarded by the tall fella and buster.

I sent Mickey to help him every now and again, while I took a look up and down the road through the window, there were no cop cars or vans thank god and the street was still clear, the time had slowed down and the pressure was now off.

We were only halfway through the job, the last 25 minutes had been exhilarating but at the same time excruciatingly stressful, my heart was beating like crazy and my adrenaline was pumping through my veins at a speed of knots.

I checked on the South London boys who were with Dez on the second floor, when I got there Dez was bringing out the bags into the hallway, he had made a long line of bags, which meant we were now halfway there, he had laid out ten full bags which left ten more to go, we had allowed for twenty bags to do the whole job.

I went back to my position monitoring the road and front desk from the landing window, so far no problems, let's hope it stays that way I told everyone over the coms, up to now we had been so lucky , professionally lucky that is.

Frankie then came back on the Radio and said two geezers are walking towards the front door, "ok, don't panic" I said.

"Let's see what they want" I didn't call Dez or the other guys as I didn't want to spook them, plus I could clearly see from my vantage point that these two guys were technicians as they were carrying tool bags, well I assumed they were technicians, so called down to Frankie and told him to buzz them in, "let them through mate" which he did.

If they come to the second floor we will just have to deal with them , I positioned myself in front of the lift doors and called Mickey up to watch my back just in case they stopped at our floor and gave me any trouble, the tension was palpable, my heart was beating , I heard the lift doors open and then shut, they were now on their way up.

Frankie was in the monitoring room watching them get in the lift, He then informed us that they were on their way up. "Be careful mate, they are big lumps."

"Ok brother"

I took another deep breath, then a sigh of relief as the lift passed our floor, thank fuck I thought; we had run out of cuffs, which meant we would have had to use shoe laces to tie them up.

I looked at Mickey who was now smiling back at me, we had dodged a bullet by one floor.

Frankie watched them go into a room on the third floor, we could now only hope they wouldn't venture out again anytime soon but to be on the safe side I told Frankie not to take his eyes of the ball.

The tall fella was asking for a time check and Dez said his team were almost finished, we had ten minutes left , if we were gonna walk out of here at ten o'clock as planned.

We had to completed our mission to get every motherboard out of room 992.

The fixer had stipulated that nothing should be left behind, his consortium had paid for the complete annihilation of all the evidence that linked them or their banks to any fraudulent activities.

To come this far and fail now was not an option that I favoured, we couldn't give them an excuse not to pay up.

Nothing could be left behind, our money had already shrunk to three hundred thousand pounds each, because we had given Frankie an equal share which was only fair, as he was taking the same risks as us.

Dez buzzed me and said his guys were almost ready, "it's time to pull out brother"

"Nice one mate."

I got back on the coms and said "everyone apart from the tall fella up to the second floor now."

Everyone needed to grab two bags, Dez and I took 3 each, as we had to carry the tall fellas since he had the dog.

"Ok slowly does it guys"

Mickey took his bags first, then Frankie, then one by one the south London boys took theirs, we all slowly walked down the stairs I was surprised at how heavy the bags were.

By the time I reached the ground floor I was feeling the pressure, this was the last hurdle. Getting out of here without drawing attention to ourselves.

Everything had to look natural; no running or panicking we had to look like we owned this building.

I positioned myself on the landing so I could see the oncoming traffic and when I was sure it was ok I gave Mickey the signal.

"Are you in position mate?"

"Yes!"

"Ok ready, go now mate"

Mickey opened the side door of the van.

Then the South London boys put their bags in, they calmly crossed back over the road to their car and pulled away, they had done their job they were staunch guys.

We gave them a few minutes to get clear before I informed Dez that it was our time to make our exit.

Dez took his bags out, next Frankie; Mickey and Frankie then calmly got in their car.

"Well done boys!"

I called the tall fella who came out smiling, I held the door open for him and buster, put my three bags in, shut them both in the back, calmly got into the front passenger seat and smiled at Dez and said "home James, let's get the fuck out of here"

We pulled onto the main road and did a sharp right into Royal College street, up Kentish town road and as we neared Holmes Road police station, all hell broke loose as four police cars pulled out in front of us, followed by two to SPG vans, full of wooden tops (police).

It was 10.06pm and the scream had already gone up.

Blue lights were flashing all down Kentish town road and for a second I thought they were on to us.

My stomach was doing somersaults, I could hear the dog barking in the back and the tall fella telling buster to shut the fuck up.

Dez was concentrating on the road and looked as cool as a cucumber; as always.

At Parliament Hill fields the tall fella got out with buster and disappeared into the park so he could give the dog back to its owner, he still had all his police gear on but it was covered up under his rain mac.

We continued up to Muswell Hill where we unloaded all the bags into a garage.

Mickey and Frankie took the van.

We followed them in their car to the drop off point, parking the van and car side by side, before walking away leaving Mickey to torch them out.

We all jumped in the car and drove to Dez's house, it was dark and it had started raining which was great, because rain, fog and the darkness are the best camouflage for the criminal after a bit of work.

When people are cold, all they want to do is get home in the warm and mind their own business.

When we finally arrived at Dez's house the tall fella was waiting outside, he was smiling and looked ready to burst.

We all went through the side gate and into the house, first thing we had to close all the curtains.

Than we all gathered in the front room just looking at each other smiling, all at once we started jumping up and down celebrating.

"Yes!"

"We did it!"

"Fucking hell, I can't fucking believe it"

"I didn't think that cunt was ever going to open the door!"

"I know" Dez was laughing as he responded.

"Did you see the look on that guy's face?" I asked.

"Especially when you hand cuffed him, Tel and then dog wouldn't stop licking that fucking guys face, did you see it?"

"Yeah" I laughed back in agreement with the tall fella.

"Mate I shit myself when the old bill pulled up behind you"

"Me too!"

"We didn't see him either, not until his fucking siren went off."

"Who shouted abort?" I enquired to the whole room.

"It wasn't me" Frankie had responded but not very convincingly.

"You cunt" I was jovial in my response but still a little annoyed as this could have blown the entire job.

"I could hear you on the phone, Verizon security here can I assist you sir?"

"That was the worst bit for me!"

Dez then took command of the room "Listen up guys, I'm so proud of all of you, that was fucking awesome, it was something else"

I then took the opportunity to take over.

"It really was.

It was like an out of body experience walking into that lobby and seeing all their faces looking up.

I was sure one of them was going to twig on and start performing or press their fucking panic buttons, but when you asked them all to stand up and face the wall and they did, well that was it , I knew then that we had this in the bag, it was brilliant.

Tall fella; well what can I say?"

"I'm the best dog handler in the Met!"

"No really! I'm honestly honoured to have been involved in this."

"Mate my heart was fucking having palpitations but I loved every second of it, standing in that staircase seemed like a fucking eternity but they were all convinced we were real old bill so none of them gave me any shit, it was fucking class, that's all I can say, fucking brilliant"

"Frankie?"

"Mate that was the best experience of my life, I'm so thankful to you all for inviting me to be part of something that was so fucking unique and special.

I thoroughly enjoyed it, it will stay with me for ever"

"Mickey?"

"I especially liked burning out the van and the car!

Right from the start when you suggested this I thought you were all fucking crazy.

And I still do!

Joking aside, I'm being serious now, I love you guys and doing this job has galvanised my respect for you all, even more than before, I am just amazed that we actually fucking done it"

"Speech! Speech! Speech!" the chorus rang out.

"Fuck off you lot!

Ok look, first of all it has been my pleasure to work with you all, not just tonight, but for the last two years.

I never thought in a million years that we would do this or I would ever do anything like this in my lifetime.

The sheer audacity of what we just did hasn't even computed yet, but when I wake up tomorrow and for the rest of my life, I will always remember this moment in time for all the right reasons and remember it with pride, the perfect job for me is when no one gets hurt or traumatised by gratuitous violence.

You all showed restraint, respect and when we pulled away tonight your professionalism was evident and that's why I say this, I'm honoured to have made my mark on the world with you guys standing shoulder to shoulder with you, well what can I say apart from Its been emotional you cunts, thanks, love yea!

Now let's get pissed, I know a little place nearby, in Southgate that's open all night."

When we got there the tall fella bought four bottles of Champagne and we toasted each other into the early hours of the morning; drinking champagne, beers and finished on the shots (sambuca).

The night had been one to celebrate, we partied hard and as I watched the tall fella laughing and joking, Dez and Mickey talking in the corner, I couldn't help but wonder if we could ever top this moment or the camaraderie we felt for each other after doing this job.

We all woke up at Dez's house the next afternoon, Mickey had left to pick up a van, as we had to pick up the motherboards and drop them off over at Kenwood house, I'd arranged to meet the fixer and one of his drivers.

I showered, shaved and changed my clothes, then shrugged off last night as best I could as we still had work to do.

Mickey and the tall fella loaded up the van and brought it back to Dez's, then both went home to sleep off their hangovers, Frankie had gone home last night.

Which left Dez to drive the van, as I tailed him in his car.

We drove along Spaniards road onto Hampstead lane, did a right into Kenwood house car park, Dez stayed with the van, I went and met the fixer who was having tea in the Brew House at the side of Kenwood.

"Hi"

"Fucking hell, looks like you've had a busy night mate, did you leave your phone in the car?"

"Of course I did, what do you take me for?"

"Have you seen the papers yet?"

"No, I haven't, I've just got up!"

"Here let me read this to you, apparently there was a robbery last night in Camden town!

Listen to what the London evening standard wrote:

£1 million Ocean's Eleven style heist.

Robbers disguised as police stole over £1 million worth of computer equipment from a data protection centre with state-of the art security in a daring Ocean's Eleven-style robbery, by using dogs and convincing guards they were investigating reports of intruders on the roof."

"Fucking brilliant! I hope they get away with it" I laughed.

"Listen to this one as well, it's from the Metropolitan Police this is the new revised version out today they have just confirmed that a multi-million pound robbery by a gang of ruthless villains impersonating police officers got away with (£5,000,000) five million pounds of motherboards and communications equipment.

Here's the best bit, detectives from the serious and organised crime command (SCD7) have taken over the case from CID investigators, so if anyone's got any information ring crime stoppers on
0800 555 111, no arrests have been made as enquiries continue."

"What's the reward?"

"It doesn't say, they think it's a foreign firm with military training , as this sort of job is too sophisticated for a British firm, apparently we are too dumb to pull something like this off.

Ok enough of that how do you want to do this?"

"Well my guy is over there." I pointed in the general direction of the car park.

"Where are the motherboards?"

"First where is our money?"

"Well Tel as soon as my guy drives off with them I will transfer the money Into all those accounts you gave me"

"Here's another account too as we had to take another body with us, so it's £300,000 each across the board ok?"

"No problem Tel, you've got some bollocks mate, I honestly didn't think you would be able to pull this off.

You've helped a lot of useful people out and earnt me some money to boot too, we won't forget that!

Just out of curiosity how did you manage to break Verizon's security?"

"Well, it was pretty straightforward really every data centre has the same security.

The physical security is addressed with macro segmentation using a six layered approach, the perimeter is the first level of defence, the second the clear zone; the facade and reception, then the service corridor, the data hall, into the data mainframe system cabinet, we just joined up the dots, by using the information you supplied us and good old Irish good luck.

The biggest risk for us on any job is that everyone attached to the security will actually do their job properly, if they did we would be found out and the siren would go up."

"Brilliant fucking brilliant!

Now where's the motherboards?"

"They're in the car park, a blue van, the keys are in the ignition and my guy is keeping an eye on it"

"Ok shall we walk up?"

"Yeah, I could do with some exercise"

"Come on let's go"

The fixers guy jumped in the van and true to his word he wired us our money the minute he was gone.

Dez gave me a thumbs up from across the car park, the money had landed in the accounts.

"It's a pleasure to do business with you Tel"

"Likewise mate"

We shook hands, job done!

I told Dez that I was going to walk back, as I could do with some fresh air and stretch my legs.

"Mate thanks for everything it's been fun"

"I'll see you in a month or so, as I'm going to take a little break"

"Yeah me too!"

"Give the lads my regards and be careful, the serious crime command (SCD7) are on our tails brother and these cunts won't let up, not until we are all banged up."

"The job was clean, no violence, so no problem" Dez laughed, he knew as well as I that dressing up as the old bill and pulling off such a big job under their noses would piss them off.

"See you later"

"Yeah Tel."

I was walked through Hampstead heath I received a call from one of my pals who said "have you heard about that job last night in Camden, St. Pancras way?"

"No, what's happened?"

"Well a firm went in there the other night and stole a fucking fortune in motherboards, they were all dressed up as old bill, they took a right fucking liberty on our manor, even used a fucking dog!"

"No mate I've been in bed with the flu for the last couple of days"

"You know what Tel, when I first heard it on the news I thought it was you!"

"Don't be such a fucking idiot, I wish it had been me mate , but no such luck, I'm fucking on my arse at the moment , I could do with a few quid, if it wasn't for my bird looking after me at the moment I'd be living on the streets.

Anyway what you up to Kev?"

"Not a lot Tel, a little bit of this and that , but fuck all really Tel"

"Ok mate, I'll talk to you later"

"Bye mate"

The trouble with this game is that there are always people fishing for information, you really can't trust anyone, no matter how much you think you know that person.

It's really important that you let everyone think you are either skint or working legit, that way you will last longer, plus loose lips sink ships.

Talking of ships, I had arranged to take the kids away before Christmas, I'd also promised them that I would turn my phone off and have three or four weeks of peace and quiet with them,
do something different with them.

I got on the phone and called a boat hire company in Leighton Buzzard, Bedfordshire.

By the time I got off the phone from speaking with the guy, I'd talked myself into renting out a canal boat, for three weeks, a 50 foot long narrow boat, four berth, with a double bed and three singles.

All fitted out, kitchen galley, TV and central heating. I called the kids mum and asked if I could take Chloe who was now 11 and Terri 14 , away with me.

Thankfully she agreed, Charlene and Kyle who were 19 and 20 would join us the following week.

I told the kids it was a birthday treat to myself and I wanted to share it with them, I bought myself a captains hat, I also bought all of us some warm clothes, which I packed into three suitcases.

I bought hats, gloves and nice warm jackets each, I booked a taxi, drove round to Kelly's and picked up my new ship mates.

The journey up the M1 took just over an hour but to see the kids' faces made it all worthwhile, the boat was blue and red and really clean and tidy.

Before I was allowed to take it out I first had to do an induction course, which consisted of me piloting three hundred yards in a straight line, through a set of locks, before turning it round, reversing and mooring the boat up.

Which I did to the delight of the kids, I was now the captain of my own ship and competent enough to navigate myself through the minefield of locks .

We brought all our belongings on board unpacked before heading off to get some provisions, it was still early, 2pm, I was told not to pilot the boat at night for obvious reasons, also given directions to the nearest Sainsbury's supermarket that was about an hour away.

Apprehensively I started her up, the girls were at the front of the boat and I, their captain gave the order to cast off.

It was plain sailing until we reached the first lock, all I knew was that I had a big metal key that I had to insert into the lock gate mechanism, then wind it up to open it, back down to close it.

It took me a couple of minutes to fully understand how the water flow and the lock gates worked but thank God it was pretty straightforward and before we knew it we were through and on our way.

As captain I steered the boat and the girls opened and shut the locks, it was slow going but they loved it.

By the time we got to Sainsbury's we were really hungry, I popped ashore and quickly bought us all a Macdonald's each.

The Sainsbury's store backed onto the canal, I picked a trolley and basically did a supermarket sweep of the place buying everything I could lay my hands on that I thought the girls liked or needed.

Soups, breakfast cereals, bread, bacon ,sausages, sandwiches, cakes, crisps popcorn and chocolates, we bought everything and quickly stored it all away before casting off and heading up to Northampton.

It was cold but we had a coal fire to keep us warm, it also heated the hot water and supplied the central heating.

The TV worked off the boat's batteries.

Going through the towns and small villages, such as Milton Keynes was certainly different, it gave me a better perspective of living off the water ways, it was idyllic, peaceful and the scenery was breathtakingly beautiful, at night we all cuddled up in front of the fire, eating crisps, cakes, chocolates and drank fizzy drinks.

It was a far cry from the normality of my chaotic life robbing data centres, and living on the edge.

The Grand Union Canal holds so many hidden gems, just ten miles outside Milton Keynes is Stoke Bruene, a small village in south Northamptonshire that has a fantastic marina, but getting there was hard as we had to navigate ourselves through Bisworth tunnel, apparently it's the 9th longest canal tunnel in the world at 3075 yards long.

The kids and I got soaked to the skin going through there, because every forty or fifty yards there were access holes that let in light but also water from the hills, which acted as showerhead cascading down on us every time we passed an opening.

The girls had rain mac's and hats and every time we passed under one of those holes, I could hear them laughing.

The tunnel was also dark and there was only enough room for two narrowboats to pass at a squeeze, it was at times like this that I convinced myself that my life was perfect, especially when Kyle, his girlfriend and Charlene finally turned up.

We went to the canal museum first, Kyle stayed in a bed and breakfast, while Charlene stayed on the boat with us, we all spent a couple days there before deciding to head back towards London's regent's park and Camden lock.

The journey down was great fun we ate in every little village's pubs and restaurants, some were really quaint, the people were really friendly, it was a massive contrast compared to the hustle and bustle of London.

When we reached London, Regent's park after opening and closing forty or more locks, we all banked into London zoo, we did this by mooring bang in the middle of it.

Afterwards we went on to Camden town where we were met by the kids mum, it had taken us three weeks but the experience was memorable and one I hoped they would never forget.

It took me another week to get back to Leighton Buzzard, I took it slowly, I even managed to read a book, took in all the scenery and by the time I arrived back with the boat, I was reenergized and ready for whatever came my way.

I'd been away just over a month but no sooner had I turned on my phone when message after message came through.

Dez and one of our pals had been arrested after four of them were given a bit of work, that specified it had to be done straight away, the information they'd received was that there was a safe with two hundred thousand pounds in it, ready for the taking, apparently the guy who had it was going on holiday that afternoon.

There was no time to do any surveillance or any home work on it, it was only a little terraced house, the guy had a safe under his stairs, it was supposed to be a two minute job.

They had gone there at 6.30am, gaining entry within seconds they had just emptied the safe, when there was a knock on the door.

To their surprise it was the real police, also being in police uniform they thought they would style it out and opened the door.

The following is what happened next, this was from the horse's mouth:

"It's ok officer we are dealing with this"

The officer looked at him and curiously said "what station are you from?"

With that Dez's pal whacked the officer on the chin, grabbed the other one and threw him over the wall, just as a police van pulled up.

It was a chaotic scene as there were old bill running in all directions, in the confusion Dez slipped out of the house, across the road through some gardens and over a wall.

The area was quickly sealed off, one of Dez's pals was arrested at the front door in full police uniform, he was six four, so they just cuffed him.

Dez unfortunately wasn't so lucky as they sent a dog after him over the back gardens, he managed to punch the dog out, before getting away again.

As he came out into the streets he was cornered by 10 police officers who cuffed him and laid him on the floor.

The bastards set the Alsatian on him, biting his head and taking a lump out of his shoulder.

Dez and his pal were the only two arrested ,the others managed to escape.

A couple of days later I woke up about 5.30am as I couldn't sleep, so I got ready and made myself a cup of coffee.

My girlfriend was still asleep so I decided to have a fag on the balcony just as I was about to open the door I saw a young bird and a geezer walk past and the girl looked up.

It just didn't feel right so I ran through to the kitchen, out the back door, jumped up onto the roof, I couldn't go anywhere else as we were four floors up.

I ran across the roof until I came to the end, I climbed down the emergency ladder, dropped about twenty foot to the pavement.

I had jeans on, a blue fleecy jacket and a baseball cap.

I pulled the collar up, the cap down and walked across the road.

As I looked up the road, I saw about twenty old bill going into my block of flats.

I didn't even have time to warn my girlfriend but at least I was free.

I had also managed to grab my rucksack which had twenty grand in, unfortunately I'd left behind my passport, bank cards, car keys and fucking everything else I owned, including all my banking details , what a cunt I am, I'd panicked and left everything.

I quickly made my way to Hampstead and jumped on a train to west Hampstead where I bought myself a throw away phone, called a pal, who was able to get me some ID at short notice; a driving licence in the name of Eddie Jones.

I jumped on train and ended up in Luton where I hopped on a bus to Dunstable.

I called another pal who was able to rent a little cottage out for me in the country, it was a lovely little place with a big garden, it had a little gym in the garage, it was a perfect place to put my head down and keep a low profile.

I joined the local gym in Dunstable to occupy myself , I trained every day trying my best to keep fit and healthy.

Dunstable was only a little place , so I also rented out a little room in Leagrave in a shared house, as I wanted to be near the station, I told the landlord that I was a fast response driver for the police and would be in Dunstable for about six months, I showed her my police ID and hey presto I was in, no questions.

I also found out from a pal that I'd been put in the frame because I was friends with one of the guy in Dez job.

Because we were all well known as friends, my photo was shown to all the security guards at Verizon, where I was subsequently picked out as the ringleader and the person who did all the talking.

The game was afoot and SCD7 (the serious crime unit), set up to catch us, were working overtime.

They had a specialist team of 70 men hunting me and they weren't taking any prisoners, everyone I was associated was either raided or being watched.

It was crazy, they were even plotted up in a house across the road from my dad's place, or so his neighbour told him as he had given the old bill a surveillance position to watch him from.

It was three weeks until they gave up and packed away their cameras.

I was worried though as I'd thrown away my phone, I'd also brought myself ten new throw away phones, which I only used once or twice before lodging them.

I met a new girlfriend who was a champion bodybuilder and a hairdresser we got on so well that after a month or so we started up a hair salon together.

I was seeing a nurse from Luton at the same time who got me a job as a personal trainer at her gym.

I had a false identity, a driving licence in the same name, I'd brought myself a little Range Rover to get from A to B, which I insured through a pal's company, I was now Eddie Jones - personal trainer.

My girlfriend's brother had his own gym and a food supplement shop so I was training and eating well, I was even going to body building competitions and creating a new life for myself.

I was working with a couple of pals so money was still coming in, but I was getting reckless, I was visiting the kids in Hampstead and on a couple of occasions, I even took the kids to one of my fitness classes.

It was really funny because I'd dyed my hair blonde and was training all these fat Indian birds, my daughters couldn't stop laughing.

Chloe and Terri were in hysterics, it was great to see them laugh.

I was also doing Mickey mouse jobs for ten or fifteen grand a time.

One night I got a call from a pal who said he had a job in Camden, Marigold foods in Camley Street, he said he knew someone who worked there and guaranteed me that there was 25 grand in the safe.

Like an idiot I came down, three of us drove in there and I ended up tying up three bods on my own, the third one was a lump of a guy who couldn't speak any English, he was opening boxes in the factory cold room when I walked in and asked him to follow me, he looked confused, then all of a sudden he pulled out a machete and nearly took my head off.

We ended up rolling around on the floor until I overpowered him and cuffed him, unbeknown to me in the scuffle I dropped my police ID, it must have happened when I pulled the handcuffs out of my back pocket, a stupid mistake.

My second mistake that evening after leaving the warehouse was when I got on the train back to Leagrave station.

I stupidly forgot to put my cap on, this was a massive oversight on my part, as most stations now have CCTV and photo recognition in operation which could have pinged me.

I now had potentially given the old bill their first two proper leads on me in 8 months.

The loss of my police ID was devastating as it was confirmation that it was definitely me doing these jobs, dressed up as pc fucking plod,
it was a bad start to September and one that I hoped I wouldn't regret.

This moronic behaviour had come about because I had acted rashly and taken the word of a pal, believing he was up to the job, when in fact he was fucking useless.

When we got inside the factory this evening, my pal had gone straight up to the office, forgetting we had to restrain all the employees first.

This left me to do all the work , I captured the first employee fairly easily walking through the factory, the second was no drama either as I collared him coming down the stairs, I handcuffed them to a metal stand, the third one I come across him in the walk in fridge, he had a big fuck off machete in his hand, I asked him to put it down but he didn't understand me as he was foreign.

He just looked at me then without saying a word he swung the machete at my head, I quickly ducked down whilst at the same time grabbing him round the neck to wrestle him to the floor, it was while I was trying to hand cuff him that my police ID fell out of my Jean's pocket, it was a shit end to a fucking shit night.

My pal had gone home with some money in his pocket, none the wiser to what he had done.

He called me the next day but I turned off my phone and threw it in the fucking bin.

It was time for me to definitely leave the country so I called my pal Geoff in Thailand and arranged to fly out as soon as I could arrange a false passport.

He had a bar in Koh Samui and was married to a Thai girl, he could put me up for as long as I wanted, I thanked him and said I'm on my way, just give me a week or two.

As soon as I got off the phone to him I phoned another pal who knew a guy who worked in the passport office, he promised to get me a passport that would pass any scrutiny but it would cost me ten grand with five grand up front so I quickly arranged for the money to paid into his account through another pal of mine.

He called me back an hour later to confirm the money had arrived.

Promising me that my passport would be ready in about ten days, so with that confirmation I booked a plane ticket for Thailand leaving on 17th September.

At my cottage the first thing I did was to get rid of everything that would incriminate me or anyone I knew, I chucked all my clothes and wiped the place clean.

I moved into my little room next to Leagrave Station as it was only one stop away from Luton airport which meant it was only one stop away from my new life.

I chucked away everything I owned as forensically I didn't want to leave anything behind.

Over the next few days I went down to London to see the kids, I took them over to Hampstead to the little cafe near the bandstand, we walked around like any other family, the kids were blissfully unaware that I was now one of Britain's most wanted criminals.

I cut my hair and had deliberately grown a tidy beard and moustache for my passport photo which I'd had done right next door to Kentish town police station, two doors up from Macdonald's.

After having my photo taken I had walked back up the Crescent to give it one last goodbye, I strolled along Pond Street, before taking a walk through Hampstead heath with the girls.

I would be sad to leave my old stomping ground, all my friends and family, I had no other alternative left open to me, it was either go or end up in prison here.

Koh Samui, Bangkok, Hong Kong, Thailand or Cambodia, I could definitely lose myself in anyone of those places.

It was now the 10th September, in seven days I would leave my beloved London town, the nostalgia of a place that has brought me so much happiness and pain.

I was still relatively Young at 42 years old so, starting over again would be easier now than in my 50 or 60 s.

My only regret was the kids, leaving them was my biggest worry as I loved them so dearly, more so than I ever let on.

I think it's because I always had to be strong and never show them my feelings, but seeing them leave as I walked away was heartbreakingly difficult, I almost cried on the train home thinking about them.

I regained my composure as I needed to go shopping in Luton to buy some suitcases, I also had to buy some new clothes, it was just what I needed a bit of retail therapy,

I passed the day shopping and in the evening I stayed with Kia my nurse girlfriend.

I didn't tell her that I was leaving in a couple of days, as I didn't want to upset her plus I could do without any more headaches.

I also went to see Karina, another girlfriend, we had dinner in Luton as she knew all the best backstreet traditional Indian places to eat, after seeing her I met Carol, another girlfriend of mine.

We had a memorable night and I left quietly the next morning, I had said all my goodbyes without actually saying goodbye, it's what this life is about smoking mirrors and deceit.

I would be glad to get out of England and get myself a real job in my mate Geoff's bar.

It would mean no more having to look over my shoulder and lying to every girl I met, I had decided to spend the last couple of days staying in my room on my own it would be safer that way.

I sent some money ahead to Thailand hopefully it would be enough to get me through the first couple of years, I had a thousand pound in cash on me and tomorrow morning I would be off.

My bags were packed and my passport would be here at 8.30pm.

This would be my last full day in England It was 2pm in, the 16th September, I was restless and confused; there were so many thoughts going through my head at once.

Would I ever see my girls again Terri, Charlene or Chloe?

Would I get to say goodbye to my mum and dad before it was too late?

How would Kelly, Natalie and my sons react to the news that I had disappeared off the face of the earth?

It didn't bear thinking about, but there I was thinking about it.

It was now 3.30pm so I decided to pop out and go over to the chicken shop for something to eat, it was only a couple of streets away so it wouldn't be any harm.

I put my lucky blue Nike cap on and jacket.

It was cold outside but it felt good on my face, I would miss the English weather but not too much.

I looked up and down the street everything looked ok, the streets were empty and quiet not too many people about.

I crossed the road then walked up to the mini roundabout, took the first left, I was on the phone to Mickey and just shooting the breeze when all of a sudden a car mounted the pavement heading towards me.

"What the fuck?" I shouted down the phone before lodging my phone over the wall.

I turned my head to look behind me but another car was hurtling towards me so I jumped in the air and both cars smashed in to each other.

They narrowly missed breaking my legs and as I landed on the floor a van pulled up beside me, the side door opened letting out six or seven masked old bill.

All dressed in black combat gear before I knew it I was being battered with truncheons until I fell to the ground again.

The whole street had come alive with old bill, I lost count at 25 as I was now face down on the floor.

All I could hear was "it's definitely him"

"We've got the bastard"

"Well done"

"Brilliant work guys"

"Finally we got the cunt"

I was brought to my feet and asked my name.

"Maybe you should have asked me that before nearly running me the fuck over, my name is Eddie Jones and what the fuck is going on here?"

"The games up Terry, we know who you are, actually we thought you would be little taller."

"Look you know you've got the wrong man don't you?"

"No we haven't Terry Ellis, you're nicked" they then read me my rights.

It was ten minutes before they eventually got permission from Luton Constabulary to take me back to London, to Kentish Town police station, but not before they produced a photo of me and held it up to my face.

"GOTCHA!"

I had to smile at the irony of the situation, I was one day away from my new life but now these bastards had intervened and chosen their version of my new life for me.

Unfortunately their version didn't consist of sun, sea and blue lagoons or even a new Thai wife.

Well shit happens.

I was placed in the car between two plainclothes officers with two more in the front, to be honest it was a relief to finally be caught, in fact I felt rather calm as we drove back to London, even though this was possibly my last look at freedom from the M1.

When we drove into Kentish town police station it was dark and pissing down with rain.

I was led handcuffed in to what can only be described as a roll call of honour, but not for me, everyone was clapping and cheering as we walked into the holding area.

The desk sergeant, eight wooden tops and the four that were with me , which made 13 plod in all, all giving it large with Hi-five's and hand clapping , shouting and saying well done to each other.

When they eventually calmed down I was standing in front of the desk sergeant who said "take his cuffs off"

"What's your name?"

"No comment!"

"Very droll Mr Ellis, you have been arrested for your involvement in robbing Verizon Business and Global Communications IT company on St. Pancreas way, you will be held here for questioning as to your involvement in this crime, do you understand?"

"No comment"

"Do you want to call a solicitor?"

"Yes"

"Would you like to inform a family member?"

"Yes"

I called my dad and appraised him of my situation , he wasn't too surprised as he understood that this day would eventually come I suppose, I asked him to call my brief, we had a short conversation about my wellbeing I said I was fine and not to worry.

I spent three days in Kentish town police station but said nothing not even my name, so they remanded me to Pentonville prison, a cockroach infested shithole on Caledonian Road.

I spent the first week in the block as I refused to share a cell with anyone.

I was placed on to D wing and put in a single cell.

The wing was infested with cockroaches so I spent the first week catching them and putting them in a large HMP bag which I hung up on my wall, that first week I managed to catch 120 cockroaches.

Why you may ask?

Well when I was down the block I spoke to the Governor about the Cockroaches and the conditions I was living in, he sarcastically remarked back to me saying "well Mr Ellis don't tell everyone or they will all want some"

So for that comment I had decided to show him how it felt to live in these conditions, as luck would have it one day the Governor was right outside my door sitting up against the wing pool table, he was talking to a large group of prison inspectors mostly women which looked to be going rather well, so I took the bag off the wall, looked through the crack in my door to see where all the screws were and to my surprise there was only three with him that day.

They were standing against the opposite wall, so I slowly opened my door, took a deep breath, walked out behind him and tipped the bag of cockroaches over his head.

It only took a fraction of a second but it felt great , all the women started screaming and running up the landing.

The Governor screamed like a little girl, I just stood there laughing before I was jumped on by all the screws before being carted off to the block, I ended up with a couple of digs but nothing too severe.

Two weeks later I was put on a production order and requested to appear at Kentish town police station, where I was questioned about a number of robberies but once again I made a no comment statement before being taken to Islington Police Station.

Unfortunately when we got there we were told that we couldn't come in due to building work being carried out, so it was decided that we would go to St. Anne's ID suite for me to go on an ID parade.

They handcuffed me again, for some reason this time they hadn't put the cuffs on properly, as I could feel that one was loose, as we drove along I managed to pull one of my hands free, the other one just wouldn't budge, no matter how much I tried to force it.

I wasn't too concerned about that as I still had one good right hand free, we had about twenty minutes until we reached St. Anne's in Tottenham.

I kept thinking about was how good it would feel to escape from these mugs, to actually be free again to continue with my departure from England.

This would possibly be my last ever chance to make good an escape.

First I had a mountain of obstacles to overcome, the first being I had to somehow overpower my guards, which wouldn't be easy, secondly I needed some Ellis good luck, most of all it would need a lot of effort on my part, which unfortunately meant banging out my escorts.

Something I wasn't keen on doing as the last thing I needed was a GBH charge added to the list, I really had no choice as my escape depended on me overpowering one or more of my guards.

The journey seemed to take for ever so I took the opportunity to put my captors at ease by making some small talk.

They seemed pleased that I was now talking to them, as I hadn't said one word to them since I'd been arrested in Leagrave.

One of them even offered me a deal of six years if I grassed up my pals, I told him to fuck off and that I was thinking of breaking out of the van that evening and fucking off to Thailand.

My joke seemed to make them all laugh one even quipped back by saying it's going to be a very long time before you ever see the light of day again, let alone the red light area of Patang.

I just smiled at his sarcasm as I believed my freedom was just round the next corner and in a few minutes these mugs would have a rude awakening.

As we pulled up to the gates I noticed that the wall was about 15-feet high but the gate we were driving through was only 10-feet high which looked easier than I imagined, God all I needed now was a good run up to get over it, or I could use one of the cars parked up against the wall.

A part of me really wanted to do this but there was another voice inside my head saying don't be such a fucking idiot, it was a battle between good and evil and by the looks of it evil was definitely going to win the day, because all I could hear was you can fucking do this Tel.

As the gates opened and my adrenaline started to flow, this mixed in with the butterflies in the pit of my stomach was all I needed to get myself ready.

"This is it Terry boy, get ready son!"

The car following us parked up against the wall and as I looked over at them I noticed that none of them were getting out, this was my first bit of good luck, maybe these idiots thought their job was done.

Then my driver got out and walked over to the back door entrance, he rang the bell waited a minute before being buzzed in, fuck that was my second bit of luck.

I was now on my own with my two escorts in the back of the van, both in their late forties, they wouldn't be a problem to me.

Just as I thought about nutting one of them in the back of the van, the one nearest to me slid the door open and stepped out, while the other one just sat there reading a paper behind me.

What luck!

It was time to make my move, I jumped out of the van, spun round and banged the copper on the chin putting him on his arse.

I started running towards the front gates, but just as I turned the corner two uniformed old bill came through blocking my escape.

I looked back over my shoulder I saw all my escorts jumping at the van and cars pursuing me.

I quickly jumped up on to one of the car bonnets, ran up the window screen, leaping onto to the wall grabbing it with both hands.

I had fucking made it, see you later you fucking mugs!

As I tried to pull myself up the handcuff dug in the wall bending my wrist backwards and made me lose my grip which gave them vital seconds to make up some ground towards me.

It was now useless as I tried to pull myself back up, I felt a whack in the middle of my back, then a second across my head, someone grabbed hold of my legs and as I hung there one of them jumped on my back with his arm around my neck, choking me, until I lost my grip.

All three of us fell to the ground, with them falling on top of me.

I was facedown with my head in the dirt being spread-eagled on the ground with my hands once again cuffed behind my back.

I was then placed back in the van with my face on the floor being taken back to Pentonville where I was charged with attempted escape and put in the yellow and green patches (a striped escapees suit).

As luck would have it I eventually got a not guilty for trying to escape as the old bill mistakenly put the wrong police station down on the charge sheet, in their haste they said I tried to escape from Kentish town police station instead of St. Anne's police station, so the charges were dropped on a technicality and I was moved to Wandsworth prison immediately.

This was exactly where I wanted to be as my good pal Dez was there, what seemed on the surface as a punishment, turned out to be a blessing in disguise.

It is a well-known fact that Wandsworth is seen as one of the worst prisons in London in as far as the screws run it like a military operation.

Having Dez there more than made up for that, plus he would be in a position to update me on any current investigations that the old bill were actively pursuing against us.

It was great to see him after almost nine months, he looked fit and healthy and was in good spirits considering where he was and especially when you took into account that we were both now looking at long custodial sentences.

But he was upbeat nevertheless.

He said that almost every police force in the country had been down to interview him under caution about robberies that involved police uniforms since he'd been arrested, the evidence was mostly circumstantial as there was no DNA or CCTV evidence linking us to anything, so that wouldn't stand up in any court of law.

Apart from Verizon that is, as the CCTV footage was crystal clear especially of us.

It would still be a 50 / 50 chance if we took it to trial, because our caps covered our faces and the photo recognition evidence wasn't conclusive either.

They had no idea who else was involved, the south London boys, Mickey, the tall fella and Frankie were all in the clear, so out of ten people, only two of us would pay the piper.

"We have bigger problems though Tel, the FBI and MI5 are actively investigating links between us and our connections in Ireland and America."

"What do you mean?"

"You won't believe it if I tell you, this is fucking massive and me and you are right bang in the middle of it all.

It's been crazy, MI5 will definitely come and interview you, so you better be ready, as they know that you are the main Protagonist in all this bollocks and definitely the one who organised it all.

You can see quite clearly from the CCTV that this was no fucking ordinary robbery!

It was well planned and carried out like a military operation, they also think we had inside help, that's why they aren't pursuing anyone else, they are particularly interested in the involvement of certain banking officials, who they believe pinpointed specific information and the precise location in London(i.e. Verizon) where valuable information was stored, regarding certain banking irregularities by some of the world's leading banks, companies and financial institutions.

They believe they were involved in the prime mortgage scandal, they mentioned Royal Bank of Scotland, Northern Rock, Lehman Brothers, AIG, Fannie Mae, HBOS, Merrill lynch and Freddie Mac.

The information we stole would have been vital for them in securing prosecutions against some of the CEOs of these corporations and banks."

"Fuck! Are you kidding me?"

"No, honestly you couldn't make this shit up Tel. We are for all intent and purpose well and truly in the shit my friend!"

"Well let's get me sorted out first before we take on the establishment, I need a phone, a job and a single cell.

Can you help me Dez?"

Yeah no problem Tel, I can get you your own mobile hopefully by this evening and a job on the hot plate if you want it?"

"Yes definitely brother"

"But you have no chance of getting a single cell, they are like gold dust in this fucking shit place"

"Mate it's so good to see you"

"You too mate"

"Come on let's have a catch up"

It was a week before I had my first visit from the kids and their mum, a visit that made me realise that they would all be grown up women before I got out.

My barrister had already informed me that I was likely to get double figures probably 16 or 17 years but could be more.

I couldn't tell the kids that or their mum, so we talked about school and them going to college then eventually off to University.

Charlene had already made her mind up that she wanted to be a hairdresser, Chloe said she wanted to be a nurse and Terri wanted to do psychology and criminology.

The visit was good spirited and even enjoyable, I think it's because my kids are a lot like me resilient they take everything in their stride.

I've never seen them despondent about anything especially on visits, I've always had that devil-may-care attitude and maybe they understood me more that I realized.

I was sorry to see them go.

Chapter Forty Eight

MI5 - The interview

"The game of life is a lot like football. You have to tackle your problems, block your fears, and score your goals when you get the opportunity."
- Lewis Grizzard -

The next afternoon I was called to the visiting room believing that it was my solicitor, but it was the police from three separate police forces.

They had a mountain of paperwork, that they implied implicated me in several unsolved robberies that had taken place throughout the United kingdom, they even professed to have overwhelming evidence to support their cases and because of that they wanted to interview me under caution.

They asked how would I feel about them talking to me today without my solicitor.

"Obviously, you are joking!"

"No we are not!" quite an emphatic response to leave me in no doubt they were actually being serious.

"Ok let me tell you this then, if you lot have any evidence that categorically puts me at any of those robberies, then charge me now, otherwise fuck off, I also want all your badge numbers for my barrister and what police station's you are from"

I stood up knocked on the door and asked the screw to take me back to the wing. I just hoped now that the information that Dez had given me was accurate and that these officers didn't have any concrete evidence on me, such as DNA or CCTV footage.

The good thing was that our case had been fast-tracked so if they had anything on me then they only had a very short window of opportunity to charge me and present their case.

I could only assume that if they hadn't charged Dez with all those robberies, then they weren't going to charge me either.

They were just going through the motions hoping I would crack and give the rest of our team up.

I could also only assume that Verizon was their priority, their trophy scalp, they have to be seen to convict us, sending out a message that crime against big business will not be tolerated in London, so to dilute their case with robberies that they couldn't possibly prove would only muddy the waters.

We hadn't used any guns or violence, but we had taken something that would potentially have serious ramifications if they ever managed to resurface or get into the wrong hands ever again.

We would ultimately be the scapegoats in all this saga and our sentences would reflect that.

The authorities also had to make the Verizon heist look like a computer theft, or a simple burglary, because to admit that major companies, corporations and banks throughout the world had instigated and conspired with each other to share information, that could well bring down some of the wealthiest capitalists in England, Ireland and America, that would be unthinkable especially to all those bankers in powerful political circles.

Surely they wouldn't allow that?

Bankers, unlike criminals, can steal hundreds of thousands, even millions and possibly billions, and the consequences for their indiscretions would simply be a fine, retirement, or a bailout from the government and that's the real hypocrisy in all this.

For me and Dez we were just Mino's in a sea of corruption, that was definitely above our pay grade.

We had done our small part to protect the guilty by doing the Verizon job for a Consortium of corrupt bankers, but at what cost to us?

What was coming our way?

What would be covered up by the dark arts or whatever was at play now?

There was nothing that me or Dez could do to stop it now.

I was settling in at Wandsworth, I had a good job on the hot plate and was sharing a cell with a guy called John from Newcastle, I'd also started an affair with one of the DHL girls.

I was seeing her once a week but phoning most nights and on top of that, I'd formed a relationship with my forensic psychologist who had been assigned to me because of my escape attempt, the incident with cockroaches that the Governor hadn't particularly been impressed with and the serious nature of my crimes.

Which made the monotony of prison more bearable as I'd finished with Carol and kea.

So these ladies were a pleasant distraction and the catalyst for me starting to write poetry.

I also started reading every psychology and criminologist book that I could lay my hands on in the library which helped me immensely to articulate certain hypothesises with my forensic psychologist friend.

This morning started like any other I'd been on the phone talking to my brief, we were still working on our strategy, we still weren't sure what we were going to do yet.

After the dinner bang-up I could hear the unmistakable sound of an officer's boots echoing outside on the landing, once you zone into that sound, no matter how many times you hear it you think it is coming to your cell.

However, this time I was correct, it was.

I heard the keys jangle outside my door, then in the lock, before it was opened and I was greeted by two prison officers.

"Ellis?" Every officer puts on a more masculine tone when addressing an inmate, but this time it seemed far more forceful than normal.

"Yes Guv" it's the standard response especially from me towards the officers, but in reality though I was thinking "what fucking now?".

"You've got visitors Ellis, let's go"

"Wrong Ellis Guv, I don't have any visits today either from my family or defence team, so you've got the wrong Ellis Guv."

Dopey bollocks wouldn't listen, he just insisted saying that he was right and I was wrong,

I wouldn't normally object, to going to the visits hall, but I knew they were mistaken.

But he insisted again.

"I beg to differ Ellis now let's go" The way he answered was much more assured this time.

So, I decided rather than stand arguing with him, I would go and make him look like the idiot he was, it was the only thing I could do given my situation, hopefully, when he finally realised that he'd made a genuine mistake, he would eat humble pie and escort me back to my cell,

So If I achieved nothing else today, apart from mugging him off because of his own stupidity, then so be it, it would make my day anyway.

"Tell me then Guv, who is this visitor I know nothing about? it would be great to get some background information" The sarcasm in my voice must have shone through, but to their credit, both officers remained unusually professional.

"We don't know who it is, we just got told to come and get you and bring down you to the interview room"

"Interview room? I ain't talking to anyone without my solicitor, so I will save you and whoever it might be some time, by letting you know that I will be saying NO FUCKING COMMENT to all their questions, is that clear enough Guv?"

"Tell us that as much as you like, we have been told to take you there so that is where you'll be going"

Naturally at this point everything goes through your head, the police can be sneaky fuckers, they try to get you to admit to crimes you never did to make themselves look better, it helps with their clear-up rate, normally you get wind of something like this beforehand from your solicitor, but this time I've heard nothing.

"Guv, can you at least tell me if it's the police that we are seeing, I am pretty sure you have to let me know so I can have legal representation"

"We don't know Ellis, we got a call to come and get you that's it, we have no idea what it's for, who it is, what it's about or anything else, the Security Governor just said we needed to come and get you and bring you down here. That's it"

"Ok Guv no problem, tell the security governor then that unless my solicitor is present the answer is no comment"

I had waves of emotion running through me, I have never been a guy to turn on anyone, I go into every job accepting the fact I might have to do a bit of bird, especially if the worse happens, it's the unwritten rule, no deals.

I can only assume that this is some soppy plot by pc plod to get me on their side, it won't happen though. I am about to go into this interview in full defence mode.

"In there Ellis, sit down"

"Why?"

"Just sit down, that's a direct order."

"That's an incredibly mundane response!" I suppose my two escorts hadn't exactly been a barrel of laughs up to this point so why should I expect anything more from them now.

"Stay there and be quiet, someone will be with you shortly"

"I can't exactly go anywhere can I" A nod to the fact we had had to walk through several locked security gates.

"Guv, since you interrupted my busy day of doing fuck all, can I please get a cup of coffee?"

I knew this was probably another pointless request but occasionally you'll get an officer that does their job and helps you out.

"We'll see what we can do" That's Prison officer speak for, I will walk away and do fuck all.

Ten minutes later to my surprise and utter shock, officer truculent bollocks walked back in and gave me a coffee, this was another indication that something wasn't quite right, anyone that has been in prison knows that something is off when officers do something for you.

"There you go" He placed the coffee in front of me, as the door was propped open behind him, I could see down the corridor two blokes in suits talking to the security governor, they might have been police officers but I got the feeling they were something more important.

It was making sense now, why I had gotten the Ritz treatment receiving this shitty, lukewarm black coffee, they were more important than your normal C.I.D or (plod) police officers.

Still, who am I to complain, I was getting to spend an hour or more off the wing, out of my cell and with any luck, I will also get the opportunity to piss off a couple of police officers or MI5.

I assumed that after seeing the officers talking to the security governor they would be in pretty quickly.

I can't express to you how pissed off I was becoming, because even after an hour I was still sitting there, still locked in this fucking room and still none the wiser as to why I had been brought down here.

I am pretty sure I had heard Dez being escorted past, that was my biggest indication that this was about the Verizon but I still didn't know why because the court case was ready, we had already been charged and the solicitors already had full disclosure so surely they can't be trying to add on charges this late in the day.

Whatever the reason, I should not have been sat here for the last fucking hour, I know its tactical to get me annoyed, keep me waiting, so I agree to anything just to get out of this claustrophobic interview room, especially this room as it stinks of piss - probably the last poor bastard that they had down here waiting for hours just to say no comment.

Finally, I could hear footsteps coming towards the door, the shadows darkening at the small gap at the bottom, this was their way of announcing their presence

As the door opened, I couldn't help myself.

"About fucking time!"

"ELLIS!" clearly, I had rubbed the screws up the wrong way, but that was nothing new for me, he hadn't even managed to put one foot in the room before I had pissed him off, there was more where that came from, they had kept me waiting all this time, so I would react in kind by pissing them off at every opportunity I got.

The two guys in the suits talking to the security governor that I had seen earlier now made their way in, it was unusual that the security governor and not the prison officers had brought these two to me.
Something was amiss.

"Ellis, these two gentlemen have a few questions for you" The security governor didn't give me a chance to respond, he just put the two of them in the room and left.

"Where are you two from? Which police force?" knowing where they were from normally gives you some indication about which crime they are going to ask about.

"It doesn't matter where we're from"

"Well, it does because I won't answer anything until I know, also why have I not been allowed a solicitor? That is my legal right, isn't it?" I was already irritated by the wait, it was now definitely showing in my tone.

"You don't need a solicitor because we are not police officers"

"MI5 possibly?" he smiled "gotcha" I thought.

"Well, if you're not police and it doesn't matter who you are, then why the fuck should I speak with you? Bring the screws back and we can end this nice and quickly"

"Mr Ellis, we have a series of questions we would like to ask you about, regarding the data robbery from Verizon, it could be very beneficial for you to help us answer those questions" they both looked the same, with the same cheap suits and shit Poundland haircuts.

"Let me save you the time and give you all my answers now - No Comment"

"Mr Ellis, your cooperation would be greatly appreciated and we can assure you that nothing you say in this room will be used against you, if you help us the time you serve could be greatly reduced"

"No comment"

"At least hear us out"

"Look, until you tell me who you are and what you are doing here, my answer is no comment, what kind of spooks are you anyway, you haven't cautioned me, you haven't read me my rights, you aren't even recording this"

"Exactly"

"What do you mean exactly?" They had tried unsuccessfully to confuse the fuck out me with all their cloak and dagger bollocks. But it wasn't working,

"We aren't from the police; you are not under caution and nothing is recorded. We simply have a few questions for you, we work for the Government."

"What department?"

"We can't tell you"

"Well, in that case, You can definitely both fuck off then" I had even less time for spooks (MI5) than I do for the police.

"Mr Ellis, we are only interested in the details surrounding the stolen hardware from the Verizon data centre, if you can answer our questions, we can look at getting you a seriously reduced sentence, you could be back home with your children in 3 years, think about it, back with your family and home for Christmas"

"No Comment"

"Can you tell us about why you chose to steal the data hardware from Verizon?"

"No Comment"

"Were you aware of what was contained on the hard drives before taking them?"

"No Comment"

"Can you talk us through how you obtained that information?"

"No Comment"

"Were you working for someone?"

"No Comment"

"Can you explain to us how you came to be working for that person?"

"No Comment"

"Mr Ellis, I put it to you that neither you nor the person you were charged with had the intelligence or foresight to pull off such an audacious robbery, so if you can help us to identify the person or persons who were in charge, then we can genuinely help you out, you scratch our back and we can scratch yours"

"Are you guys for fucking real? Scratch my back" I laughed at them.

"Let's talk about the person who ordered the job shall we?"

"No Comment"

"We know that you were working for someone Mr Ellis, it is crucial that we speak to you about who that was"

"No Comment" Eventually you get tired of saying the same thing over and over again but the key is to only say that, as any deviation and they will use it against you.

Whilst they claim not to be police, it is obvious that they are from the intelligence branch because his face went red when I mentioned he was MI5.

"Can you tell us about when you first came into contact with this person?"

"No Comment"

"Did you meet them in a professional setting?"

"No Comment"

"Perhaps you met them in a bank?"

"No Comment"

"A pub?"

"No Comment"

"Was it only over the phone?"

"No Comment"

"Maybe you met through a third party?"

"No Comment"

"Was it in this country?"

"No Comment"

"Are you prepared to discuss how you would make contact?"

"No Comment"

"Mr Ellis, you are not helping yourself here, we know who you were working for and we know why you were working for them, all you need to do is simply tell us what we already know and you can return to your life in a much shorter space of time"

"No Comment"

At that point the two of them got up and walked out of the room, I can remember thinking that I had broken them a lot quicker than most police, they normally drag it out for hours and it can be a real test of wills for who gets bored first.

After five or six minutes though they both returned, I was fully expecting them to try and do the clique good cop, bad cop routine, such was their predictable approach to questioning me.

"Mr Ellis, let's try a different approach"

I fucking knew it, I thought to myself, good cop, bad cop was about to start.

"How about we tell you what we know and you just answer yes or no?"

"No Comment" I could see one of them rolled his eyes, you should never show that I thought, I'm getting under your skin mate.

"You were working for a fixer"

"No Comment"

"This fixer was connected to a bank"

"No Comment"

"You were given detailed plans of exactly which hardware to take and where that hardware was located"

"No Comment"

"Those plans were given to you by someone connected with a large bank"

"No Comment"

"Mr Ellis, I don't think you understand the opportunity you have in front of you right now, a little cooperation from you is all it will take to help yourself out immeasurably, help us to locate where the hard drives are now and we can make your life so much easier for you moving forward"

They could dangle whatever carrot they wanted in front of me, it would make no difference because I would not talk or break my own golden rule, I puffed out my chest, paused for a second, as though I was going to speak, this had the added bonus of raising their hopes and then leaned forward and said "No… Comment!"

"Mr Ellis, we already know that the information passed to you was done so either directly or indirectly by an insider in a major world bank, it is very important that we locate this hardware, so I will ask you again for assistance in this matter"

"I told you already, No comment"

At this point the two of them got up and walked out again, I could see that they were putting two and two together and coming up with fifty, otherwise, there would be extra charges, they had planned on speaking to Dez, otherwise why else would he be down here too.

After about five minutes the Security Governor appeared, "Hallelujah" I thought, finally they've given up, he had another coffee with him.

"Here you go Terry" He placed the coffee down in front of me,

"Thanks, Guv, but what the fuck is that for?" Governor's in my opinion are even lazier than the screws so having one as your own personal waiter is odd, to say the least.

"It's just a coffee as you have been down here a while, I wanted to speak to you about your cooperation with these gentlemen regarding their questions, these guys need your help and I wanted to make sure you understood that whatever you say to them won't leave this room"

"I know Guv, but with all due respect" and of course by saying that I meant with absolutely zero respect at all. "They have come here to ask me questions, they won't tell me where they're from, they won't let me have a solicitor and you have suddenly become a waiter, in a failing attempt to get me on side, as I said from the outset my answer is no comment, so why don't you go back out there and tell them that and I can get back to my cell and prepare for my court appearance"

"Just consider speaking to them, Terry "

I had to admire everyone's persistence but their efforts were futile and the very first thing I would be doing when I got back on the wing would be to speak to my solicitor and ask him to put in a complaint about this kangaroo court style ambush.

I hadn't even had a chance to drink my coffee before MI-69 and his cock-sucking sidekick came back into the room.

"Great, you two again"

"Terry" They had obviously decided to get more serious because they had dropped the formalities of calling me Mr Ellis, so I was fully expecting that this would be the "trying to relate to you" tactic. I have been in a couple of interviews over the years so I know how they operate.

"Terry, we want to help you but for that to happen we need you to confirm the details of the robbery, we don't care at this point what you made from it, we don't care about your motivation for doing the robbery and quite frankly we don't care if you have done 100's of other robberies just like this one, but what we do care about is the location of the data stored on what you took and who ordered the job"

I didn't even bother answering this time, I was drinking my cold coffee, so just shrugged my shoulders and smiled.

"Can you confirm that the job was ordered by someone inside the Lehman Brothers bank?"

Royal Bank of Scotland?

Northern rock?"

Again, I just looked at him, for a moment I wanted to ask him for some KFC or McDonalds but judging by the line of questions now, I guessed, that boat had sailed.

"Terry, what you took contained highly sensitive banking data that, in the wrong hands could have very significant repercussions around the world, we need you to help us relocate them and tell us who ordered the job"

"No comment"

"This is your last chance, you are currently facing a very long sentence, what we are offering, is to reduce that to six, you will serve three and would be out on licence before you know it, surely that is worth telling us who ordered the job?"

"As I have said already, No Comment"

They both left the room again I thought I was going to end up with a trip down the block after this, the security governor had made an effort to speak to me in person so I can only assume he wouldn't take my refusal to co-operate very well.

When I was eventually joined by two new officers who were tasked with taking me back to the wing, I said I wanted to go and speak to the security desk, this is where all visitors sign in as they book out the interview rooms and keep a detailed log of all the visitors.

As we approached, I had already prepared what I wanted to say in my head.

"Can I get a record of who just came to visit me please, I believe it is my legal right to do so"

"What visit Ellis?"

"The one I was just in, obviously Guv" it was a particularly stupid response but one I hadn't expected from a serving prison officer.

"No visits have happened today, look" The screw showed me an empty visitor and security sheet.

"Well then Guv, you haven't done your jobs properly, because two blokes just spent the last hour or so wasting my time, and I would appreciate a record of that"

"There were no blokes in with you Mr Ellis"

"No problem Guv"

With that, I was escorted back to the wing, I asked the escorting officers about the two blokes and they said, "what blokes, we saw no blokes".

As soon as I got on the wing, I rang my solicitor to get him on the case, but all he said was that it all sounded a bit strange but it is possible that the guys were actually from MI5, but that would only happen if the information contained on those hard drives posed some kind of risk.

The coming weeks would show that perhaps the information on our motherboards was more to do with the financial sector then we ever imagined.

It had been 3 weeks since those two bob Government spooks had secretly visited me in Wandsworth, I was still perplexed, as I couldn't fully understand what they expected of me, did they honestly think I'd flip over on my pals after being tortured with two cups of cold coffees and a lecture from the security governor to assist them with their enquires, I think not.

Even though they had left empty-handed, their faces and demeanour said it all, I was definitely in trouble now, I hadn't given up any information that could help them convict those that had procured my services.

So I wasn't too surprised at their leaving Salvo, they left me in no doubt to what they had in store for me eventually.

The one who had done the talking mentioned that I should expect nothing less than double figures at my sentencing, my response to that and them was a cursory finger gesture and a smile as they shut the door.

There had been no repercussions from the security governor or the screws, they knew the eventual outcome of me not cooperating with the investigation, I was going to be caged up like an animal.

42-years old and looking at a long sentence that would take me well into my fifties, a daunting prospect at any time of life, but more so now because I'd miss the most important years of my kids' lives, growing up, their transition from childhood to adolescence, a consequence of my actions that I had never envisaged or considered until this very moment.

It was the most important period of their lives and I wouldn't be there for them, I felt sorry for them which is a father's prerogative, but I couldn't feel sorry for myself, even though I was responsible for this whole sorry saga because that's just not what I do.

I have to believe that my life trajectory is exactly how it was supposed to be now and sitting in this cell was just another life lesson that would eventually make me the man I was always supposed to be.

Prison has always been an afterthought for me, but never a deterrent because how can I fear a system that holds no fear.

As a kid they threw everything at me apart from the kitchen sink, they brutalised me, isolated me and even locked me up and called it the care system, in reality it was a child's prison.

I saw prison now as nothing more than a place of safety, my old home and the rest of it was just a waste of time.

Prison has never been a place for rehabilitation, just a warehouse for society's so called human detritus.

But never-the-less it was now my new reality, a reality of life that would either break me or make me, that would still be determined by the length of time I would eventually do behind bars and the games the authorities wanted to play with me now.

I was informed that morning that I was also being charged with a drugs offence, my finger prints were apparently found on a carrier bag that contained a large amount of cocaine up in Doncaster, even though I'd never touched the bag or had anything to do with it.

The drugs were supposedly found Inside a spare wheel of a car that belonged to a pal of mine who had given me and my pal Steve a lift to Manchester a year or so before.

I'd now been charged with three counts of robbery and a drugs offence which in the big scheme of things wasn't the end of the world.

They could theoretically have charged me with between six and ten robberies, they hadn't simply because of how English law works.

If I am found guilty they would sentence me individually for each count, but they had to run them concurrently, a consecutive sentence on top of my highest sentence would be extremely unlikely, but it was still a possibility.

The worst case scenario for our crimes would be between ten and twelve years, simply because we didn't use any firearms or violence and under British law we would only have to serve half that sentence,

So our attention to detail with regards to not using guns or violence would see us out on the streets earlier rather than later I hoped.

I had spoken with my solicitor and he had intimated that 10 or 12 years was a possibility and the lowest sentence we could receive under sentencing guidelines which seemed to alleviate the pressure, also the IPP Sentence had been taken off the table.

It would have seen both myself and Dez receiving life sentences, so considering the fact we had nicked somewhere in the region of five million pounds in motherboards and potentially hundreds of millions of dollars in data, we could actually now end up with a slap on the wrists.

For example if we had done just one armed robbery while waving guns around, we would most probably have received life sentences, so thank god for British law.

However my brief had warned me not to get too complacent as the FBI, MI5 and the police had a real hard on for me so would try their best to throw a spanner in the works, especially because I'd punched a police officer in the face and no motherboards had ever been returned.

It would be very unlikely that I would get off with a short sentence, especially one that MI5 considered to be punitive.

They had also served me this morning with a private prosecution on behalf of JPMorgan's lawyers for hidden assets, stipulating that if I ever came into money I would be liable, meaning I would have to pay the five million back in full.

My briefs exact words were "Terry whatever happens in the future, don't win the fucking lottery or they will come after you and for it"

"Don't worry, any lottery tickets I buy will be in my girlfriend's name trust me."

He then told me that my court date was on the 30th of July 2009 at Blackfriars crown court which was only seven months away.

I had to get Christmas out the way first, Dez's court cases might be on a separate day, as he had been charged with the Croydon robbery and another one in St. John's wood.

It was felt we would both be better off on our own, which on the surface seemed a realistic option as my previous convictions would certainly jeopardise his trial, plus he was ex UN army peace keeper, who it could be argued, had made a terrible mistake.

I, on the other hand was seen as a seasoned underworld criminal who had a history of violence, armed robbery and drug offences, So I couldn't blame his defence team if they wanted to separate our cases, I would have done the same in his position.

We had now both decided to go guilty, so we could get a third reduction in our sentence, as we felt to go to trial would have been futile considering the weight of evidence they had against us, it was overwhelming.

I'd also asked for a Newton hearing, which meant the judge would give me an indication of the sentence I would likely receive, with a guilty plea or a not guilty plea.

It was between nine or ten years for guilty, but if we were found guilty after going not guilty then it would possibly be 15 years.

We really didn't need any persuading on that front as It was a no brainer, the metropolitan police and operation Grafton had basically said that they wouldn't pursue a longer sentence as we hadn't used any guns or violence, plus they were satisfied with the fact we were off the streets, MI5 and the FBI were not officially involved , but their influence was inevitable, especially as we had pissed them off with our no comment interviews.

As their parting words to Dez were basically "laugh now, cry later, you're gonna regret this you prick"

Which was their way of telling us they would definitely have the last word, no matter what the outcome of the case was.

However there was nothing we could do about that now, it was almost Christmas and I had to make it one to remember so me and my cell mate John had arranged a parcel for Christmas, it would be thrown over the wall, some puff, weed, cocaine, some Subutex and a couple of mobile phones, it would be my last Christmas party before sentencing.

There were three teams of hardcore guys on our wing, Johnny and his firm from Bournemouth that consisted of 15 guys in all, Tony's team from South London - 12 men, and North London with me, Dez and of course my cell mate Newcastle John.

We had all come together and decided to throw all our parcels over the wall at the same time, regardless of the screws, the idea was that as soon as the parcels landed in the exercise yard, we were going to surround our gear with thirty of us, thus hopefully confusing the screws and the CCTV operators, something that Wandsworth or any prison really, wasn't used to, organised convicts.

We had come to this decision because for weeks parcels were coming in over the wall and would be intercepted by only 3 or four screws, whose job it was to guard the exercise yard.

That would all end today as we had agreed to work together in the first multi organised crime force inside prison.

We had agreed to smother the exercise yard as soon as the food (drugs) hit the floor.

The atmosphere was electric as we went out as usual on the yard, instead of walking round we all stood against the fence then I gave the signal for Johnny to phone the throwers, call one was to let them know that we were all in position.

Call two was to tell them to lob over drugs.

"Go, Go, Go" six packages - bam, bam, bam, bam, bam, bam.

It was brilliant the screws didn't know what day it was, they looked confused at the amount coming over, they were so used to only one package coming over at a time, but those days were over.

And before they could respond we all stepped away from the fence blocking their view, they were mortified, flummoxed that we had taken back the power.

They tried to style it out, as one of them pulled out his truncheon but we all moved towards them, Johnny my cell mate put it on one of them by saying "try it you fucking mugs".

The screw looked scared which emboldened us, as we all started chanting and jeering it felt good, this was our very own little victory,
the gear was quickly plugged up a multitude of arses.

The screws were pissed and over the Radio we could hear the security governor calling for an immediate lockdown on all the wings.

He redirected all the screws to C-wing's exercise yard, sixty or more screws confronting us but we stood our ground no one budged an inch until the acting governor came out and said return to your cells.

We had our gear so we reluctantly lined up to go in, not before being searched, every now and then the screws pulled out someone who they thought were ring leaders, me and john slipped quietly in before we could be pointed out by the CCTV operator's.

We were allowed dinner before being banged up over the dinner period, this gave us all time to bottle our phones and gear, it's surprising how much you can put up your arse when you want to , especially when you're expecting the whole wing to be searched.

The lock up period over dinner was noisy as everyone was shouting out the windows and banging on the doors, they had won a small victory that they could dine out on throughout their prison sentence as they were now mavericks.

But me and John knew different, we processed what had happened and both knew the screws wouldn't take this laying down, no they would be working hard to find the culprits before they clamp down on any dissention by all means possible.

Unlock came and went then the key went in our door the (S.O)senior officer was standing in our doorway with a clipboard in his hand , "Ellis, Skelton, pack your gear Ellis your off to B-wing , Skelton your off to D-wing."

"Fuck off we ain't going nowhere" said john as he pulled a table leg out from under the bed, he ripped off this clothes and covered himself in baby oil.

The S.O pulled the cell door shut and said "we will be back in twenty minutes with the mufti squad (specially trained officers dressed as Robocop's with crash helmets, shields and batons) so fucking get ready"

It was a Mexican stand-off , Johnny wanted a battle and the S.O wanted him to come out peacefully and I was fucking right in the middle of it.

I couldn't leave my pal, but on the other hand it would be a bloodbath if I stayed.

It took Johnny over an hour to calm down and see sense but reluctantly he did, the S.O thanked me then he called for me to come out of the cell.

As I slowly edged my way out of our barricaded cell, I looked to my left and then my right, fuck there was forty odd screws on the landing all staring at me, they all looked up for a fight.

I almost backed back into the cell but the S.O noticed my unease and said "just walk down to the holding room Terry and wait in there nothing's going to happen to you, I promise."

I took another deep breath and fronted it out, I walked the hundred or so feet to the end of the landing until I came to a room where I was pushed in before it was locked behind me.

Five minutes later John came past escorted by eight screws, he looked over briefly and smiled as he was taken down the segregation unit.

I on the other hand was not taken to B-wing but F-wing where I was given a single cell and a charge sheet, I'd apparently been nicked for dissention.

I would be up in front of the Governor tomorrow morning at 10.15 am.

I still had half an ounce of cocaine, the same in weed and twenty Subutex and my phone so all in all not a bad day, I even had a single cell and was on one of the best wings in the prison.

Dez on the other hand was on K-wing doing a three month course, some sort of psychological therapy based rehabilitation program.

I was on F on my own, it was Tuesday, 16th December, 8 days before Christmas, thankfully my girlfriend on the DHL had arranged a Christmas present for me, a bag of cigarettes, tobacco, cakes, crisps, biscuits and soft drinks. That would last me all over Christmas, love her she had left the bag on my bed, as I was down the block waiting for my adjudication.

I'd been down the block since 8.30am, it was now 12.30pm, there had been a delay seeing the Governor.

This meant I had to sit in a cell with a camera monitoring me, which in itself is not a problem, but I had a mobile phone and all my gear up my arse which was now killing me.

I was sweating but I had to look as if nothing was wrong, the pain was excruciating.

When I finally got in front of the Governor my concentration was limited and unfortunately it came across as me being insolent, so the governor gave me two weeks no canteen, two weeks loss of association, then to top it off he put me closed visits until further notice for security reasons.

This meant closed visits all over Christmas, wanker!

When I got back to my cell I was fit to burst, the pain was killing me.

As I was retrieving the offending items I swore to myself that I would never hide a parcel up my backside ever again.

I decided to dig a little hole in the wall next to the door in my cell, I made some Papier-Mache and then filled the hole, I procured some paint from wing cleaner and hey presto the phone had a new home, I swept all the dust and fag butts into the corner ,because I knew the screws were a fickle lot and wouldn't put their hands in it.

My first job now was to get rid of my Subutex, I still had twenty left.

I gave them to a pal who sold them for me, Subutex are like gold dust in prison, they sell for about forty quid each which made me £800 pounds, this would now give me enough money for my canteen until July.

My pals and girlfriends outside were also topping up my phone once a week, which was only a tenner so I could speak to the kids every night, my girlfriends too, both had their individual qualities, my DHL girl Cyndi was sexy, witty, funny and could speak for hours on the phone.

Melanie my psychologist was intelligent, sexy and extremely pragmatic she was always trying to psychoanalyze me.

I enjoyed our talks and over those months we really made a connection, in as far as me now wanting to turn my life around, she had switched me on to the fact that I wasn't just a waste of space criminal.

She had seen the real me and understood that my environment had a lot to do with my life choices up to now.

She recommended books and literature that she believed would enhance my understanding of psychology and the benefits of possibly signing up to Grendon Underwood one day.

HMP Grendon has been at the forefront of therapeutic/psychiatric intervention since 1962, the prison is in Aylesbury, Buckinghamshire, it houses 240 B-category prisoners, who are some of the country's most dangerous prisoners.

But the work that they supposedly do there has been recognised as life changing, but only if you're prepared to face your demons, it was by no means an easy ride.

But It did appeal to my sense of Adventure an exploratory journey into my psyche, at what cost though?

I would be surrounded by the worst prisoners in the system, paedophiles, rapists, child killers, serial killers and all manner of other deviant crimes and criminals you could imagine.

But there were a few notable armed robbers that have taken part in Grendon such as Noel razor Smith, Ray Bishop and an old pal of mine Mickey Gorman.

So I thought it couldn't hurt to put my name forward and fill out an application form, I probably wouldn't get in or accepted anyway as they have a long waiting list.

But like Melanie said I had to be pragmatic, I had to try and navigate myself through this sentence, so it was important I take all the opportunities opened to me, plus it would be worth a shot, especially as I was now looking at a substantial sentence.

I might as well give myself the best opportunity to change if that's possible.

Christmas in prison can be a lonely time for most men, but not for me, especially as now that I've got a single cell it will be bliss, especially with all the Christmas carols and old films on the tv and radio.

The screws have a skeleton crew on over Christmas, which means lock up and more lockdown so they leave us alone.

Unfortunately though the cat and mouse games will still continue regarding them trying to catch us using our mobile phones.

The night screws still creep around night after night with their hand held scanners, all playing at being Robocop, trying their best to pinpoint hot spot cells.

They would then report them to the mufti squad who love nothing better than steaming into your cell and catching you on the phone, especially over Christmas, sadistic bastards that they are.

For half an ounce of tobacco a week I pay one of the guys on the wing to text me every time a screw comes on the landing, which is cheap especially when you consider that a phone costs between £900 and a £1000 a time, so the last thing you need is to lose it.

For many men their phone is a life line to maintain contact with their families and girlfriend's, it's paramount in maintaining family ties.

Some men like Smoking weed it keeps them mellow and they also sleep so much better, unlike Charlie, as that makes you paranoid, skitty and gives you the Horrors.

I made that mistake on C-wing, after taking it with john one night I was so paranoid that all I could see was the sniffer dogs walking past my cell with slippers on, it was fucking mental, we had a great time
but I can honestly say never again, I'll just stick to the odd puff every now and again.

The new year came around quickly and before I knew it I was singing Auld Lang Syne with Jools Holland and watching the fireworks out the window, my life had been reduced to this.

On my own on New Year's Eve and day, the thought of having to do ten or more years of this was torturous.

I would be in my fifties and an old man, it was feeling more and more like a nightmare now that I had settled down to prison life.

I was having the same conversations and listening to the same old jokes and the monotony of it all was at times more than I could comprehend.

I just wanted the court case over so I could plan my future, I wanted to be able to think of a time when I could get my life back.

The uncertainty was mind numbingly exacerbating, I found it hard to concentrate let alone read or talk to people, I hadn't even been sentenced yet but I was contemplating that day when I would leave prison a free man, if only I could turn back the hands of time and start my life again.

Hindsight is a wonderful thing it gives you an opportunity to address your behaviour and answer those questions that you should have asked yourself before taking the road less travelled.

I should never have done this, why did I choose this life, why didn't I just choose education instead of this lazy idle behaviour and hedonistic lifestyle? "Oh please God make this all fucking go away, let it be a dream, let me wake up tomorrow in my own home with my kids, a normal life , please God"

This mental self-flagellation is common, I suppose we all go through it, firstly we blame ourselves and when that doesn't work we blame God, the government and everybody else, but ultimately it was my laziness, greed and just being a selfish tosser that got me here.

I always told myself that I would never be like my dad and abandon my kids, but I've done exactly that, I've gone against everything that I promised that I wouldn't be or do, I had one job to do and that was to make my family safe and loved, but I couldn't even do that; I've let them all down.

They were my strength, they kept me grounded, but all I've ever done is leach off their love and affection.

They have always been the strong ones; not me.

How many times have I been in this position in my life, promising the kids that it will be fine; daddy will be home soon.

How do I make this fucking right now?

How do I make this mess go away?

I can't, I'll just have to keep telling myself that we will all get through this together, only time will now give us the answers.

I'm off to court tomorrow for pleas and dee's (guilty or not guilty) the outcome will still be the same - prison.

The money saved by not having a jury in attendance or being found guilty is roughly 3 or 4 years, so I'm definitely going guilty.

The journey through the streets of London in a sweat box (prison van) is something else.

Every woman looks so pretty and beautiful, the streets more colourful and vibrant, yet people are oblivious to this.

They rush about their lives not noticing its splendour, this precious commodity that they all take for granted; freedom.

These epiphanies only happen in the back of a sweat box, they bring home to us the futility of the risks that we take in the pursuit of money, life is so precious and to waste even one day should be an affront to life itself.

It's so ironic now to think that I would give every penny that I've ever made out of my crimes to be standing on that pavement right now looking in as it drives past, I'd give up all the houses, birds and all those so called good times, just to hold my kids in my arms right now.

This is the beauty of prison, it opens your eyes, at least for period of time you are there, as I had proved from past sentence's the epiphany's are soon forgotten when the vices are dangled in front of you again.

Blackfriars crown court is a nondescript building that I've only ever seen from a van, I could just about see the metal shutters going up as we drove in, to be welcomed by 3 G4S security guards, one a tall woman and two men, both in their forties.

The sweatbox door I'm in is opened up, but only a little way as there is a security chain on the door, I'm asked to put my right arm out through the gap, the guard then hand cuffs himself to me before the door is fully opened up, I'm escorted by all three escorts to a cell,
offered a coffee then locked in again.

It's a bleak experience, the room is painted magnolia, there are names graffitied all over the walls with dates, fuck only knows why anyone would ever want to put their name up on the wall, it is beyond me.

It's now 11.00am I'm supposed to be in court at 1.30 PM, its eerily quiet until the guard comes back with my lukewarm coffee, he explains that my barrister will be along shortly, but it's an hour until he eventually turns up.

All he's able to say is "don't worry, everything will be fine, it's just a formality today, there's really nothing to worry about Terrence"

He sounds like me talking to my kids everything will be fine, it's no wonder I don't believe him.

At 1.20pm I was unlocked, taken to court no3.

I thought it best not to tell anyone I was coming to court today, so I was surprised to see my dad and the kids sitting in the gallery, the kids seemed more concerned with the occasion than looking at me though, when I did finally get their attention all I could do was mouth to them, that everything was to going to be fine and not worry, as I smiled woefully at them.

They just gave me a thumbs up and smiled, my dad on the other hand seemed nervous but that's understandable as he had once sat where I was now, he winked and said "you ok?"

"Yeah dad!"

Then bang on half past one the door at the back of the court opens up and everyone is asked to rise for the honourable judge what's his name as he comes in.

He gives me a stern look before telling me to sit down.

The atmosphere is cordial but his authority is absolute, the prosecution go first and outline their case, they go straight for the jugular as if I'm public enemy no1 saying that they will be asking for a maximum sentence for me as I'd used gratuitous violence and threatening behaviour against staff, with the help of my fellow conspirators and a vicious German Shepherd dog, which they argued was the equivalent of me using a gun.

"Fuck" I thought "is he having a laugh" I mouthed to my barrister, but he just shrugged his shoulders and again told me not to worry.

"Also Mr Ellis has shown no remorse or regard to his victims, his criminal record is testament to his criminality, he has a long history of armed robbery, gratuitous violence and larceny and his record spans three decades.

He has an attempted escape whilst in custody, he has assaulted a police officer in his duty during the failed escape attempt, it was only because of the officer's colleagues that he didn't sustain more serious injuries."

I wanted to shout out and say "are you for fucking real, you're making me out to be some kind of animal.

But instead I called my barrister over and said "are you going to defend my good character or not because this cunt is making me out to be Genghis fucking Khan"

"It's ok Terry he's just presenting his case"

"But it's all fucking lies"

"We will have our opportunity in due course to present our case so please don't worry"

This was fucking bollocks, but what did I expect, I had banged out a copper, admittedly though I'd done it to give myself an opportunity to get away but not to hurt him, realistically how could I defend the indefensible.

In their eyes I was a vicious criminal who was prepared to use violence to get my own way, I'd bashed that copper to get away, I'd robbed Verizon and tied up ten security guards, I had a criminal record as long as my arm, so who was I kidding, why did I feel so affronted by the prosecution's remarks, was it because the kids were here or was it because the truth hurts?

I have always had an idea in my head of who I am, but to hear it said this way was fucking awful, I saw myself as a loving father, kind considerate and respectful to the elderly, I don't hurt people.

I've always had a romantic notion that I was one of the good guys, a sort of modern day Robin hood, but listening to this cunt today it was like pulling teeth, listening to a description of someone completely different to who I am or at least who I thought I was.

It was now my barrister's turn to outline our so called defence regarding my actions by way of mitigating circumstances and hopefully make me look like a victim.

In this game of subterfuge and smoking mirrors, he tried his best but his protestations felt weak and lacked any real substance or conviction, he was definitely no match for the crown prosecution and their team.

I could only thank God this case wasn't going to trial now.

The judge then asked me to stand up.

Asking me how I wanted to plead "guilty or not guilty?"

I waited for a second as there was no point in trying to drag it out "Guilty your honour"

"Just to confirm the sentencing date will be the 30 July, 2pm is that convenient for all parties?"

"Yes my lord "

"Yes of course"

"Ok, Mr Ellis we will see you back here on the 30th July"

"All Rise" said the Usher as the judge left the court room,

As soon as he left I was given a minute to say goodbye to my dad and daughters, I couldn't hug them or kiss them goodbye.

So I just said I loved them all and told them whatever happens, I would be ok, reiterating it's going to be ok, they said their goodbyes and left with my dad.

I thanked the two security guards for giving me that time with the kids, before returning to my cell, it was now 2.15pm, I'd been in court for just 45 minutes, but it felt longer, it also felt like a complete waste of time, I couldn't understand why they just couldn't just sentence me today and get it all over with.

My barrister popped his head in afterwards and gave me the obligatory pep talk before he went back to his chambers.

It didn't help as he didn't give me any straight answers regarding the sentencing guidelines, as it seems that the judge has the ultimate discretion and can bend said guidelines to suit his own agenda depending on his mood, so I was none the wiser for my excursion here today, the judge for all intent and purpose, was judge, jury and executioner.

Just as I was contemplating today's events the hatch on my door opened and a voice that I recognised said "hello Terry how are you?"

It was that guy who had visited in Wandsworth the MI5 fella, the so called government official.

He said "that looked quite ominous in there today Terrence, the prosecutor was pretty harsh, he's definitely gunning for your blood, and the judge seemed awfully biased if you ask me, it's not looking very good old chap is it?

Maybe you need a friend like me in your corner?"

"Ok what do you want?"

"Well you scratch my back and I'll scratch yours, I want everything Terrence, I want the fixer; his contacts at the bank and I want the motherboards back, plus your accomplices.

This deal I'm prepared to offer you ends today, you can either walk out of here or stay it's your choice Terry.

It's a one-time special offer that will see you out with your beautiful daughters, your family, it's a chance to start all over again while you're still relatively young.

So let's stop playing silly buggers, it's time to do the right thing by them Terry"

"It's a tempting offer and you say I could be back on the streets today?"

"No, no it will be 3 years Terry."

"Why 3 years?"

"Because we can't just let you walk scot free can we!"

"Wow!"

"That's still a very generous offer"

"And all I have to do is grass all my friends up, give you everything, the fixer, the motherboards and the bank official, sounds like a plan.

Unfortunately old boy it's not my plan, you see I'm not your kind of guy, I've already accepted my fate and I've made peace with it and my family.

So for you to even think that I would even contemplate your offer is an insult to me and my integrity also to everything I hold dear to me , my loyalty can't be brought with a promise of freedom you Judas cunt, So fuck you and your offer, it's been emotional, now piss off."

"Terry you're a stupid man, this was your only option trust me, you will live to regret your decision."

"I stand by my decisions, it's why I did Verizon, so see yea brother, You obviously know the way out"

He slammed the hatch close then hurriedly left, it seemed he wasn't too pleased with my rebuttal to his offer.

As much as his offer on the surface looked appealing, my standing amongst my friends was unbreakable, as a criminal we have to stand by our own actions and decisions.

I choose to do Verizon and all the other jobs, no one ever twisted my arm, to grass would be a selfish act of betrayal, a betrayal of everything I stand for, so believe me when I say this, it wasn't a hard decision for me to make.

As soon as he left I pressed the bell to summon one of the guards, when he arrived I asked him for the name of the gentleman who had just visited me.

He said "what gentlemen?"

"The one that was just talking to me through the door, I want his name"

"I'm sorry I didn't see him"

"Then who did?"

He shut the hatch and walked back into the office it was probably above his pay grade.

The van didn't arrive to pick me up until 4.30pm and by the time I got back to Wandsworth and in my cell it was 8.30pm.

I'd been up since 6am just to spend 45 minutes in court, it was bloody ridiculous, however when I got back there were police everywhere outside the prison, blue lights flashing and the whole prison was on lockdown.

I asked one of my pals what going on, he said apparently a guy leaving Wandsworth after visiting someone had been assassinated by a guy wearing a smart suit and a crash helmet, the dead guy was shot four or five times in the car park.

The contract on him had been arranged over the phone by one of the guys on my landing who had called the hit man fifteen minutes before to let him know that said target was on his way out, to shoot an unarmed man is a cowardly despicable act at the best of times,
so I hope that whoever did this or were involved gets what they deserve.

We were banged up for two days until all those involved had been moved to HMP Belmarsh.

But not before the whole prison was searched, all because a live bullet was found on the exercise yard, it was pandemonium, the screws were running around like headless chickens, the security governor was having kittens, until a specially trained unit of officers with sniffer dogs were brought in.

Which in turn stated off a tsunami of panic by some of the inmates, as toilets could be heard flushing at a rate of knots all over the prison as one by one everyone got rid of their phones or whatever else they had hidden in their cells.

I was brought out onto the landing while my cell was ripped apart, the screws missed my phone, which I still had in my secret hiding place, I had to chance leaving it there, because I couldn't bottle it as it was too painful.

It was a calculated risk but one I was willing to take, to be without my phone would have been a nightmare.

Simply because the phones on the wing were always occupied and were filthy, especially with hundreds of guys using them every day , spitting down the phone, the thought of using them made me feel sick.

After everything had calmed down, I put myself on a six week carpentry, plumbing and decorating course which consisted of 2 weeks on each module (trade).

The course was very basic but got me out of my cell, I was also having one to one counselling sessions with my psychologist which had become the highlight of my week, simply because I got to be the real Terry Ellis again.

A man who had thoughts, feelings, was funny, gentle and romantic.

It was a form of escapism that made this prison experience so much more bearable and rewarding, I was learning so much more about myself and why I was the way I was, I had come into prison to be punished, but instead I had met someone who was able to penetrate my armour with just a smile and unlock the trauma that had tortured me since childhood, experiences that I had normalized to protect my own sanity and self from.

I had to reconcile with the fact that maybe there was some small glimmer of hope, that one day I would be given the opportunity to explore the intricacies of my mind and find the answers that had alluded me all my life.

But first I had to minimize the damage that the attempted escape had bestowed on me and reinvent myself.

At my barrister's request, he had suggested that I do all the rehabilitation programs that were on offer to me.

Especially before my court date, to show the judge that I was more than my past, so I had no other option but to play out the charade that was prison rehabilitation.

Even though I knew it was a pointless exercise, I had to maintain the illusion that I had turned my life around and was now someone of good character who was prepared to put his life of crime behind him.

So I did everything I could, maths, English and even the six week multi-skills course, I even received the certificates of completion for them, but only God knows what having them will eventually do for me.

Time in prison seems to be a law unto itself, the last 9 months seem to have flown by, I only hoped the rest of my sentence would be as productively quick, because in two more days Dez and myself would face the final curtain.

We had been celebrated in prison by our peers and put on a criminal pedestal as being at the top of our game, we had revelled in the fact that we had accomplished the impossible and accepted all the accolades that were bestowed on us as testament to our endeavours and professionalism.

But none of that would matter after tomorrow as we would join the same long list of red top celebrity criminals who have had their fifteen minutes of fame.

We would now be denigrated to the annals of time as those guys from Camden town who did the Verizon heist, what's their names?

After the court hearing we would be convicted criminals and shipped up north somewhere, away from our families, friends and loved ones to be warehoused in a dispersal prison until a prison became available to us, probably Swaleside as most of the London contingency end up there.

I had spent my last sentence there so didn't relish the prospect of returning to Isle of Shepley, the island prison was either boiling hot in the summer or freezing cold in the winter, there were seagulls everywhere and getting there was a nightmare for your visitors.

My last sentence was 6 years and I had to do four years of it and if I'm honest it was relatively easy, but nevertheless it still seemed to last for ever.

Now the prospect of having to do it all over again was mind numbingly exacerbating, Deja-vu times a million and Groundhog Day part 2, it's a nightmare scenario, a consequence of the life I'd chosen.

30 July 2009

Doomsday was this the day that I got to reset the clock and wipe the slate clean?

Under British law now any jobs that they suspect you of doing or being involved in has to be disclosed whilst you're in custody.

So in my case the authorities have had nine months to build a case against me that could potentially see them introduce historical evidence or information that could link me to a cataclysmic amount of unsolved robberies all over the country involving police uniforms, dating back to God knows when.

So for me this would be their last chance to open Pandora's box or forever keep it shut.

The process was called gate arrest, but thank God it's no longer an option in case like mine, historical robberies that is; murder, rape or any sexual offences are not exempt.

Gate arrest used to be the old Bill's favourite tactic, they would let you serve your sentence then arrest you at the gate as you were released from prison, recharge you, remand you, then resentence you; It's a nightmare scenario especially if you've just finished a long stretch, not just for you, your family as well.

I'm told that its absolutely barbaric and simply torture, a totally out of order practice, that only the British establishment could think of and use, so thank God they've now stopped it.

But as I've already said it's still used in historical sexual cases and murders which is rightly so for obvious reasons.

So regardless of whatever happens in court today, I will walk out in hopefully the not too distant future with a clean slate,
to re-enter Society and try and make my mark on it once again.

For now I have to face the music that I'd helped compose, as I entered the reception area Dez was already waiting there.

We had been separated and put on different wings , so I hadn't seen him for the last two months or so, but nothing had changed he was his normal self, relaxed and nonchalant about our impending kangaroo court appearance.

We had both arranged for new suits to be sent in , so we could at least look dapper.

Both suited and booted in front of our families, I tried my best to hide any anxiety and apprehension I was feeling, but my stomach had other ideas, I looked the picture of equanimity but inside I was shaking uncontrollably, it's hard to describe Impending doom.

It's like being in a car crash without having a seatbelt on, that feeling you have at the fair on the big wheel, just as it goes over the top when your stomach turns over.

All I kept doing this morning was pissing, it was driving me crazy, I've been to the toilet ten times already, it must be my nerves.

Chapter Forty Nine

D-Day - Sentencing

"All who sin apart from the law will also perish apart from the law, and all who sin under the law will be judged by the law."
- **Romans 2:12** -

Dez and I have decided to go guilty.

So we will both be sentenced together today in the same courtroom,
the van ride was uneventful but for some reason, we had been given a police escort, a special team of police who had been sent with us, because they still couldn't fathom, how I got out of my cuffs the last time, so now I was on Houdini watch.

All my clothes were searched thoroughly this morning, I was also strip-searched even my shoes were put through a metal detector, they also took my belt off me, these guys were not taking any risks today.

Dez would be going in a separate van, mine was followed by a plainclothes old bill in separate vans and cars, that made up our security detail for today, It was a bit OTT but to be expected I suppose.

When we arrived at Blackfriars Crown Court we were searched again and I was given my belt back, we were then taken to a holding room/cell.

It was the first opportunity I'd had to talk to Dez without any screws or old bill about this morning.

I told him about the offer of the six years that MI5 had made me, he said they had also done the same with him, "3 years and out" he said.

"Yes same offer mate" we both laughed.

It was Dez's first offence so they couldn't really put any pressure on him.

The maximum they could give him, would be ten years and with time served on remand he would be out in four years, I was hoping for the same as we hadn't used any guns or violence.

I was only hoping for a couple of years more than what MI5 had offered me.

We could at least hold our heads up high, regardless of any inducements, we were the only two nicked and that says a lot about us.

After about 20 minutes Dez was called out to see his legal team and 5 minutes later I was sitting in a room with mine.

The strategy was simple we would offer up mitigating circumstances such as family, the rehabilitation course we had done since both being arrested.

Dez would go first as his army record would hopefully impress the judge, Dez had been part of a UN peacekeeping force, his record was exemplary, he had a good family, this behaviour would be construed as being out of character for him and would hopefully be seen as the only blip in an otherwise blemish-free career in the armed forces.

My record on the other hand was like a Wikipedia page of armed robbery, larceny, GBH (Grievous Bodily Harm), Theft, Burglary, TDA (Taking And Driving Away), an encyclopaedia of criminal endeavours, a sociopathic habitual criminal, my resume (curriculum vitae).

I wasn't just being sentenced today for my part in the Verizon heist, I was being sentenced on history it would ultimately be factored in regardless of all the multi-skills courses or maths and English certificates I had and nothing would change that little fact.

The cell door was eventually opened at 1.45pm for us to take the long walk to courtroom 3, we took our positions in the dock, as I looked around the courtroom, I could actually smell and taste it.

Behind us stood four security guards, we were all encased in a small space with bulletproof glass as I looked forward and directly in front of me, I could see a coat of arms, on the wall behind the judge's bench, the royal court of arms appears in every courtroom in England and Wales demonstrating that Justice comes from the monarch and the law court is part of the royal courts, hence the name.

In front of the judge sat the clerk of the court, to his right stood the usher and directly facing them were four desktop tables, to the left was the defence barrister, behind him was the defence solicitor, to his right sat the prosecution solicitor and in front of him sat the prosecuting barrister, then us, the defendants sat behind them.

To my left were four rows of benches, with all my family on, to the right of the aisle sat Dez's contingent all in all there was about twenty family members and friends, behind them sat five specially trained officers yes our security detail, who were all in plain clothes, you never deeply reflect on life until you're standing in the dock of a courtroom seeking out your families faces.

Seeing the finality of your situation in their expressions as they wait for the shout to go out by the clerk of the court.

And so it begins.

"Could everyone please rise so the presiding judge can enter the room and take his anointed seat at his bench, to start the proceedings"

The tension is something to be experienced as there's nothing quite like it.

Your demeanour says hurry up and let's get on with it, but inwardly you're saying goodbye to each family member while pleading with them and God to forgive you for your life choices and indiscretions.

Begging for leniency in your subconscious, at the same time you're wondering if you and your accomplices could overpower your guards and make a break for it.

There are so many thoughts going through your head at this time that it's almost impossible to think straight.

The reality is I had my chance and fucked it up and because of my failed attempt to escape, there was now no way out past this small army of security guards and plainclothes police officers who were now blocking my path to freedom, it was a situation that I had created by my own stupidity.

I was in trouble and there's nothing I could do about it now apart from resigning myself to the fact that today is an opportunity to reflect on my life experiences and challenge myself to change them,
so I never have to stand in another dock like this ever again.

Hindsight is a wonderful thing because it's always right, but we rarely give it a second thought until it's too late, like today.

The clerk was preparing himself as he's just stepped forward, here we go.

"Please rise for the right honourable judge"

Everyone stops talking all at once and stands to their feet, even me and Dez as our compliance will ultimately determine our fate, because our future is now in this judge's hands and his alone.

He looks old and impressive in his traditional gown and wig, his subordinates, barristers, solicitors, and court officials bow in obedience to his presence as he takes his place behind rimmed glasses and an expression that says I'm in charge.

The time for pleasantries was now over and the dance of the judiciary was just about to begin as the king of pomposity was in his rightful position presiding over his minions, he smiled then said "sit down everyone".

It was now time for the prosecution to outline their case against us, thus giving our families their first-ever insight into who we really were and what we were capable of doing, through the eyes of our victims.

Up to now they had only ever heard our watered-down versions of events that always portrayed us as the heroes in this game of subterfuge.

However, if we thought this was only a formality before sentencing, then we were wrong as the police and prosecution were out to paint a picture of Dickensian barbarity that would expose us and open up Pandora's box.

Dez's case summary was laid out first.

"He was a trained soldier who had gone rogue using his tactical skills to put together a team of ruthless and highly trained individuals to do his bidding, which culminated in him committing an aggravated robbery in Croydon where an undisclosed amount of money was stolen by him and his accomplices who have never been traced let alone apprehended.

These men gained access to the premises by the front door, waking the occupant who they then overpowered, Mr. Collins was physically wrestled to the ground, handcuffed and then intimidated into revealing the whereabouts of the keys to the safe, that held his companies monies.

It was only because of Mr. Collin's neighbour that this man was apprehended and brought to justice but not before an attending office was punched in the face and kicked to the ground, whilst his colleague was pushed over a wall and repeatedly kicked in the head, Dez (although the prosecution used the formal Mr Whatever) was seen making off through the gardens, in Warlingham Road, pursued by a number offices and a k9 unit who subsequently cornered him.

Even when confronted, he preceded to punch the dog repeatedly around the head and body, it was only because of the k9 units handler and other officers stepping in that the dog wasn't seriously injured.

Then on the 6th of December 2007, Dez and his accomplices pulled off what can only be described as an audacious heist at Verizon Telecommunications and IT business data centre in king's cross, where several members of staff were attacked and forcibly manhandled before being wrestled to the ground and handcuffed.

One was so traumatised that an ambulance needed to attend, other members of staff were treated at the scene for shock, technical staff were threatened with violence and intimidated before being handcuffed and marched into a stairwell on the ground floor, also four women cleaners were treated appallingly and received medical assistance after being manhandled with threats of violence before being handcuffed and threatened with a dog unless they kept quiet.

We will be seeking the maximum sentence with time served and a third off for a guilty plea your honour for Mr. Dez, that's the prosecution case against the defendant number one your honour.

In Case summary two, against the accused Mr. Ellis we will be presenting evidence in regards to several offences relating to drugs, robbery and an attempted escape and assault of an officer in the course of his Duty."

I'd been charged with escape and assault on an officer whilst I was in Pentonville prison and was found not guilty because the charges were written out wrongly so the case was dismissed and I was taken out of (patches) the green and yellow jumpsuit that escapees have to wear, but it seems now the prosecution wants to introduce it as evidence, as if the charge was still actively alive which they were not.

I only hoped my defence barrister would rectify that before I was sentenced.

He should highlight the fact they were playing games in here today to muddy the waters because now in the eyes of the judge and everyone else in this courtroom today, it was plain to see I was prepared to use violence and anything else to get my own way, which was the case, but that wasn't proven at the time, so why were they allowed to bring it in court, I couldn't even defend myself, because we had already gone guilty and today was supposed to be all about sentencing and not a character fucking assassination.

I was on best behaviour but it seems the prosecution was playing dirty.

"Our case against Mr. Ellis is further evidenced by his involvement in the distribution of drugs in a case that has already been proven and now sentenced for in his absence whilst he was on the run for his involvement in the robbery of Verizon and Marigold foods in Camley St. where he again stole a large amount of monies after handcuffing four members of staff single-handedly with threats of violence.

In the case of Mr. Ortega whom he punched in the face and forcibly took to the ground whilst he handcuffed him, subsequently in the scuffle Mr. Ellis dropped his police identity card in the name of Darren Brown.

He also jumped across a desktop and forcibly Restrained the owner of the premises by punching him in the stomach and placing him face down on the floor again as he handcuffed him.

The other two employees were handcuffed together, then cuffed to the metal handrail on the stairs, the owner and his employees were all treated appallingly and needed hospital treatment for shock.

Two stolen cars were also used in the course of this crime and subsequently destroyed by fire.

Mr. Ellis' accomplices have not been traced or apprehended, he also refused to cooperate with the police investigation to recover the stolen property and monies.

On the 6th December, he played the leading role in the Verizon heist that had Mr. Ellis' DNA written all over it, gratuitous violence, threat of lethal force in the shape of a German Shepherd dog, which he used to maintain control over his victims.

He is seen orchestrating every aspect of the robbery, the entry, the orders came from him, this is evidenced from the security CCTV footage, his involvement was instrumental in ensuring the success of the Verizon robbery.

The victim's accounts suggest he was the ringleader, the head of security at Verizon Mr. Adebola states Mr. Ellis forced him and MS Adankwo into the staircase with threats of violence and forcibly handcuffed them to a metal banister Rail.

He also gave orders to his henchman to handcuff the supervisor and his team of CCTV operators, then coerced him to call three security personnel to the main reception area where he threatened to set the dog on them unless they complied with his orders.

He then restrained them with handcuffs.

He was also seen handcuffing Mr. Abayomrunkoje who was thrown to the ground where he sustained bruising to his torso, this altercation left him needing hospital treatment afterwards.

In respect to the technical staff and cleaning ladies, he was overheard to say if any of them give you any trouble, set the fucking dog on them.

Concerning the conversation between Mr. Ellis and Mr. Evans the head supervisor at JPMorgan's independent security services, Mr. Ellis impersonated a Verizon employee in establishing a plausible excuse for the shutdown of the network.

In closing summary, we recommend that Mr. Ellis receives the maximum sentence for his involvement in count 1 the Verizon heist,
Count 2 robbery of Marigold food, count 3 possession with intent to supply Class A drugs, and count four Benedict Court, again we will be also asking for the court for the maximum penalties that the guidelines permit."

It was now time for Dez's defence team to present an argument for mitigating circumstances, his barrister was confident but it was plain to see he was between a rock and a hard place in as far as trying to mitigate Dez's involvement down to a one-off act of stupidity when he could be clearly seen as a willing participant in both robberies and had nearly killed the dog in his attempt to escape capture.

His army record was exemplary, he was a UN peacekeeper and had done a couple of tours in Northern Ireland, he was a family man and had a strong family network.

He'd also kept his nose clean in prison by enrolling in several rehabilitation programs, his criminal record was non-existent, so his barrister asked for this to be taken into consideration, when sentencing him.

It was now my barrister's turn to try and bail out a sinking ship with a sieve, maybe I should have stayed downstairs in the cell, as being character assassinated like this all seemed a senseless waste of my time to me.

Of course, I understood the process, this wasn't for my benefit, this charade was for the victims and society in general, to send out a message to anyone thinking of following in my footsteps.

However It was for this reason that we had deliberately not used any guns, because no matter what they implied or said about us they couldn't give us a life sentence.

Still, these barristers would argue otherwise, yes we used intimidation and were heavy-handed and forceful with our voices, which has wrongly been interpreted in here today as forceful and in gratuitous violence, how can I defend myself and the indefensible?

My fate had already been chosen, my sentence already determined, this mock trial for all intent and purpose had turned into a kangaroo court about nothing else than our characters.

I wanted to shout out and say fuck the lot of you, whilst doing an Irish jig in the middle of the dock, but my kids were in court and they needed to see justice served, so I couldn't deny them that, so I kept schtum, it would be an important lesson for them to learn for their futures.

My barrister God bless him tried his best but I had zoned out by now I couldn't listen to any more of this gobbledygook or his platitudes because they made me look as if I actually gave a shit about getting a reduced sentence, I would hold my head up high and take whatever they threw at me, I would embrace it and turn it round to my own advantage because that's what I do, I turn a negative into a positive.

My barrister closed his summing up with a whimper, I could only thank God that I would never have to go through this palaver again, the months of waiting to be sentenced were nearly over, it had taken eight months. Coming to court for pleas and dees and the visit from my solicitor and barrister which had drawn the whole process out, it had been tortuous agony.

The clerk then stood up and said:

"All rise"

It was now time for the honourable judge to take his leave he would now return to his chambers so he could reach a final decision on the evidence he had heard in here today, but we knew better.

MI5 had promised to fuck me, as they had missed an opportunity to take down some major companies, corporations and banking officials, in Ireland, America, England and across Europe and for that they blamed me, so I could only imagine that there was a letter sitting on the judge's desk when he got back to his chambers.

Written on it, was for your immediate attention, Mr. Eills needs to be made an example of and we suggest that the full weight of the crown be placed upon his head.

We were told that the judge would retire to his Chambers for about fifteen or so minutes to make amendments to his sentencing, after hearing all the barristers closing summaries.

I gave the kids a thumbs up and a wry smile but they knew the gavel was just about to be banged down on my head.

So we just all smiled, everyone looked pensive but Dez and I just said "Whatever happens in here today, it has been emotional brother, we did the impossible and we are still here.

What can they really do to us?

Plus it ain't an armed robbery, there was no violence"

"What do you reckon Tel?"

"Ten years for you"

"Yes all day long"

"I reckon that's about right and with time served you'll be out in four years"

"What do you reckon for you Tel, I'm hoping for the same mate"

I laughed "let's see brother, when the judge comes back, let's stand tall and show no emotion, remember you're out in four years with time served"

The reckoning was here.

"All rise for the honourable judge"

"Please sit everyone."

The judge sat down and ruffled his papers while he made some notes before he gestured to the clerk.

"Can the defendants please stand" The clerk ordered us to stand and the courtroom fell silent.

It was our time, our day in court, but it really wasn't our day, it was theirs to do with us as they pleased and in the next couple of minutes the police, prosecution, MI5, and judge would get their pound of flesh.

"Mr. Dez and Mr. Ellis, On December 6, 2007, the circumstances surrounding these crimes arouses disbelief and it is difficult to imagine the stress you perpetrated on your victims, the fear was intensified by the use of a German shepherd dog and the brutality you used.

I have read the victim's impact statements and the effects on them will be long lasting, the contrast between you and them could not be more vivid, your arrogance has been breath-taking, not once during the police investigation, did they detect a Flicker of emotion pertaining to your victims, from either of you.

It was only thanks to the dedication of the forensic scientists and the police investigation, assisted by your victims, that you were both brought to justice.

Despite your guilty pleas no monies, motherboards, or your accomplices have ever been traced or recovered.

That is your right and I will not increase your sentences because of it.

However, it is symptomatic of your staggering lack of remorse, that affronts me in this courtroom today.

Your defence teams have said all they can on your behalf, entirely in keeping with the exemplary way this hearing was conducted on both sides of the bar, all matters of fact which could reasonably be agreed were and the issues were well focused.

It doesn't go too far when I say I was shocked by the contents of the criminal justice social report and consultant forensic psychologist, MS Winterbottom.

Each of these reports suggests you carried on with your criminal activities and behaviours whilst inside prison.

Mr. Ellis this is in regards to your attempted escape from custody and your violent assault on a police officer in the course of his duties, a charge of mutiny and dissension were brought against you, where you were found guilty of good order and discipline.

These reports paint a clear picture of the cold, callous, calculated, dangerous, remorseless individual you are, I do not intend to go into every detail of these reports because I think it would be detrimental to this case.
However I think the public should hear the flavour of its contents which the prosecution barrister has already outlined.

You were not under the influence of any substances, so your actions were purely of your own choosing.

Two other aspects of the reports are worth mentioning, you were not suffering from any mental disorder or syndrome of any kind.

You are lacking in any victim empathy, the social reports noted your cold calculating manner, therefore the only sentence I can impose on you is custodial.

Mr. Ellis a lot of work will have to be done to change you before you could be considered for release, even that may not be possible in your case.

The period I select is known as the punishment part of the sentencing as its purpose is to satisfy and requires retribution and a deterrent.

The parole board will deal with the protection of the public, I have to take into account the circumstance of the offences and everything said on your behalf and in sentencing you, your reintegration back into society should also be taken into account.

However, the weight to be given to the various sentencing considerations of the cases and the nature of these appalling offences and what I read in these reports make it clear to me, that reintegration and rehabilitation, while these are important considerations, they are a remote possibility and neither your best interests nor anyone else's will be served by a speedy return back to society, none the less the punishment would have been substantially longer if you had used firearms, but notwithstanding that your Cavalier approach and attitude leaves a lot to be desired.

No sentence I impose will alleviate your victims anguish and if it wasn't bad enough on the streets of the capital, you chose to impersonate those that are here to protect us; the police.

You were both lynchpins in the organisation of these robberies, you used police uniform to con your way into the Verizon building, in the process putting your victims through a traumatic experience and stealing five million pounds worth of motherboards and potentially hundreds of millions of pounds worth of data information that could be used in various criminal activities.

JPMorgan's lawyers have applied for an international confiscation order on Mr. Ellis for the return of their data equipment or monies to the amount of five million pounds, the crown will be seeking a hidden assets order to the equivalent amount; also of five million pounds.

So it is the decision of the court to sentence you today.

Mr. Dez

On count 1 you will go to prison for 9 years.

On count 2 you will receive 8 years to run concurrently.

On count 3 you will receive 7 years which will run concurrently.

Take him down."

Dez had received 9 years and the other two sentences the 8 and the 7 years would run concurrently which meant they would all run together at the same time which was a great result for him.

As he walked past me on the way back to the cell he couldn't himself from smiling, as he mouthed "result!"

"Well done mate, see you in a minute."

"Yep, no problem Tel"

Dez had already served a year so with good behaviour and a third off his sentence, he could be home in three and half years and that my friends is why we never use guns.

It's the difference between 9 years or three life sentences for what we did, I've known men get 25 years for nicking 25 grand, all because they used a gun or a knife.

Dez had definitely dodged a bullet and rightly so, but good luck to him, I have nothing but respect for him, he's been nothing but a stand-up guy throughout this escapade, he kept his mouth shut, which is a testament to his character and the man he is.

"Terrence David Ellis by your own admission you have pleaded guilty.

Mr. Ellis, the court has thoroughly reviewed and considered your records presented by the prosecution and your defence team.

The court has evaluated and weighed the aggravating factors beyond reasonable doubt and mitigating circumstances established by the evidence presented.

I must say that in all the years of serving on this bench I've never encountered anyone quite like you, you have a blatant disregard for authority and a devil-may-care attitude, that has elevated you above the laws of this land, your criminal beliefs and behaviour are inherently entrenched.

Your crimes were carried out without any moral justification or thought for your victims and your record speaks volumes regarding your character.

Whilst in the commission of these offences you were prepared to use gratuitous violence, intimidation, and manipulation for your own gratification, you have shown a callous disregard towards the investigative team and your victims.

You recklessly and without any thought or consideration assaulted a police officer in the course of his Duty.

I find it extremely difficult to find words appropriate to describe the dreadful crimes to which you have pleaded guilty to and I question anyone who did what you did to seriously ask this court for leniency.

You have traumatized countless victims and done irreparable damage in impersonating the Police, you display the action of a cold, calculated, ruthless criminal and I'm in no doubt that you and you alone were the mastermind behind the Verizon heist, you are and were a prominent underworld figure and your criminal activities still stretch far and wide throughout our community.

Now through your counsel, you claim to be remorseful but remorse was only expressed for the first time when you pleaded guilty, the perusal of the criminal justice report may have carried more weight if you would have communicated that earlier.

An important matter of law was raised to whether I was initially entitled to impose an IPP sentence for public protection.

I have found this an extraordinary submission that the prosecution and defence had agreed with the contents of this narrative which has tied my hands so I cannot enhance my case for an indeterminate sentence.

Regrettably, I was not asked to be part of that discussion, as the crown for some reason decided not to persist in seeking a conviction on that charge despite detailing in the agreed narrative the many factors that would have fully justified such a sentence, the lord advocate submitted I would still be entitled to as an aggravating factor and he referred to several cases he submitted that supported that approach but this was out of the scope of the indictment.

However, because of your earlier guilty plea, I am obliged to consider a level of discount, I will limit that discount by way of a consecutive sentence.

The sentence will however be backdated to when you were first remanded in custody.

You will therefore be sentenced in accordance with the law.

The sentences I will impose should give you ample time to consider the ramifications of your actions, it should also be a time of reflection and reformation, that I hope you grasp with both hands.

On Count 1 I will sentence you to 9 years in prison.

On Count 2 I will sentence you to 7 years 9 months consecutive.

On Count 3 I will sentence you to 8 years to run concurrently.

And on Count 4 I will sentence you to 7 years to run concurrently.

"Take him away" he then smiled and got up and left the courtroom.

And there lies the rub, the powers that be have conspired against me and given me the same sentence as Dez.

On top of that, they felt it necessary to top me up with a consecutive sentence, which now means I can't appeal it on the grounds of disparity of sentence.

We both got the same amount of time, which now means that I have to complete the first 9-year sentence, before I start the seven years nine months, meaning my total sentence is sixteen years nine months and with a third off for my guilty plea and the eight months I've already served on remand.

That now leaves me a grand total of seven years eight months and two weeks to do, the totality of my sentence is 8 years 4 half months behind the door.

Everyone in the gallery was shocked, I suppose to them it must have seemed like I'd gotten more than most murders get or someone carrying a gun on a robbery.

I just smiled and said "it's going to be ok."

I turned to the guards and asked them to take me back to my cell.

Once I got through the door I allowed myself a moment just to stand there and wallow in self-pity at the enormity of my sentence, but only for the briefest of seconds as I couldn't let anyone see that I had been affected by it, it's not what I do.

- The End -

Follow my journey through the prison system:

HMP GRENDON - THERAPEUTIC PRISON:

Living amongst the beasts: The rise and fall of the Grendon experiment
by Mr Terry Ellis, Mr Christopher Alston, et al. | 26 May 2020
★★★★★ ~ 141

Paperback
£10⁰⁰

Get it Monday, May 3
FREE Delivery by Amazon

Kindle Edition
£0⁰⁰
kindleunlimited
Free with Kindle Unlimited membership
Learn More
Or £7.00 to buy

HMP SPRINGHILL - RESETTLEMENT PRISON:

The Final Countdown to my Freedom: Resettlement Diaries
by Mr Terry Ellis and Mr Christopher James Alston | 1 Dec 2020
★★★★★ ~ 10

Paperback
£9⁹⁹

Get it Monday, May 3
Eligible for FREE UK Delivery

Kindle Edition
£0⁰⁰
kindleunlimited
Free with Kindle Unlimited membership
Learn More
Or £6.97 to buy

GENERAL ADVICE AND GUIDENENCE FOR NEW PRIONSERS AND THEIR FAMILIES:

HMP - Help Me Prepare: A guide to prison for first timers and their families
by Mr Christopher James Alston, Mr Terry Ellis, et al. | 10 Aug 2020
★★★★☆ ~ 14

Paperback
£9⁹⁹

Get it Monday, May 3
Eligible for FREE UK Delivery

Kindle Edition
£6⁰⁰ £9.99
Available instantly